Where Grieving Begins

Where Grieving Begins

Building Bridges after the Brighton Bomb

A Memoir

Patrick Magee

Foreword by Jo Berry

PLUTO  PRESS

First published 2021 by Pluto Press
345 Archway Road, London N6 5AA

www.plutobooks.com

Copyright © Patrick Magee 2021; Foreword © Jo Berry 2021.

The right of Patrick Magee to be identified as the author of this work has been
asserted in accordance with the Copyright, Designs and Patents Act 1988.

British Library Cataloguing in Publication Data
A catalogue record for this book is available from the British Library.

ISBN   978 0 7453 4177 4   Hardback
ISBN   978 1 7868 0686 4   PDF eBook
ISBN   978 1 7868 0688 8   Kindle eBook
ISBN   978 1 7868 0687 1   EPUB eBook

Contents

Acknowledgements

I am grateful to David Castle and to his colleagues at Pluto Press for their insightful editorial stewardship of my memoir in trying times for all. The manuscript was submitted to Pluto before the spin-off impact of COVID-19 on the book trade, causing the publication date to be moved back from September 2020 to February 2021. I also regret missing the very enjoyable visits to their offices in Highgate, but much was seamlessly accomplished at correct social distancing.

Gratitude is due to many in grappling with the struggle to make sense of the past described herein, not least by far to my mother whose own recall was shamelessly plundered during my sadly too-infrequent visits in the final years before she died. I also honour my father's influence and the personal accounts of other relatives.

Others no longer with us, but whose memory continues to inspire, include Martin Meehan and Ann Gallagher.

I received valued feedback and positive critique from the following who read early chapter drafts: Danny Morrison, John Loughran, Aly Renwick, Peter Berresford Ellis, Paul Kavanagh and Fionntán Hargey. A particular thank you to Fionntán's mother, Anne Hargey, for her memories of the old Market.

I also greatly appreciate the wisdom and support of Dr Maeve Stokes and Dr Brian Glanville.

A special thanks is due to Brian Warfield, the chorus of whose brilliant indictment of imperialism, 'The Ballad of Joe McDonnell', heads chapter ten.

Never least, I thank Jo Berry and Harvey Thomas, who will always inspire me to question.

And lastly, for Tessa, for her tireless support.

A memoir is such an idiosyncratic endeavour that, despite the value added by all of the above, and more, I must take full responsibility for any and all of its failings.

Patrick Magee

Foreword

by Jo Berry

It is both an honour and a challenge to write this foreword; it is unusual to be asked to write a foreword for someone who killed your father. Yet I have for the last twenty years been in dialogue with Patrick Magee, the man who planted the bomb at the Grand Hotel in Brighton which killed my dad, Sir Anthony Berry, and four others.

This book is Patrick Magee's memoir, from his early memories to his vision of Belfast today; he charts his joining the IRA, the appalling experience he and others endured of internment, his active engagement, his imprisonment and his release. It is eye opening for us who have only heard of this time in history from the English perspective, revealing some harsh truths that I think it is important we learn about. The last six chapters describe our first meeting and the work he has since done with me and others from around the world, engaging in peace and reconciliation.

Please read this story as one of the many truths of the conflict; no one has the objective truth of what happened. Everyone who was present has a valid story that we can hear – even if we don't agree. I have empathised with people who have been enemies to each other, and some to me, and I can see that if we had lived each other's lives we may have made the same choices as the other person did. It is easy to judge, make someone wrong and someone right, but the question for me is how we can listen to one another and learn from the past so violence is not used again.

I appreciate the honesty of Patrick's writing and I could feel the challenging situation he found himself in Belfast. I think it is important for those outside his community to see something of the harsh reality some Catholics experienced. There are parts of the first half of the book that I found hard to read; there is much suffering and pain. I cannot help but reflect on how different my experiences were at that age. I have never felt comfortable with justification for violence and there is much in this book. The nuances and uncertainty that Patrick has sometimes expressed in our talks do not feature but I understand that he is writing for some of his community who do not feel heard. For some people he may have gone too far, for others not far enough.

His description of our first meeting captures the intensity well, and to help the reader understand my motivation, I will share a little here. Twenty years ago, I arranged to meet Pat Magee as a one-off encounter so I could look into his eyes and see him as a human being. I did not need an apology, for that wouldn't bring my dad back; I knew from meeting others who had been in the IRA that he would come with a sense of righteousness. They were the oppressed, those without power, the marginalised – my dad represented power and the elite. I knew Pat would see it as a righteous war and one they had had no choice in. He did start by justifying and talking from the generic 'we'. I listened and asked open questions to find out more of his personal story. I remember the moment when I looked into his eyes and saw how much he cared for his community; at that moment, he was no longer a faceless enemy but someone with his own story and humanity. An enemy is just someone whose story we haven't heard.

I was about to end the meeting when Pat had what he now calls his 'epiphany' moment. I remember the difference – he was no longer justifying or saying the word *we*. He was speaking from his heart, being vulnerable and asking me about my father. He was visibly shaken and emotional; his voice had more depth and I knew I needed to stay longer. It was dawning on him for the first time that my dad had been a human being and he had killed him. He realised he had lost some of his humanity and was guilty of demonising *them* in the same way he accuses *the Other* of demonising republicans. He could hear the impact of his actions.

I had reached my limit of being able to listen after another hour, and that was when he said 'I am sorry I killed your father.' He spoke with great feeling and conveyed how this weighed heavily in him. I say, 'I'm glad it was you' – the words just popped out, and twenty years later we are still discussing what I meant.

I was acknowledging that I did not think many would have opened their hearts at that point, to feel the emotional cost of their actions. Pat has said that if I had started the meeting with blame and finger-pointing, he would have stayed within the safe place of righteousness. Instead he was disarmed by the empathy I showed. I was more curious and interested in who was behind the rhetoric than seeking revenge for what he had done to my family.

Pat recognised he had lost something of his own humanity by being violent. He is still on a journey and the book conveys this. People sometimes ask me why we still meet – is it not repetitious to still share our story together? I reply that it is always different, as we are both still changing. Maybe it is even harder for Pat – the more he knows me, the more the distress in him grows.

Pat moves from a tribal perspective in the first half of the book to a more holistic global perspective. His last paragraph shows the impact of our work of the last twenty years on him:

> *We need to transcend division; to leave Otherness behind as a useless, debilitating, myopic and self-destructive state of mental negation. I think it is profoundly inappropriate to speak of winners when so many from all sides have experienced loss. Nobody wins until we all win.*

Pat has been a teacher for me, sometimes very challenging and also very transformational. We now have twenty years of shared experience, and for that I am deeply grateful. I salute his courage to have become vulnerable, to feel the cost of what he has done and to write about it in this book. His actions for me show his strength and his vulnerability. He chooses to meet despite what I represent – I am no easy option, instead a difficult mirror and a reminder of the choices he made. He trusts me and together I believe we show what is possible.

My final thoughts: can we let go of our hatred, find the courage to listen to those we do not agree with, find alternatives to violence and build a world founded on compassion and empathy? I believe we can, and my hope and wish is that this book adds to a new conversation.

Introduction

'... knowing thyself as a product of the historical process to date, which has deposited in you an infinity of traces, without leaving an inventory.'
— Antonio Gramsci, 1891–1937

The reader may know of me only from the tabloid branding, 'the Brighton Bomber'. Drip-fed, this has served to cloud the need for deeper scrutiny of a complex struggle; an example in a long lexicon of 'thought-terminating clichés'* in service to power, such as 'terrorist' and 'godfather'. A key Irish Republican Army (IRA) operation, the targeting of Conservative government ministers, politicians and their financiers, part of a wider campaign against the British state and its terrorism against an historically oppressed community in Ireland, is personalised and thus reduced, as if the bombing of the Grand Hotel in 1984 was a matter of individual volition, not a strategic action drawing on the vastly more limited resources of a guerrilla movement against its powerful adversary. The off-the-peg labelling cultivated by the media points to the work of 'a fanatic'. Look no further. No cause to consider motivation, strategy or context. The political establishment and its attendant media would have the world understand that operation as the consequence of an individual psychopathology, or as a British judge in summing up at my trial concluded, the actions of 'a man of exceptional cruelty and inhumanity'.

One aim in writing this memoir, therefore, is to counter this limiting view and to instead offer an alternative appreciation of the movement I joined as a young man and in which I served as a volunteer for nearly three decades, whether on active duty or as a prisoner of war (POW).

For an Irish republican, the task of writing about the past, of one's own lived experience, is a fraught affair, like balancing on a high wire above a minefield. There are the obvious legal hazards. Released under the terms

---

*Robert Jay Lifton, *Thought Reform and the Psychology of Totalism* (W. W. Norton & Co., New York, 1963).

of the Good Friday Agreement (GFA), as a former Irish republican POW, I remain on licence and therefore subject to recall. Many in positions of power in politics, in the media and in academia continue a crusade of criminalisation and would seize on any revelatory slippage to undermine what has been hard gained by republicans after decades of sacrifice, some detail that might trigger a witch-hunt. The movement's task – the ending of British rule and the creation of a rights-based democracy – is far from completion. We must be aware of not giving away hostages to fortune. Therefore, I should also state from the outset what this memoir is not about. Anyone expecting to glean substantial hitherto-unrevealed detail about the planning, logistics and execution of the Brighton Bomb may be disappointed. Discussion of the operational side of that, or indeed of any actions I was involved in as a volunteer in the IRA, lies outside the purposes here, of which I will say more presently. At an unforeseeable juncture the story of Brighton may be told, though not necessarily by me.

This memoir is, therefore, less an account of events (and indeed of much private family detail) than a reflection on key influences, experiences, motivations and intent, and of the circumstances in which these have shaped the course of my life, the essential context being the conflict between the British state and partitioned Ireland.

In 1921, Britain partitioned Ireland, ignoring the democratic mandate of an overwhelming majority in Ireland who voted in the 1918 general election for Sinn Fein's demand for an Irish Republic. The resulting hived-off six-county sectarian statelet imposed on my grandparents, their children and on my generation was a gerrymandered 'political slum',* an act of violence, political and actual, perpetrated by the powerful upon the weak, the outplay of which impacted egregiously on our communities and, more specifically in this account, upon my family. It was the defining historic event of our lives, setting the scene for the eruption of violence in the late 1960s. As Martin McGuinness famously put it, 'We didn't go to war. War came to us.'

We do appear, despite current uncertainties generated by Brexit and the fears within unionism of demographic change, the extension of human rights and the continuing electoral rise of Sinn Fein, to be moving slowly

---

*Cal McCrystal and the *Sunday Times* Insight Team, 'John Bull's Political Slum', Sunday Times, 3 July, 1966.

but inexorably towards a more just, more democratic future, one in which the recourse to armed struggle ought never again be a morally justifiable and legitimate option in the Irish/British context. The resulting closure on that option will clear more space for former republican combatants to reappraise the conflict and express our collective trauma (the trauma of the communities we defended and to which we integrally belong), certainly in ways barred to previous generations of republicans. Some republicans may disagree, and not solely from within 'dissident' camps. There is a deep-rooted culture of silence within the republican movement, and there are those who will rigidly abide by that code no matter what the future political dispensation. I do have some sympathy for that position. I recall, with pride, the reticence of older republicans from the 1920s, 1930s, 1940s and 1950s to talk about their involvement. Their silence was a badge of honour. And wise. They were conscious of the future and of unfinished business. And while we may achieve further democracy here, and it will certainly have to be defended, there are other theatres of conflict in the world, where oppressed people may gain from our example and experience. Ours is an anti-imperialist struggle, after all. Nothing about strategy or tactics should ever be revealed that could possibly assist the powerful in their imperialist quest for the subjugation of the colonised. With peace embedded here, however – a sustained and sustainable peace within this island and between these islands – the truth may yet out. That will still require a long-overdue acceptance of due culpability for the conflict from all sides, whether republican/nationalist, loyalist/unionist or state force personnel and their political masters. We are not there yet and attitudes and interests persist as obstacles in the path of a fuller, more open account. I do believe, nevertheless, that it is beholden on all sides of the conflict to address the past with as much candour and empathy as allowed within the shackles of British law. The reader will understand, however, if I am a little guarded in discussing operational matters.

I am trying to figure out the whys and hows of my life. Why did I, for example, born in Belfast but raised in England, decide to join the IRA? For me this involves a searching appraisal of my motivations and beliefs, because the older I get the more questions surface about why I chose that life course. Could all that followed from the choices made, and those life turns not pursued – could they be ultimately linked? The what if's are there to haunt, however sure I can be in all honesty that there were no other choices open for me. And we must not forget the political necessity of looking back over the past. For isn't there an obligation on those of us who made hard choices to share our truth, collectively gathered from a troubled, experiential struggle within an oppressive, restricting reality?

I know that during the conflict there were choices, however reduced by contexts and events. For even while options seemed so few in the lived moment, I could in theory have chosen to do nothing, to walk away, but that path never figured as a real option for me or for many others who chose to resist. There is that story (apocryphal, one might assume) told of South Africa's Truth and Reconciliation Commission: two men present themselves before their local hearing –

'What did you do?'
'We did nothing.'
'Then why … ?'
'Because we are ashamed. We did nothing.'

To have done nothing was to be a part of the problem. Given the context of Belfast in 1972, I elected to volunteer. Thousands like me, constrained by the context of our lives, acted similarly. But there is the personal awareness, shared I know by the many involved, that the playing out of our choices had a massive impact on others, near and far, on families, friends and foes. I also reckon I was capable of, and possessed, sound judgement and was never easily led. Certainly not since my early teens. But even now I can't be sure of all the trace forces that helped forge me, nor of where my sense of right and wrong or political outlook originates, except that Belfast, or my conception of it, is mixed intrinsically into the whole churning cycle. I am, in that sense, derived. A product. The Italian Marxist Antonio Gramsci argued that we should 'compile … an inventory' of these traces and, to the extent that it is possible, this is one of my aims in writing, for my recall is not a seamless flow but an incomplete mosaic. How, for example, did I arrive at the huge personal decision to return to Ireland at the start of the Troubles, and why, within a year, did I throw all my energy into the IRA? How and why did I quickly perceive that the armed struggle I volunteered to further was the only option open to me and to the beleaguered nation-alist working-class communities I found acceptance in and pride in trying to defend? I will speak of motivations, of context, of communal, familial and personal suffering and sacrifice and grief, but also of a transcendent spirit stemming from the struggle against oppression, discrimination and injustice. I am witness to what is achievable when ordinary people pool what little they possess in common cause. Having that knowledge, that insight, I will always hold to optimism, especially in difficult times.

I also believe conflict damages us all – all victims, all combatants, all protagonists, all caught in the crossfire, no matter the uniform or the political ideology or allegiance. It is part of the legacy of all conflict. And if you have been involved in causing injury and suffering, there is an obligation, a moral imperative, to address past actions, to reappraise, to reflect and, when circumstances allow, to explain. Even before my release in 1999 on licence under the terms of the peace settlement, I knew that there was at least the possibility that one day I would meet former enemies, whether British squaddies, the Royal Ulster Constabulary (RUC), Special Branch torturers, loyalists or the various factions within republicanism – perhaps even British politicians. I was prepared also to meet victims of IRA actions – of my actions. This is a state of mind largely lost in conflict.

In November 2000 I met Joanna Berry, the daughter of Sir Anthony Berry MP, who was one of five people killed, one of the five people *I* killed, in the IRA bombing of the Grand Hotel, Brighton. We have met on more than two hundred occasions since then, sharing platforms in universities, schools, conferences, prisons; reconciliation events in Ireland, north, south, east and west; in England; and further afield, such as in Lebanon, Rwanda and Israel/Palestine. That we continue to meet, that Jo trusts me to be honest with her, however fraught the occasion, is a humbling but also a healing recuperative experience. All this contact despite the fact that I killed her father.

Another significant purpose in writing, therefore, is to chart lessons learned from these meetings, several of which were filmed for a BBC documentary, *Facing the Enemy*, first broadcast in December 2001. The documentary tracked our meetings over an eleven-month period and seemed to touch many people with its message that we need not remain locked in a cycle of hatred and recrimination, and that inclusion and dialogue should prevail over discrimination and politically fostered ignorance about those whom the powerful would exclude. It is also clear that the documentary raised more questions than it answered. For all the production's merits, the very nature of the documentary format, of this televisual treatment of complex issues, often precludes a fuller analysis. My hope is that herein I can flesh out many of the issues generated – for example, the controversial matter of forgiveness – and perhaps reveal more about me as an individual. Neither Joanna Berry nor I would suggest that our experience is a blueprint or map for others to follow. Our journey of reconciliation is not prescriptive and is perhaps better understood as an exploration. At times it has felt like an experiment in uncharted reaches of the soul. I believe our experience can offer the absolute conviction gained that much is possible when there is a genuine will to understand the other's perspective. Not to condone or agree with, although the search may reveal a considerable overlap despite profound differences.

While keeping these themes and issues to the forefront, I will attempt to track those critical hinge moments in my developing understanding. In all our lives there are key dates, successes and failures, shaping events; points which open up or shut off new opportunities. We each will have known many such moments. I will examine several in my life. Many qualify as ports of entry. In the dock at the Old Bailey? Releases from detention and imprisonment? On the threshold of meeting victims? Further back, to me, aged four, on first experiencing the shattering impact of removal, dislocation, from all then dear? For that reason, I will try to explain the course of my life in a roughly chronological order, setting the scene for my later involvement in the freedom struggle. I would also wish to address the widest possible readership, for Britain's propaganda reach is extensive and the world has been primed to see the struggle through a distorting lens. To this day, the British public remains woefully misinformed, underinformed and disinformed about what successive British governments inflicted upon Ireland in its name.

In large measure I write in response to the reductionism that, in service to power, persists as the pervading discourse about the conflict some two decades after the signing of the GFA, a discursive drag on our ability both to reach a genuine understanding of the past and to achieve an enduring peace and reconciliation. My overarching purpose in writing this memoir, therefore, is to examine: context, motivation and intent. For the politically contrived ignorance of the British public in particular is a serious block on efforts to create a shared sustainable, peaceful future.

If we are to grieve collectively, and therefore to move ahead together, we should begin with an openness to each other's truth.

1

Trace Memories

My given names are Patrick Joseph. Dad chose them in part to honour my great uncle, Patrick Joseph Magee, who had been killed on the Western Front in 1916. I say 'in part' because my baptism was the second occasion to do so; the first had a tragic outcome. My paternal grandparents, Joss and Susan Magee (*née* Steenson), wanted their firstborn son to be so named, but the child was stillborn. That was in 1923, while Joss was interned by the British for his part in the struggle against partition. Six years later, and after the birth of a daughter, Rose, Dad was born and was christened John, for baby Patrick was alive still in their hearts. The legacy skipped to me. My name therefore stands for both losses.

Dad's line, the Magees and Steensons, and my maternal lineage, the Donegans and Robinsons, lived in pre-partition Ireland. My parents were of that first generation born within the six-county statelet. I was born in 1951, thirty years after its imposition. I therefore come from a blighted generation born into political impoverishment.

No one voted for partition. Actual violence and the threat of greater violence from the British and unionists created a gerrymandered political entity in which the Catholic/nationalist population (to use a convenient shorthand) was in a perpetual minority, bereft of the political muscle to counter the injustices facing us or to resolve our grievances through constitutional means.

Partition wept like an open wound through every decade of its imposition. The socialist republican leader James Connolly, writing in the *Irish Worker* (14 March 1914), had predicted that partition would cause 'a carnival of reaction North and South ... would destroy the oncoming unity of the Irish labour movement and paralyse all advanced movements'. Partition created two confessional, socially conservative political malformations. In the North, the bigotry, austerity and oppression of unionist misrule limited all and caused many to emigrate, thus offsetting the higher birth rate of the Catholic population. I was raised in England from the age of four after Dad crossed the water in search of work. This had later consequences. But I will start with those first remembered years of my Belfast infancy, for their influence on me and on my sense of self was a vital shaping factor in my development.

Mum was Philomena Donegan. She was pregnant when she married Dad, and they took a room in 29 Little May Street, where I was born in 1951. In those days, many young married couples had to lodge in neighbouring homes because of the overcrowding endemic to the poorest areas of the city, be they nationalist or unionist. Mum had grown up around the corner at 8 Catherine Street North, another small red-brick terrace on the edge of the Market district, beside the telephone exchange and close to the city hall. Due to the comparative grandeur of some Georgian features, a distinction was drawn between this side of the Market, the upper or city side, and the huddled backstreets behind Cromac Square, the lower or bridge side (given its proximity to the Albert Bridge). However, the houses in Little May Street were smaller than those in the once more fashionable Joy Street adjoining, where in the nineteenth century merchants and sea captains lodged, but still roomier, less pokey, than their counterparts across the square.

It was an area defined by and bustling with enterprise: the various markets, cattle yards, bakeries and the abattoir. Its huddle of streets housed some four thousand residents at that time. Although the housing conditions were grim, a constant refrain of locals was that nobody went hungry in the Market. A strong sense of community grew through an interdependence explicable in part by the common historical experience of existential threat. Memories of the anti-Catholic pogrom at the time of partition were a shared inheritance. Another tradition persisting to this day, despite much of the area now being unrecognisable due to the savagery of urban regeneration, is the insistence passed down that the district should be called the Market rather than pluralised, even though historically the area contained many distinct markets; for example, meat, poultry, cattle, variety and fish markets.

The Donegans originally hailed from the Mourne region of County Down, particularly from Castlewellan, Dundrum, Newcastle and surrounds. A previous generation had been farmers, but the land couldn't support them all and they gravitated to Belfast, particularly to the Market and Ormeau Road, where they became dealers and small traders, barbers, tailors and shoemakers. Others emigrated and made good lives in New York and New Jersey. Great-Grandmother Donegan and family eventually settled in the Market, where other Donegans and Robinsons had already established a presence, after she and the family were burned out of Craigmore Street in the nearby Donegall Pass during the aforementioned anti-Catholic pogrom in, I reckon, August 1920.

My father, John Magee, was originally from Osman Street in the Falls, yet another red-brick terrace in the city's nationalist heartland; identical in terms of the poor conditions they endured in subsequent moves the family made to nearby streets until they found a firmer foothold in Tyrone Street, Carrick Hill.

Magee is a common surname in the North and one shared by Protestants and Catholics – an advantage when a name might otherwise single you out for the other's intolerance. Dad insisted we had an ancestor, a radical dissenter (that is 'dissenter' in the Protestant sense) who supported the United Irishmen, the original Irish republicans who had vowed up on McArt's Fort, the giant basalt outcrop overlooking Belfast, to 'break the connection with England, the never-failing source of all our political evils'. A booklet much prized by Dad called *The Magees of Belfast and Dublin, Printers* refers, he claimed, to this family branch.* Recent interest stirred me to check whether Dad's belief in this link held substance, but thus far it remains uncorroborated. However, its veracity is of less consequence than that he felt pride in believing it. This was a proud tradition – an identity – one I effortlessly assimilated.

I've only managed to verify the already known paternal line, from Belfast street directories and censuses going back to the turn of the 1900s, to addresses in what today is referred to as the Lower Falls: Steele Court, Baker Street, Theodore Street, Plevna Street, Lincoln Street and Servia Street, all in a quarter-mile westerly radius of Divis Street at the bottom of the Falls Road. That generation were Catholics and living in some of the poorest overcrowded tenements on the edge of the rapidly burgeoning industrial city. There were further moves: Bombay Street; Ardoyne; even

---

*Francis Joseph Bigger, *The Magees of Belfast and Dublin, Printers* (1915).

a pre–World War II short residence in London. Both Mum and Dad were born in the old maternity hospital in Townsend Street.

Census returns reveal that women of the family worked in the nearby linen mills as flax spinners and reelers, the young men as flax dressers. In 1972, I briefly worked for a few nights as a cleaner in one of the surviving mills on the Falls, what is now the Conway Education Centre, and was struck by the dampness and cloying stench of the place and was moved at the thought of the poor women going back decades who had to endure those appalling conditions for lack of alternative employment, for little had changed. I knew neither of my grandmothers. They worked standing in water. Both died before I was born, of tuberculosis and of pneumonia.

When Dad sought work in England, Mum moved the fifty yards or so back to 8 Catherine Street North with me and her second born, my brother Sean, eighteen months younger than me. This is the point where my memory kicked in. My first datable memory is of Christmas 1953. I couldn't then have known how old I was. But because I can recall two Christmases prior to our move to England, I know I was two and a half at the time. I can pinpoint an earlier memory: Sean, then nine months, bleeding after getting hold of a fork. Not a serious incident but certainly my first memory of blood – I would have been two years and three months old. I remember the moment when my sister, Susan, was brought home from the maternity hospital for the first time. Dad was home, in a suit. All very strange. I was three.

Dad became a somewhat distant figure to me. Mum struggled, I now realise, and Grandad (Henry) Donegan filled the void of his absence. Growing up, I always felt closer to the Donegans.

Grandad Donegan's was one of four houses in that part of the street up to Hamilton Street. As a toddler I played on the polished red-and-cream patterned mosaic of our hallway stoop, which I'm told Henry tiled himself. On the corner of Hamilton Street was the Tyrone Cattle Yard. There was also a gated entrance to a big courtyard, accessible as well through each backyard, where an outside iron staircase led up to Jack Robinson's boxing gym, the St George's ABC. It had at one time been known as Robinson's Gym. Jack would call in to Grandad's daily. Known as Blind Jack, because of his poor eyesight, he was an uncle of my grandmother, Ellen (Lena). Jack had a son, Spike, a notable local boxer in the 1930s (and who, incidentally, later became a close friend of Joss). My uncle, Seamus Donegan, who at one time was himself an amateur boxer (although remembered to this day more for his prowess with the skipping rope), used to act as a guide for Jack. As a toddler I would scale the external cast-iron steps leading to the gym door only to be escorted back down as soon as my presence was noted by one of the hopeful contenders therein. Below the gym were stables for hire. I recall seeing circus ponies, still regaled in their fancy harnesses and plumage. Mum confirmed before her death a story she used to tell us as children that as a girl she had seen elephants being stabled there.

My maternal grandmother, Lena, is recorded as born in North Camp near Farnborough, England. Lena's mother, my great-grandmother, Annie Heaphy, was from Fermoy in Cork. Prior to partition, at one time Fermoy was the main British Army garrison in Ireland. She married a British soldier stationed there, George Robinson. Census returns confirm that the Robinsons were a peripatetic family, following the various postings of a regular soldier, although they put down firm roots in County Down and Belfast.

Directly across the street from Grandad's was the side of the Fiesta dance hall, a converted Nissen hut, which fronted Hamilton Street. I've heard that during World War II, American troops were billeted there. At weekends I would eventually fall asleep despite the music reverberating through its corrugated shell. Other sounds, and smells, came from the port and docks. The heavy odours of this busy dockland sprawl overwhelm any recall of the near-pastoral redolence of the place in England where Dad would later bring us to and where I was to spend most of my childhood, Norwich (which I will come to). Beside the Fiesta, to the corner of Little May Street, was a garage or tyre depot. There was straw in the street because cattle would frequently be driven through to one of the nearby stockyards. Front doors had to be closed to bar steers from entering. When one managed to slip the cordon, as it were, it had to be shooed through to the backyard of the house, for it was impossible to turn the beast in the narrow hall passage. Worse if the unfortunate critter mounted the stairs. I've a now faint vision of Aunt Bridget, Mum's twin, feigning comic hysterics (or maybe for real) at the top of the stairs as a bullock clambered up towards her. At night, from the pantry window I could make out work shirts and dungarees flapping on the line in the small backyard, but my

Uncle Harry, Mum's younger brother, would point and convince me the bogeyman was outside. A large tin bath hung on the wall facing the door to the yard. There was an outside toilet. When dark, a candle was needed. Rats were a problem. There was a house in Hamilton Street, still standing, where Mum would buy milk, that had a pair of 'Western' longhorns on display in the hallway.

Grandad Donegan was a shoemaker and an amateur photographer, and he worked from a room at the back of the house on the first landing where the stairs turned, or the turn room, as I've heard it called. The smell of shoe leather takes me back there, a toddler dwarfed by strange shaping and cutting machines. Mum says that her granny, who was a dealer, used to buy old shoes from one of the markets nearby for Henry to either repair or use as base material for making recycled footwear. In photos she comes across as a stern, matriarchal figure with strong features topped by steely white hair. A woman not to be messed with. Grandad slept in the parlour, his domain. Evidently, he was a busy amateur, and I can still recall the mystery of the rolls of drying film hanging from lines above. On Saturday nights the parlour hosted ceilidh sessions, and two of his brothers, Hughie and Jack, with friends, would play reels on fiddle, mandolin and accordion. I'm told Grandad played the fiddle, as did Jack, but I have no memory of this. I do have a faint recall of songs they would sing in turn: 'The Mountains of Mourne' and 'Courtin' in the Kitchen'. Most were old IRA men, although I am older now than they were back then. I would be brought into the parlour to say goodnight, indulged for a minute then ushered out so that the men could play in peace.

For Down people moving to Belfast for work, the Market was a natural first port of call. But they were Down people first and always. These ceilidh weekends helped to bind them to their roots. I used to gather the coloured porter-bottle tin tops left in the wake of these sessions and would play with them on the tiled porch. There always seemed to be music. Grandad had a gramophone, the centrepiece in our pre-television scullery, and dozens of old 78 rpm records, of Jimmy Shand, light opera, the hits of the day. Mario Lanza's recording of 'Drinking Song' from *The Student Prince* is the first song I can identify, a big hit following the release of the film in 1954.

These first memories, more a flurry of impressions, became indelibly set, strong to this day, and provided a rich seam to mine while growing up in

England, where I often sought comfort in recollection of the harmony and warmth I missed and felt wrenched away from and which I associated with Belfast, more specifically Grandad's. It was all to change when I was four, in July 1955, when Dad brought us across the water to Norwich, where he had found work. The family had no connections there. He had served an apprenticeship in the Harland and Wolff shipyards in Belfast as a steel plater, but at the end of his apprenticeship there was no job. After stints in the Barrow-in-Furness shipyards and on Humberside, he ventured south to Norwich and must have liked what he saw because, with his boss's help, he put a down payment on a house for us in Armes Street, a two-up, two-down terrace. While Dad was away working, Mum would take me to a nearby phone box to receive arranged calls with him. Grandad Donegan was scathing with her before our departure: 'Yer in for a quare gunk ... You'll never sit yer arse in England.' She also remembered him admonishing her by telling Bridget, 'Light a candle. She needs a prayer said for her.'

Mum was excited in the days before we left, which she tried to instil in me, but apparently I was resistant to the move, to the extent that I knew what was happening; and when Dad returned for us I had to be coaxed and consoled with promises of the new toys awaiting me in our new home. We left only days later. My last memory of leaving Belfast is of ships in the harbour; of seamen leaning along the entire length of the hull rail of a huge black ship.

Until I was six I assumed that the move to England was temporary. I would pester Mum about when we would be going home. I think she was in two minds and didn't herself fully regard Norwich as permanent. In the course of the next few years relatives would visit us, and there were occasional trips to Belfast, reinforcing the attachment. I would rehearse the all-day train journey in my head, Mum, Dad, me, Sean and Susan scrambling to make the 'boat train' connection at Leeds, Mum in a perpetual flap, Dad calm, organised. We would arrive at the Heysham ferry when it was dark, then the all-night, often rough crossing. Passengers would openly throw up in the passageways, and the stench of vomit and salt water was heavy on the nostrils. From our cabin window I remember seeing strings of lights way off in the blackness as the ferry passed the Isle of Man. Then the early-morning docking in Belfast. Back in Norwich, the distant sound of a goods train brought the journey to mind. I even imagined the unseen local train to be destined for the ferry. I prized a postcard from Grandad which depicted Belfast City Hall in all its Victorian splendour, and because of it being situated in spitting distance from the Market, a familiar sight to me even as a toddler. Belfast had come to assume mythic proportions.

Mum was a great storyteller, and as we – Sean, Susan and I – sat around the hearth, she would recreate wonderful events from her own childhood in the Market, even finding humour in recounting incidents from the Belfast Blitz of 1941, reinforcing my own sense of displacement and longing to be back there. Mum, then eleven, had known the horror of the bombing but turned it into a tale suitable for our amusement. For Sean and Susan, being younger, the ties back were not as tangible. Susan had only been ten months old when we left.

World War II had ended ten years previously, but there were still indicators in Norwich. The bombed-out shell of Heigham Methodist Chapel stood at the corner of Armes and Nelson Street. We – I and neighbouring kids – played among the rubble, open to the heavens. There were many prefabs close by, built as emergency housing for returning servicemen and their families. It was common to see men wearing black army berets. One who lived nearby made a precarious living from selling locally cut props for washing lines. We were that close to woodland. A schoolmate's father had a full German uniform, a war souvenir. Another, a service revolver. I found a gas mask in a collapsed air-raid shelter. But the post-war became the Cold War, and air-raid siren drills were quite common, a welcome disruption to the school routine. Another occasion for a day off was when the Canadian Mounties came to town, escorting the English queen's cavalcade past our school – St John the Baptist, Junior.

One day, Mum gathered us around in the kitchen – I was six. We were no longer to call her Mammy, the Belfast practice, and instead use Mum, like the English kids. Sean and Susan had much less of a problem with this change than I did. To me it sounded daft. Mammy was Mammy. Years later, returning to Belfast as a young adult, I would reflect that the Belfast usage now struck me as childish, especially from the lips of other adults who would still use Mammy when talking of or addressing their mothers. The generational markers were set different and you would hear guys in their early twenties still being referred to as 'wee lad' by those perhaps only a few years older. I have since wondered whether Mum's concern was less about her wanting us to assimilate than fear about some anti-Irish mood at the time. Had somebody remarked? The IRA's border campaign had begun in December 1956. The IRA had organised raids for weapons in England prior to the campaign. I asked Mum before her death whether news of events in Ireland had stirred up any prejudice, one of many questions to her while gathering this account. All she could recall was having had a row with a guy in the next street. He was a tax inspector. I remember him always wearing a bowler hat. I knew there had been an incident. I attended the same infant school as his son, Nelson Street Infants, a former army depot. We often played together in our adjoining streets. When Mum, feisty, went round to his house – over what, who knows, but I suspect that I was in the frame – he called her an Irish bastard. She 'pulled him through the kitchen window', and Dad later confronted him.

I was a nervous child; a bit hyperactive; a nail-biter. Now I can understand that this was due to the wrench from the loving security I had known in Belfast. I was displaced in England. My parents also seemed unhappy, particularly Mum. We were poor. It is one thing to be poor when everyone around you is poor; but compared to Belfast, Norwich seemed a relatively well-off place. They would argue at weekends, home from the pub, Mum screaming, 'Why did you bring me here?' She could be a real spitfire. Arguments were more often about money, even though Dad was a hard grafter, very rarely out of work. Every Saturday I would go with Mum to the pawnbroker to collect Dad's suit for the weekend. On Monday the suit would be returned to the pawnshop. From about nine it was my responsibility alone to do this weekly errand. Her wedding ring was another frequent pledge.

Dad worked nights and slept during the day, as he did through long stretches of our childhood – too tired then to take much of an interest in us once he was home from a hard shift and for the most part intolerant of our racket. As the oldest, and probably the rowdiest, I bore the brunt. We would see him shaving before leaving for work in the early evening, or on his return next morning while we were getting ready for school. He would listen to music on the then Third Programme, such as Tchaikovsky's *1812 Overture*, or a movement from a Mozart symphony, inculcating a much later realised love of classical music in me, though at the time I was resistant.

One Christmas stands out. I was ten. Dad had lost money. There's also some account that he was mugged in the town after a drink. There was nothing in for Christmas, no food, no presents, all preparations apparently having been planned for the last minute. On Christmas Eve, Mum said gently, 'Hang your stockings at the end of the bed anyway, we'll pray for a miracle.' Heaven mocked and the electric went out. There was no shilling for the meter. Mum had a solution: we would all go to midnight Mass, more in hope of borrowing money while there than to petition for divine intervention. Next morning our socks hung limply at the foot of the bed. Around midday, nuns from the Little Sisters of the Assumption came with a box of food. Many of the nuns were Irish – Teresa, Mildred, Rita. They were frequent pastoral visitors and very kind in the way they talked to me. We were invited to come by the convent later to select from a by then greatly depleted stock of donated toys. After I was sentenced in 1986, some twenty-five years after this time, nuns from the convent who remembered us were interviewed by the Norfolk press, one of whom, when asked for a comment, replied that she would pray for me.

The only times I can recall Dad ever having a close talk with me were when he and Mum would return from the pub at weekends. He would check on us. I looked forward to this. He would express his hopes that I would do well at school; if not, I might end up as a dustman. He set the bar. With an education I could be a journalist or a draughtsman. Vicarious aspirations, I later felt. These conversations developed in me a positive attitude towards drink. Adults seemed at their best and friendliest when drink was taken.

I never for a day forgot I was Irish. Nor was I allowed to forget. Someone or something would remind me. At home and in my head I was Pat, but everywhere else I got Paddy, which at best was patronising but at worst, I sensed, hostile. Half the kids at school (St John's being a Catholic junior) had Irish surnames, although they were second or third generation. The IRA versus the Black and Tans was a playground variant of cowboys and Indians. I was drawn to outsiders, becoming friends when seven, for example, with an American kid named Russell (his given name) whose father was an airman stationed in one of several American bases in the region. At nine I befriended an Australian girl, Peggy, new to the class. And yet I grew up watching British war movies: *The Dambusters, Reach for the Sky*. Contradictions piled up. Being born in Ireland marked a difference. I felt this clear demarcation between me and my classmates. I was stubbornly Irish. I was bullied. I could also be a bully, although more sinned against than sinner (later, as a teenager, I developed an aversion to violence out of shame and regret, a convert to pacifism, then a fashionable creed because of Vietnam and the inspiration of Martin Luther King).

However, my sense of Irishness was underinformed. I recall a music lesson at school. The class was asked to identify the country of origin of various national anthems from an LP. I would have been about twelve and was asked to single out the Irish anthem. I can't recall having ever heard, or heard of, *'Amhrán na bhFiann'* ('The Soldiers' Song'). I chose the Welsh anthem, 'Land of My Fathers', thinking it the more melodic, conforming to an idea of Irishness I'd somehow garnered. Mum used to recite prayers in Gaelic: *'In ainm n'Athair . . .'* ('In the name of the Father . . .'). Being an Irish Catholic was an extension of this sense of difference. Encouraged by my parents, I became an altar boy. I sang in the church choir, served at Mass before school and twice on Sundays. Mum thought it would bring us luck. We went to Mass on Sundays as a family. Mum would also regularly attend novena services. If anything, I think Dad was even more devout. Later, when I was about twelve, I began to have doubts and dropped out of the choir and from serving as an altar boy, a decision that Mum claimed led to much bad luck for us as a family, although I can remember precious little good luck before then. Before turning thirteen I was a fully fledged and priggish atheist, given to arguing against religion with teachers, and to shock the young Irish priest Mum invited round to talk some sense into me.

I had been a late developer at school, hyperactive in the classroom, what today may have been diagnosed as some form of attention deficit disorder. I learned to read and write at seven, two years after everyone else in my class, practicing by myself, writing out simple sentences by rote and checking for an elusive spelling, pestering Mum by shouting downstairs from the landing. I was in the B stream, marked for failure. A new teacher, Miss Rudden, recognised some spark of wit in me and encouraged me to read more. Then the 11-plus was upon us. I passed the first part, the only child in the class to do so – much to the amazement of Mr Clark, who taught Class A, for some of his boys had also failed. Then the day of the second paper arrived. Afterwards Mum asked me how it had gone. I thought I had done well. I told her about one question I couldn't answer. What was an eighth of one pound sterling? Mum tutted at my foolishness at not recognising the fractional value of a half-crown, eight to the pound in the old money. Fractions had never been explained to Class B. I failed. Failing meant a choice between two schools. At the state secondary school (in those pre-comprehensive days) I might still get into the O-level stream. But that was a 'Protestant school'. The Catholic secondary modern could offer only CSEs, but the headmaster (Miss Rudden's father, incidentally) persuaded Dad that these were as good. By thirteen I couldn't see the point, although I can't put it all down to having failed the 11-plus.

The two subjects at school at which I seemed to do well were English and History – the History as taught of English kings and queens, of Hastings and Waterloo, of empire. But some of that turgid rendering did inspire me to read beyond the received account and to seek a wider understanding. I loved books. My favourite retreats were the main library in Norwich and a nearby rickety bookshop, where I became aware of, if not more informed about, broader or alternative views.

*   *   *

If you skip my parents' generation, relatives on both sides of the family had been active Irish republicans in the 1920s. I knew this but cannot pinpoint how I knew. Obviously, there was talk, to which I wasn't privy but which I somehow absorbed. I had a hazy notion that Joss Magee had been imprisoned in Crumlin Road Prison (the Crum) and interned on the prison ship *Argenta*, anchored in Belfast Lough near Larne, because of his involvement with the anti-Treaty IRA in Belfast. His cousin, Harry Magee, was held there too. Grandad Donegan had also been involved. His brothers, Hugh and Jack, were interned on the *Argenta* as well. Dad was proud of the fact that his mother, Susan, had carried guns under her shawl during the Belfast pogroms. Mum's mother had similarly contributed to the defence of the Market. But that background never got much of an airing while I was growing up. I knew of it, but this awareness carried little appreciable purchase and I bore no pressure to think in terms of a family tradition. There was much I wasn't told. I only learned quite recently about the Donegans having to flee their home during the pogroms. These horrors were never mentioned, or certainly not in front of the children. Was this to spare us the burden of bitterness? Irish history seeped into my consciousness. At school, aged twelve, when listening to a teacher's recital of the Louis MacNeice poem 'Carrickfergus', my ears pricked up at a reference to a prison hulk – 'Somewhere on the lough was a prison ship for Germans/A cage across their sight' – I thought of the *Argenta*.

If anything, I was more aware that Joss had served in the British Army before joining the IRA. As already mentioned, I share the same name as his older brother, Patrick Joseph, who was killed instantly when a shell he was stacking exploded while he was serving with the Royal Irish Fusiliers in France on 13 December 1916. He is buried in the St Pol British Cemetery in St Pol-sur-Ternoise, France. He was nineteen. I have a feeling that Joss may have enlisted because of his death. Then again, he might have enlisted to escape the poverty of Belfast – a form of economic conscription. Or perhaps he bought into the Redmond pro-conscription line, as thousands of young men did, that Britain would honour Home Rule in Ireland, deferred until the war was over. I can only imagine his mother's horror at his enlistment so soon after losing her eldest son (his father died in 1909). And the huge conflict of affiliation that many of that generation must have endured; three of my great-uncles were killed during the Great War: Patrick Joseph, as mentioned, but Joss's future wife, Susan Steenson, lost her younger brother in May 1915 – Charles, who died in action in the Fromelles region; an older brother, Thomas, also served on the Western Front; another great-uncle, John Robinson, also died in France; and a further two uncles served in France. Joss and Susan had that loss in common. His mother, despite the loss of Patrick, supported him during his IRA involvement. This is a common heritage, shared across the divides.

As I was his oldest grandson, Joss talked to me more of his past, but I didn't feel I was being burdened with an old wound, or a chalice being passed down. On one of his visits to Norwich, he used marbles to illustrate various military manoeuvres on our front room floor; how to outflank or sneak up behind the enemy. He referred to his time in the British Army, never his days in the IRA. This reluctance of republican veterans to talk about their roles in the struggle is something I've encountered throughout my own involvement. There have been occasions when I might have asked someone of Joss's generation, had they known him, but held back from doing so, so strong was this culture of silence. It just wasn't done. The sense of siege solidarity was deep laid. I do recall one piece of advice from him: never get a tattoo. Joss's knuckles were tattooed (all my life imagining 'Love' and 'Hate'; but not so, for apparently he had 'SUSAN' squeezed into the space more usually allowed for four letters). A tattoo made you easily identifiable. The voice of experience but a strange warning to a ten-year-old. Was I being somehow prepared? I've learned since that this was a common piece of wisdom passed down from the 1920s and 1930s. These days the lack of a tattoo might more readily set you apart.

Recently I've begun to research Joss's military involvement, both in the IRA and in the British Army. A cousin in Australia sent me a typed copy of a testimonial letter, dated 2 February 1919, dictated, it seems, by Joss's commanding officer while he was serving as a clerk at battalion HQ in northern France:

For over a year Lcpl. J. Magee, has worked as a clerk at Battn. Headquarters. And during that period his work and conduct has been excellent and reliable.

In appearance he has always been clean and smart.

He has a good knowledge of Office Routine which should be a good basis for similar work in civil life, after further training and experience he will develop into a first class Clerk. And also into a man any employer will confidently place in trust.

[Signed] W. J. Gordon, Col. DSC, 12th R. Irish Rifles, FRANCE [sic].

There is no record extant to prove that Joss had ever reached the dizzying rank of lance corporal. Perhaps he embellished, as many a CV is today. However, instead of leaving the Royal Irish Rifles and returning to civilian life, after the Great War he transferred to the Connaught Rangers. He served in the Punjab and played some role in the Connaught Rangers mutiny in 1920, leading to the forfeiture of his two service medals. The mutiny was sparked when the squaddies, with few exceptions Irish, started receiving letters from home detailing Black and Tan atrocities there. The Rangers were in India defending the British Empire and that same Empire was killing and torturing Irish people in their own land. The protest was initially peaceful. They raised the Irish tricolour. The mutiny spread to a neighbouring encampment and at its height nearly three hundred men were involved. In ensuing developments two of the mutineers were shot dead. One, Private James Daly, was executed. About another eighty received various sentences of imprisonment. Joss doesn't appear to have been among the main mutineers. Apart from the forfeiture of his service medals, his punishment was limited to four weeks in detention, although you would think he personally scaled the flagpole to raise the green, white and orange the way the story was handed down. So, there was evident family pride at his role, which I had seamlessly gathered as part of my heritage.

After India, Joss returned to a Belfast in the throes of major upheaval – the expulsion of Catholics from the shipyards, the rampages of unionist murder gangs – the Belfast pogrom. Joss joined the anti-Treaty IRA, or the Irregulars as they were known to supporters of the Treaty. The Anglo-Irish Treaty (December 1921) had effectively partitioned Ireland, split the IRA and led to the Civil War. While still only twenty-one, in August 1922, Joss was one of a group of about thirty men lifted during a raid on an alleged meeting of the IRA's C Company in Currie Street Hall in the Lower Falls, Belfast. Then in September 1922, he was interned for about twenty months. I obtained a copy of his internment file from the old Public Record Office in Belfast. He was 'believed to hold a prominent rank'. His occupation was listed as an apprentice fitter. Several alleged offences for which he was a suspect were also listed, ranging from murder to armed robbery. The report stated that 'witnesses failed to identify him at a parade just held' but that he was 'still a suspect'. He was also described as 'one of the worst characters in the city'. It is difficult to imagine a higher accolade from an RUC inspector, worth more than any forfeited medal. I also discovered that Joss and Susan were married at Larne Workhouse Camp, part of the internment administrative fabric, while he was interned. She gave birth to a stillborn child within days, a boy – Patrick. Joss's application for a compassionate visit is dutifully recorded. Then the officious refusal before it was subsequently overturned and allowed. He eventually 'signed out' of internment. Among republicans, to do so was considered shameful: a breach of solidarity. However, this followed a series of recorded refusals to do so. I believe he eventually conceded to the signing because of concern for Susan's health. She was extremely frail from the trauma of losing the baby. Susan died in 1947, aged 49, of consumption.

You do wonder about a possible succession of events following his CO's letter of recommendation, written when Joss was eighteen, to the RUC's opinion of him as a 'worst character', by which time he was still only twenty-one. However, I think it more likely no moment of conversion occurred, marking a turn from dutiful soldier to 'murderer', and that he was honourable in both spheres. He was being perceived through the distorting prism of imperialism. It would be easy to conclude that a transition occurred during his experience as a foot soldier at an outpost of the British Raj. Perhaps, too, his imaginings of what was happening in his own country to his own people had stirred some perception of an older injustice.

2

The Politics of Place

In August 1964, when I was thirteen, Mum brought me, Geraldine, aged two, and Malachy, the youngest then at ten months, with her to Belfast. Grandad Donegan was dying of cancer. I now know it was a hinge moment in my life; one opening a portal. We had been living in England for nine years. If I hadn't returned at that age, if the time gap between Norwich and my earliest memories had further widened, arguably Ireland's hold on my affection may have loosened. Ireland seemed to embody all that was positive – in sharp distinction to the estrangement I felt as a child growing up in England. My life could have taken an utterly different trajectory. Instead, I was reforged by the return.

When Mum got the telegram she was inconsolable. Dad was quickly present. High-strung, she turned almost hysterical in her initial grief at the terrible news. Dad just sorted out what needed to be done. Her father hadn't long to live. Grandad would be dead within weeks, maybe less. Mum would take the Heysham ferry back to Belfast. As the eldest, I would be there to help her with the youngest because he couldn't take time off work. Sean and Sue, eleven and nine respectively, drew the short straws, for they would have to fend for themselves while Dad was at work. These arrangements were quickly sorted out around me.

As grave as our purpose for being back in Belfast, from my first early-morning sighting of the port and during the taxi ride to Grandad's, happy associations flooded back. I knew with crystal surety that here was where I belonged: the Market, with the broad embrace of its cramped terraces; its edgy bustle and bakery aromas; even its abattoir smells of cowhide and blood.

Catherine Street North was smaller now than my recall of it. So was Number 8. I had imagined it much bigger than the house in Norwich. Relatives crowded the scullery. We were welcomed in with hushed greetings, for Grandad's parlour was in earshot along the hall and he was resting.

Mum had to see him – to sit alone with him, if only for a moment, while I stayed minding Geraldine and Malachy in his buggy, waiting my turn.

Bedridden, Grandad looked shrivelled, weighing less than six stone. Part of me recoiled at seeing him like that, the first time I had seen someone terminally ill. Cancer of the spine. Through the tiredness, he recognised me, or acknowledged somehow his memory of me. We heard from Mary Burns, his second wife, that he slept most of the time, although what drugs could there have been then? As those first days mounted, seeing him became a duty. I would struggle to find something to say to this man who had been a father when Dad was away in England.

That first day and in the following weeks, I got to meet cousins, aunts and uncles, who would visit him then sit in the back kitchen and talk with Mum. I formed a crush for my cousin Kate. Unreciprocated, although that did not spare her from being teased with me in equal measure. I also got to meet some of the neighbourhood kids, of various ages, and helped them to collect bonfire material for the big mid-August Feast of the Assumption, the Catholic dedication to the Virgin Mary, an annual ritual (only eight years later to be eclipsed by the first anniversary commemorating the introduction of internment). I could not take it seriously, the devotional aspect. And neither did the kids. Just an excuse for all the associated mischief, for not all the requisite combustibles were volunteered. But the sense of being a part of this community rite was infectious. It clearly marked who they, and now *we*, were. For some time I had rejected the Catholicism of my parents and religion in general, matching an earlier disillusionment with the tooth fairy. I had thought of myself, since twelve, as an atheist, but in Belfast that August I reined in that priggish certainty for the sake of inclusion. To all outward intent I had reverted. To be a Catholic in Belfast was to be part of something intangibly strong. The feeling of belonging, of being accepted, was highly seductive. All in the first week. Now I look back with much shame and regret that I did not instead spend more time with Grandad. But I recoiled from seeing him so small and emaciated. I have never since been good around illness.

Belfast was so different. This was the first time that I registered the politics of the place, noting with some amazement that policemen (the RUC), or 'Peelers', all carried holstered weapons and wore military-style kepis, like American cops on TV and unlike British bobbies in their black beehive helmets. I remember excitedly telling mates at school about this on my return to England. Norwich seemed colourless in comparison, with its recently issued panda cars.

I also visited my other grandad, Joss Magee. He had moved from Belfast to a ground-floor pensioners' flat in the Diamond, Rathcoole, then a mixed estate – although the majority were Protestant – because the old national-ist enclave of Carrick Hill was being pulled down to be replaced by Unity Flats, part of a plan to rid the city of its then-worst slums. The bus journey along the Shore Road to Rathcoole afforded the dual splendour of Belfast Lough below on the right and Cave Hill a craned neck to the left. Quite a sight, undeveloped even now.

I can see him now as he was then, a half a century ago, braces over long johns, duncher worn low on his brow so that he had to hold his head high to see from under, like a miniature sergeant major. His thumbs were tucked in the waistband where his braces were attached. I stood beside him in the doorway, small myself then as now but as tall as him then, the eldest grandson, over from England. A loyalist flute band was marching through the estate. It was the fag-end of the marching season. 'Look at those dirty Orange bastards,' he delivered through clenched teeth. I was shocked. As much for his vehemence as for the meaning he was trying to impart to me. Dad had brought us up to believe that bigotry was ugly and bigots ignorant. Mum had no time for Joss. She referred to him as 'Bullet Brain', alluding, I sensed, to more than his baldness. To me he was Magwitch, straight out of David Lean's 1946 film adaptation of *Great Expectations*. I recall so little that Joss ever said to me, another generational matter of deep regret, with too much that must now go unanswered. All blunt but perversely instructional, the little he imparted has stuck, despite my rejection of its negativity, for I could think for myself. I can reason now that Joss distinguished between the late-eighteenth-century Protestant radicals of the United Irishmen and the loyalism of the flute bands, as evidenced by Dad's retention of *The Magees of Belfast*, mentioned at the end of chapter one.

Grandad Donegan died in October 1964. The consensus aired was that we were all witness to a minor miracle at his defiance of medical expecta-tions. Mum and I had to return to Norwich in September and therefore were not present for his last struggle with the inevitable. That was hard on Mum. She didn't want to leave him. All the Donegans had expected his death to be weeks sooner. I carried this extra burden of grief at having to leave Belfast. I felt torn from its arms. I cried as the ferry pulled away from the dock. But the money had run out. Dad had his work obligations. There was now no one to mind Sean and Susan. I had to go back to school. The autumn term had commenced already.

Within days of my being back in England, Belfast was all over the news. Two days of violent street disturbances broke out there. It was the run-up to the October 1964 general election, the year Labour got in under Harold Wilson, signalling change, modernity. But Belfast was experiencing a throwback in the shape of a firebrand evangelical preacher, the Reverend Ian Paisley, who had demanded that the RUC remove a tricolour (the green, white and orange of the Irish national flag, ironically signalling peace between the two main politico-cultural traditions) from a Sinn Fein election office window. It was an offence to display the Irish tricolour under the Flags and Emblems Act (1954). When nationalists protested its removal, the resulting riots led to over a hundred people being injured. Belfast made the news every night through the duration of what were termed the Divis Street (or Tricolour) Riots. Paisley's brand of sectarianism would lead to worse within a few short years. Another two years were to pass before Belfast again poured into my consciousness, making headlines when a recently resurrected loyalist paramilitary group, the Ulster Volunteer Force (UVF), murdered a young Catholic barman, Peter Ward, on the Shankill Road. That same year, Paisley tried to force an Orange march through the Market. Then things seemed to slip the attention of the press, or went largely unreported by the British media, for there were other, similarly inspired attacks from the UVF directed at the imaginary or exaggerated threat of Irish republicanism, the fear of which historically had always translated as attacks on the Catholic/nationalist population. The timing was all the more potent given that it was 1966, the fiftieth anniversary of the Easter Rising. The sectarian topography was getting a fresh coat of red, white and blue. The markers were there plain to see in the graffiti of the moment: 'No Surrender.' 'Fuck the Pope.' 'KAT' (kill all Taigs). Little of this seemed visible to the rest of the world. But my interest was stirred each time Belfast happened to grab a headline. It is an oddly vertiginous sensation to grasp now that in a mere six years after returning to England I would be back in Belfast, and soon after in the thick of it.

Dad also followed unfolding events. The evening news was sacred in our house and he would give a running commentary, talking to the set. He particularly admired the Irish politician and writer Conor Cruise O'Brien and felt pride in seeing how the intellectual O'Brien coped in a TV discussion of the looming crisis in the North. Dad was a staunch British Labour Party supporter, a trade unionist (a member of the boilermakers' union) and, for a short while, a shop steward. He read the *Daily Herald*, which morphed into *The Sun* (prior to its lurch to the right), the pre-Murdoch *Sunday Times* and the *New Statesman*. His loathing of bigotry and sectarianism was due, I think, to his own experiences growing up in Belfast and, perhaps, his time in the shipyards. Mum reckoned that most of his mates in those days, however, were Protestant.

Dad was always very calm, and careful with words: he took time to explain what he meant, epitomised tolerance and was regarded by most who ever knew him as being a well of good sense. Neighbours would call to the house to seek his advice, about benefits or how to solve this or that problem. He was also strong-minded; even stubborn. When a new neighbour, an off-duty policeman, knocked on our door presenting Dad with a petition of complaint about another neighbour's dog, he refused to sign. He offered no explanation, saying after that the petitioning neighbour was a busybody and a 'slabber'. Some old-school rule about how not to handle a nuisance neighbour was being invoked. Joss was the same by all accounts: living by his own credo; knowing the system; his opinion sought – though that's hard to tally with my recollection of him in Rathcoole and his gnarly sectarian observation.

I must have been quite opinionated because when I was still thirteen I made the provocative statement to Dad that I was a communist and indeed was reading what I could get hold of about Marxism, encouraged in this by a couple of the lads I knocked about with. I've lost sight of what response I intended to provoke; letting him know I could think for myself, I suppose. All he said was, 'you should read James Connolly', the only real indication from him of any interest in Irish history. However, much later he revealed that as a child he had known Tom Williams, an IRA volunteer executed in 1942. Apparently, Tom used to be entrusted to take Dad when

he was a boy to Mass, presumably to nearby Clonard Monastery. Dad
then lived around the corner in Bombay Street, one of many moves the
family made. The street would become a byword for intolerance when in
1969 it was gutted by an Orange mob. Dad told of one time when Tom
came to the rescue. He had dropped the house key down a grating and was
unable to reach it. Luckily Tom retrieved the key and saved the day, for
Joss was a stern father. Dad recalled these memories after we listened to a
rendering of a ballad dedicated to Tom. I did not fully realise the impact of
Tom Williams's execution on Dad until decades later when I was among
the thousands who followed Tom's coffin to Milltown Cemetery during
the re-interment of 2000. I doubt if more than a very few people outside
of Belfast have heard of Tom Williams, but on that day I experienced a
truly mass intergenerational ownership of loss. It seemed to grip the entire
nationalist population as if every family had a personal account of Tom. A
common, inherited wound. But of course, and regrettably, it was an exclu-
sively Irish nationalist veneration, and more evidence, again regrettably, of
divided communal memory.

I didn't read Connolly then (and indeed did not until my return to
Belfast, post-internment), although interested in history, curious enough
to seek books about Ireland from the recently opened Norwich Central
Library. As mentioned in the previous chapter, it became a refuge, my
favourite space, whether after school or skipping school or at weekends.
The library prized an extensive collection of Americana, donated by the
US Air Force, regionally stationed, including original accounts by early
American colonists of their struggles against the 'redskins'. Armed with
Mum's library card, I foraged extensively through all the library's many
sections for anything relating to Ireland and Irish history – curiously,
though, finding nothing on the shelves about settlers closer to home and
their run-ins with the native Irish, known as the plantation of Ulster. All
I can recall borrowing was the memoir of a former British Army officer's
involvement in the Black and Tans. His testimony left me confused, never
quite certain who was who, what was what, mixing the good and the bad
guys, believing then there ought to be an easy separation of the two.

I was an avid reader then, and not only of history. One book from
school held a particular significance: George Orwell's dystopian classic
1984, written in 1948 and set thirty-six years in the future. I read it, after

reading his other alarm cry against tyranny, *Animal Farm*, when I was about fourteen, and when 1984 seemed a remotely distant future. It was a significant book for me at a time when I was becoming increasingly aware of the adult world. How could I have known of the future personal significance of that prophecy-burdened year!

My troubles, my rebelliousness, began before I turned fourteen. In fact, from my return to Norwich I always seemed to be in trouble: with my parents, with teachers, with anyone in authority. That thirteen is a difficult age is a commonplace. I've witnessed the mood swings of my own sons as they mutated into teenagers. My unsettling, moody rebellion must have been hard for all, especially at home. From this point in time I was always in some scrape or another. I knocked about the streets instead of school. So, alienation and resentment aplenty. A rebel in search of a cause? Bolshie, certainly. I grew my hair long. I spent a meagre fortune on studs for a plastic biker jacket. My truancy often lasted for weeks – leaving the house each morning but then wandering the streets, in and out of the shops in town, spending hours in the library or killing time in parks, weather permitting, before returning home acting as if I had been diligently at my desk. Of course, the school would contact my parents. I would go back for a week or so, and then the truancy would resume. Ultimately, Dad took a hard line, dragging me into the barber's next door to our house and ordering, to my mortification, a short, back and sides. He then took me back to school, where to that point I had had the longest hair among its male register. An early teenage humiliation.

During another bout of truancy, I fell in with a bunch of lads, older teenagers. We fancied ourselves a gang, eager for trouble. As the youngest I could be relied upon to exceed their worst excesses in order to prove myself worthy of acceptance. The gang were involved in petty crime, mostly shoplifting, vandalism; mischief, in truth. Eventually, after a row with Dad, I left home (a repeat offender in that regard), I've no clue what over, and hid out with several of these new friends. This was shortly before I turned fifteen. Within a fortnight or so I was lifted by the police for a break-in at a small butcher's equipment business, where one of the gang had worked and where he claimed cash would be found in the office. Dad was summoned to the police station. I was charged and a date was set for a juvenile court appearance. I was subsequently sent to a remand centre for assessment. Eventually the court decided to put me on two years' probation, the first year of which was to be spent at a probation hostel (in London, it transpired) once arrangements had been made, but in the meanwhile I was allowed to return home.

I remember Dad's shame at the court sitting. The magistrate had as good as accused him of having lost control over me. Hard to argue otherwise. But in the weeks before the move to London, I seemed to get on better with him. I am ashamed now that I caused him a moment's self-doubt. He used to say, in rare moments when I listened, that one day I would understand. Destined then to repeat his mistakes, I now do understand.

This was 1966, the year England won the World Cup. As a family, we watched the matches every single night, clustered on the sofa and chairs in front of the television, a scene repeated in millions of homes as the country was caught up in euphoric support for its national team. We cheered England like the rest. I moved to the hostel in late September. A court-appointed probation officer drove me to London. Somewhere past Newmarket, we had to stop on the verge so that I could be sick. This was my very first lengthy car journey.

St Vincent's Probation Hostel in Brockley, south-east London, looked after about sixteen young offenders. Lads from fifteen to seventeen. I stayed about two weeks short of the allotted year. The person in charge was a former British Army colonel, Grant, who had served in India, a decent enough spud, although we had our disagreements, particularly concerning religion and politics. He was a staunch Conservative supporter and a Catholic. I felt the need to be frank about my atheism and socialist leanings. A pattern here, flexing my bolshie independence. He arranged for the parish priest to talk to me (as Mum had, previously), who grew quite exasperated at my refusal to see things as he saw them. I've learned since that Grant in accepting the job had insisted on taking only boys with learning difficulties or of low IQ – an abbreviation peculiar to the time was used: ESN (educationally subnormal). Easier to manage, I guess. On paper I must have fitted the profile. As mentioned, I had as good as quit school at thirteen. I appeared to be undernourished. Small for my age – I was around five feet and two inches at fifteen years old.

St Vincent's, or perhaps the probation service, had an arrangement with a number of factories in South London willing to employ its delinquent charges. My first job was as a teaboy in a factory off the Old Kent Road, which manufactured tubular steel furniture. I would take orders for sandwiches, tea and coffee and place bets at the local bookmaker. Not tied to the factory floor, my responsibilities took me out and about the district, visiting local cafes, corner shops and the bookies. The area, with its malt brewery and derelict canals, stirred an odour memory of the Belfast docks from childhood. I loved London. My first pay packet contained about £2 and 15 shillings, although within a few weeks this rose to £6 or more with Saturday morning overtime, which I was required to hand over to the hostel. I also earned tips which, undeclared, I kept. At weekends the hostel boys were permitted out until ten p.m. We could spend up to 21 shillings (fourteen on the Saturday, if memory serves, and the remainder on Sunday); any remaining money was put in our personal savings accounts. I often had more money than the others because of the tips. I was quite popular, and I honestly don't attribute this merely to the weight, in those pre-decimal days, of old change in my pockets. A pint of bitter cost 2 shillings. Despite being fifteen, and although small for my age, I used to have no problem getting served in pubs and would often be asked to order the drinks for some of the older boys. I must have projected a certain confidence, of which I was totally unaware back then.

Many of the factory workforce were either Irish or West Indian. Signs could still be seen in B&B windows around south London saying 'No Irish, No Blacks, No Dogs'. Returning to the hostel one evening I saw two young Irish navvies pass a West Indian woman and her child, turn and spit at the mother. I will never forget seeing the young boy, who couldn't have been much more than six, look up at the men, then at his mother. I am still shocked by that. Such shame, too, that the culprits were Irish. Where did I get the ridiculous notion of progress – that our generation was more enlightened and tolerant on a range of issues?

When I was fifteen I knew all the things I was for and against. Racism became the thing I hated most. I tried to befriend a young black guy who had recently started at the factory, a year or two older than me, and would engage him in conversation about the need for racial harmony. I have always been drawn to outsiders. This is traceable back to when at junior school I befriended those kids new to the class, like Russell and Peggy (mentioned in the preceding chapter), alone in the playground, who I identified with because of my own insecurities as a stranger – Irish; with an accent; poor. I was already empathetic to difference. I soon realised that he was smarter, better read than me, and knew something of Irish history. I was made to feel naive. I started to read more. Another workmate, a Glaswegian of Irish extraction, lent me a book, Robert Tressell's *The Ragged-Trousered Philanthropists*, which left a huge impression. I have heard and read of so many others since who were similarly influenced by that book; more recently, Jeremy Corbyn, for example, has named it as his favourite.

While at St Vincent's I was also quite often drawn into silly pranks and acts of delinquency with some of the other boys. Pathetically eager to belong. However, I also gained a fuller sense that I could think on my feet in an awkward situation (usually of my making, for I had a track record). To give one instance, I recall an incident involving the stealing of a Land Rover with two others from the hostel, both older – what today would be called joyriding. We drove the stolen vehicle to the West End and, on the way back, were pursued by a police car, eventually abandoning the Land Rover in a yard in Southwark, the police directly on our tail. My two mates jumped a wall which I was unable to scale, leaving me cornered in the yard, hiding under a van. The police were out of their vehicle, obstructing the only exit. I could hear them reporting in. They seemed to think all the occupants of the stolen vehicle either had escaped or were trapped. Next they would check out the yard. This didn't look good. I took my one chance to creep right past their backs as they waited for, I presumed, instruction. My size, and the darkness, helped. Just the sort of stunt that might convince you that you could get away with anything if you only kept your nerve. There were many such incidents. All daft. I did learn a powerful life lesson, though: never panic; hold your nerve and examine the options. What I had failed to figure out was how not to get myself into such scrapes.

Grant's wife and the other staff were excellent people (except for one, a temp, who the ex-colonel got rid of when he discovered him reading Bible tracts in the dormitory to one of the new boys – at least that was the received account), not that that was how we necessarily saw our carers then. Our freedom was curtailed and we deemed any figure of authority culpable. One of the staff, Anthony Kendall, never fitted the authoritarian groove. Perhaps recognising that I didn't quite measure down to Grant's low criteria, he would engage in conversations about politics and music. On a day out from the hostel, he introduced me to his family. They lived in a fashionable part of London (Kensington, I think). I was made to feel very welcome. His father, a former business executive with a headmasterly demeanour, set me 'homework' – O-level standard questions on Shakespeare's *Julius Caesar* – which on completion he read, annotating favourably. It is difficult to overestimate the impact of that positive assessment after my 11-plus failure, consequent low esteem and loathing of school.

After my year in London I returned to my parents' house in Norwich. I did not want to return there. I wanted to stay on in London and had an option of boarding with some workmates, but I was still on probation and the hostel wouldn't permit this, or rather the colonel objected – rightly, I must now concede. I couldn't persuade him that at sixteen I knew how to look after myself. But I resented having to leave London. Norwich held no attraction, but I got on well enough with my family from this point.

Just prior to my return to Norwich, Joss died. He was sixty-seven; I was sixteen. I had never known my grandmothers, Ellen Donegan and Susan Steenson. Both had died relatively young, before I was born. Now Joss, the last of that generation, was gone. So much had happened in those mere three years since Grandad Donegan had died. Time is experienced at a distinctly different pace when you are still a child. At about my age Joss would have heard of the death of his older brother, Patrick, in Flanders. Within a year he would enlist in the Royal Irish Rifles. I had no such depth of consciousness then. Belfast had been eclipsed by all the attendant distractions of youth. It was 1967. The Summer of Love. Back in Norwich, I soon adapted, making new friends easily enough, becoming totally immersed in being that most self-engrossed creature, a teenager – music, girls, trying hard to belong – and like all at that age I had a distorted take on time, which stretched out ahead into infinite possibilities. Painfully ordinary, wanting only to be a part of what was happening, following the bands. Quite literally, for among the acts I saw live was Jimi Hendrix, playing in October that year in a parochial hall in East Dereham, outside Norwich.

In the thick of all this innocence I found time for further mischief, getting involved in a stupid, spur-of-the-moment prank of stealing a motorcycle. I was caught, as were the others involved in the escapade, but unlike them I had 'previous' and was accordingly sent, three weeks short of seventeen, to what was then termed a Catholic senior approved school.

The school, St John's, Apethorpe Hall (long since closed under a cloud), was situated in Northamptonshire and had an illustrious history dating back to the fifteenth century. It was a major country house, a fine example of Jacobean architecture. Today it's an English Heritage property and is referred to as a palace. Kings have lodged there. During my fifteen-month incumbency, it hosted about seventy fellow inmates, aged from fifteen to eighteen and, like me, troubled – kids from London, Birmingham, Nottingham, Newcastle-upon-Tyne, some of whom, I became aware, had abusive backgrounds. About a quarter of them wet the bed. Many were Irish or of Irish descent. We slept in dormitories that once hosted royal hunting parties. We didn't leave the premises or grounds unless under supervision, as in, for example, an organised outing or field trip.

St John's provided opportunities to learn. We had the choice between several trade shops: painting and decorating, motor mechanics, carpentry, gardening, electrician. I picked the last of these, believing it the easiest in terms of effort required, but later decided on an alternative option on the basis that it offered the best opportunity to skive: the classroom. As well as basic writing and arithmetic, we could study for O-levels. I showed some talent for drawing. I had always liked to draw. Mum was good too. I was encouraged by one of the masters, an artist himself, a great guy called Anton, of Italian stock, to believe I had the necessary talent then to get into art school, for which the basic entry requirement was five O-levels, which I duly got with a minimum of effort, more I admit spurred on in the mistaken belief that the achievement would lead to earlier release. In the end, all I managed to knock off the remaining time was a mere two weeks and, while still under probation, I was freed to return to my parents in Norwich in early August 1969 and to start at art school there in September. I was eighteen.

Before the month was out, Derry's Bogside erupted and Belfast responded, in part to draw off RUC and B Specials (a special constabulary drawn from the Protestant community) away from besieged Bogsiders. I remember the news coverage of British troops being deployed on the streets. Their presence seemed a positive development and a victory of sorts for beleaguered Catholics, who made tea for these saviours. Mum shared my optimism but Dad commented, with impressive foresight, that once in they would be there for a long time. A wisdom passed down? It was reported, however, in those early days, that a worse crisis, and perhaps a civil war, was averted. I was subsequently to learn that this wasn't a view shared universally. From the perspective of some on the ground in Belfast, there was anger at the arrival onto the streets of British troops. The Bogside and other nationalist areas had withstood all that the RUC and Orange mobs could inflict. Now the British state was directly propping up its Orange statelet. And there were long memories and a culture of past resistance to oil the growing slide into conflict. What the Brits would wreak on nationalist areas of the six counties soon after their arrival in August 1969 they had done to our communities in the 1920s, and to many other poor people in their crimes of empire. Dad seemed to have inherited a sense of this shared memory of grievance, loss and of history being repeated.

Although I was interested in these developments, my attention soon refocused on starting at Norwich School of Art (as it was then), attracted more to the idea of being an art student than of studying art. But then it was the era of Hendrix and Dylan, of Fleetwood Mac, each of whom I saw live: Dylan at the Isle of Wight in 1969, a few days before I began a foundation year which potentially could have led to me gaining a diploma in art and design and a career in graphic design.

I was the least focused art student of the new foundation-year intake, turning up the first morning to see a semicircle of easels, a sheet of paper on each, around a small stage on which sat a charwoman taking a break. After some milling around, each of us selected an easel, upon which signal the cleaner stepped naked from her housecoat and assumed a pose. I hadn't a pencil to record the moment. A patrolling tutor stopped by and noted the virgin sheet of paper. I explained that I had expected only to register and had otherwise come unequipped. He dug in his pockets for anything that might leave a mark. All he could muster was a Parker fountain pen.

My art student career crashed before the finish of the first term, a casualty of too many alcohol-fuelled binges and late nighters. Drugs featured. Nothing serious compared to what's available to the kids nowadays. Uppers and downers, LSD once. Hashish was common but I didn't smoke, although much was inhaled secondarily. An inordinate amount of time was spent sitting around on bedsit floors talking what we imagined was anti-establishment subversion. The Beatles' *Sgt Pepper* and Cream provided the backing track. This short, enjoyably directionless respite in Norwich amid the drift of my teenage years held some amorphous potential. All an adventure. I hitched everywhere. As we all did then. I rationalised I was harvesting experience – that every knock, every setback and blind alley was grist for the still faintly realised me. And the 1960s weren't out. Like every decade, this had its myths, one of which was certainly true for me: work of the low skill variety was abundant. I often finished a job on a Friday and started in a new place on the following Monday. Factories, breweries, bottling plants, warehouses; holiday camps and bars; a few shifts as a grill chef; garage attendant; a stint with Irish Travellers tarmacking; another as a deckhand (deckie) learner on the trawlers (my nineteenth birthday was spent in the middle of the North Sea). I bored easily, and was never good with foremen. One of the last jobs I had in England was briefly helping an uncle (Sammy McReynolds, married to my aunt Bridget) to sell fruit from a stall in London outside Covent Garden Tube station. I used to tally the number of jobs, but would lose count around the thirty mark.

However, as the situation started to deteriorate in Ireland, as media revelations about attacks on civil rights demonstrators and sectarian shootings and bombings by loyalists began to impinge upon my rudderless consciousness, I was drawn to understand more. It would be quite a stretch to claim I was politically aware (to the point, that is, of wishing to join a party or become involved in activism), but so much was happening in the world, and a tangible sense of change affected me in common with many of our generation. The bolshiness had remained strong but lacked coherence, clarity, direction. The extent of my then-nascent radicalism was confined to pub rhetoric and rant, to often-heated discussions about the state of the world inherited from our parents. This was the early shaping of my politics. It was the era of Vietnam, of Mao's *Little Red Book*, of Martin Luther King and the black civil rights marches, of the Prague Spring, of events in Paris. Then in the middle of all this global upheaval of the oppressed, Ireland erupted. Ireland as an issue now contended with Vietnam for signalling radical credit. My sense of drift was magnified. I wanted to anchor; to have a centre of gravity. England had no further hold on this prodigal. All roads led to Belfast.

3
Unity Flats

'They were the descendants of the Communards and it was no struggle for them to know their politics. They knew who had shot their fathers, their relatives.'
— Ernest Hemingway, 'The Snows of Kilimanjaro'

After my childhood visits, I next returned to Ireland when I was nineteen. The pull had been strong, surging at times with my tidal awareness of what was happening in Belfast as reported: the drift of events of the splash headline. Since that previous stay in 1964, Belfast would surface in my consciousness at particularly newsworthy ruptions to compete with the many distractions of my troubled teens. As mentioned in chapter two, when the UVF re-emerged in 1966 and shot dead a young Catholic barman, one of several sectarian attacks in their campaign, I remember my mother's shock at the news. She was conscious even then of her own mother's anguished retelling of the family having to flee an Orange mob intent on burning out Catholics in Donegall Pass in the early 1920s. These accounts were vital. The trauma rekindled. Was history being repeated? A fear felt, surely, throughout nationalist communities of the northern six counties? For me, this counted as a temporary draw within my insular teenage landscape during those six intervening years. All distractions were to be swept aside in the storm surge of August 1971.

That first visit lasted six weeks over Christmas and the New Year of 1970–71. Short as it was, the visit stood as a more viable, considered choice when set against my youthful meanderings: the drift from factory to warehouse, holiday camp to trawlers; nights spent in doss-houses, or spikes as they were known then (I had read my Orwell – *Down and Out in Paris and London*), frequently sleeping rough. On one occasion, I recall being moved on by the police at two in the morning from one of the major London stations, probably Waterloo. Their ploy was to misdirect me to a supposed night hostel in Tooley Street, which turned out to be for women only. An early disillusionment with the police confirmed.

I then travelled with little more than a sleeping blanket, and what might pass for a survival kit, fitted into a duffel bag. My one valued possession was a roll of charcoal life studies, prized from that brief spell at art school. I had held on to them, and although of no obvious value to anyone other than to myself, at some point they were stolen. I felt their loss, my one tangible expression of a desire to be an artist. That single term at art school held a mere hint of potential amid this chequered odyssey. I was a vagabond in the self-making. Romantic nonsense really, living for the moment, accumulating, I rationalised, a sump of experience to draw on at some future pass.

So, when I arrived in Belfast in late 1970, intending only a Christmas sojourn with relatives, I saw myself as a witness to much, believing I had little to learn. I cringe now to think how naive my understanding was of the world, of the news from Belfast as reported – the delusion of myself as worldly, many corners turned. Dad used to admonish me with the withering judgement of some excuse for my latest bad behaviour: 'I've been round too many corners for you.' For there was little in my life before this moment that could have prepared me for subsequent experiences and decisions.

Glimpses of a different reality kicked in during that brief but vitally memorable six-week visit, during which I stayed with relatives and found that I could explore the city at will despite escalating political tensions. One image, although sketchy, still retains some clarity to this day, and concerns trouble on the Falls Road. In Divis Street, the then-narrow gateway between the city centre and the Falls Road, the nationalist heartland stretching west, I witnessed an attack from a side street on a patrolling Saracen armoured vehicle, widely used by the British Army. I was alone, suggesting a sense of unconcern as I headed back to Andersonstown (or Andytown, as known locally). Save for light emanating from a nearby corner shop, the area was almost in pitch blackness. Suddenly the arc of a petrol bomb cut through the dark. There was a brief explosion of light as the glass shattered in the road, having fully missed its target. The Saracen trundled on unscathed, seemingly unaware, or insufficiently bothered, and was swallowed up in the narrow surrounds. This amid the shadowy stillness. It was electrifying. Quite why this image should have survived the test of memory is a puzzle. Street disturbances were the backdrop throughout the conflict, and yet few incidents stand out with anything like the same iconic intensity. Possibly because this was my first time close to any act of violent political resistance. The sight of the Saracen in the narrow working-class streets was a forceful image of state power. It was an alien presence. Someone unseen in the darkness had had the heart to take it on. I would not have had the courage. Around the same period I saw the aftermath of serious rioting and shooting on the Crumlin Road, the unfurling by the British Army of cruel barbed wire to make crude chicanes to suggest some order of control in that aftermath. In the decades to follow, these efforts at separation would evolve into the 'peace walls'. Thinking back, I am struck by the oddly disconnected sense of being free to wander, almost at will: up the Falls, the Shankill, Crumlin Road, Sandy Row. An eye. Not a participant.

Another abiding memory is of the poverty I saw in areas like the Lower Falls, from where Dad's people all hailed. I had witnessed poverty in England (my own upbringing provided an apt measuring stick), the worst example being the slum tenements, soot-blackened red-brick acres spread out to the horizon, which I saw in Newcastle-upon-Tyne in early 1968 (before my time in the approved school). Such areas of neglect and impoverishment were rich wells of recruitment for British state forces. Belfast seemed worse in quality but not in scale; the narrow terraces, back to back, of places such as the Market and the Pound Loney, each smaller in area. In counterpoint to poverty was the given warmth of the people of these and similar neighbourhoods. I took my impressions back to England at the start of February 1971, coincidentally on the eve of two significant deaths: the first British soldier, Gunner Robert Curtis, was shot dead by the IRA; and earlier, the first IRA volunteer, James Saunders, was shot dead by the British Army (although a number of volunteers had been killed in premature explosions and car crashes, and the Brits, too, had many casualties off the official record).

IRA bomb and gun attacks against the British Army and on commercial property increased during the course of the year, the latter initially designed to draw troop numbers out of beleaguered nationalist areas but becoming a key strategy to cost the British Exchequer (who had to foot the bill), and also to make the place ungovernable. Internment was introduced on 9 August 1971. The British Army, under political pressure from the unionists, raided homes throughout nationalist areas, detaining nearly three hundred alleged republicans. In fact, the IRA had anticipated the swoop and had largely evaded capture. The press extensively covered the consequent violence. Allegations of torture emerged when many lifted were released within days. I soon learned to distrust the media coverage of these developments. A picture built up of terrible events unfolding in poor, marginalised districts in what I regarded, despite a childhood in England, as my home town. Eleven people were killed by the British Army in Ballymurphy, including a priest who was giving the last rites to a man who had been shot in the back. I must have tried to call an aunt in Andytown to find out more – the only relative I knew in possession of a phone. She talked of daily and nightly gun battles; of having to hide low behind a couch while there was shooting in the street. There was an urgency in my need to return to find out for myself what was actually happening. In my six months back in England, I had again fallen into the drift I had left prior to those few weeks in Belfast.

Somehow I had managed to get the sack from two factories and a promenade cafe; I even contrived to get a trial as a deckie on a Fleetwood trawler but failed to turn up before it set sail. I felt lost, directionless, when news broke of internment. At the time, I was in Blackpool, still adrift, working as a bar waiter. I finished the week and caught the train on the Friday for the Heysham ferry home.

At the ferry terminal I saw many people, whole families, huddled around their luggage, waiting for their connecting trains – Belfast now behind them, fleeing the Troubles (although the conflict was not called that then), part of an extensive exodus involving several thousand, most of whom fled south to specially prepared emergency accommodation facilitated by the Irish Army. An older guy I conversed with, seeing me heading for the ferry, his teenage daughters looking on, said that Belfast needed every man it could muster to defend the areas. One of the daughters, about my age and pretty, did a sort of humph, as much as to say, 'the likes of you won't be much use'. Their father seemed able-bodied. Why had he not followed his own advice? But I supposed he was worried for his family's safety. That wasn't why I was returning, although I can't be sure after all these years what exactly was on my mind. To be a witness, certainly, but not likely to join the fight – I felt a poor specimen for the task: I wasn't athletic or sporty – if anything, uncoordinated, as rare sightings of me on the dance floor attest – and prone to chest infections. It is quite conceivable that I would have failed a regular army recruitment medical.

The ferry was packed, with many fully kitted British soldiers, dozens of them, apparently crossing at short notice, suggesting some unforeseen logistical shortcomings in the internment planning. I watched when the chances came to see how they conducted themselves, not wanting to believe the catalogue of abuse and brutality that featured then in the more open media. Part of my witness was to establish, one way or the other, whether the reports that had horrified me of British Army brutality and murder could have any basis in reality. Judging by their accents, overheard in their subdued conversations, the squaddies seemed drawn disproportionately from areas of high unemployment and deprivation, such as the north of England: Yorkshiremen and Geordies. A way out from the poverty. Belfast, too, had been traditionally a rich seam of cannon fodder for the British imperial enterprise (as proven by the existence of the Catholic Ex-Servicemen's Association, mustered to help defend nationalist areas after 1969). I was then still hesitant to accept that they might act less than professionally and sceptical about accounts that claimed otherwise. I had known guys who had joined the army. It wouldn't even then have entered my thinking to see them as 'Brits'. But on that ferry crossing, a distancing was occurring within my perception of who I was, an evolving process which had begun, if it's at all possible to identify a starting point, during my last visit.

The ferry landed in Belfast late on a Saturday evening, 14 August, and passengers quickly disembarked to be greeted by apparently anxious waiting friends and relatives. There was urgency in the air. I was soon alone on the quay. The city centre, close by, was scarily empty. Of people and traffic. No taxis. No buses. The streets dark. I walked to a nearby hotel, Robinson's, near the corner of Donegall Street, if memory serves, and booked in for the night, for it was too late – and too dangerous, I must have sensed – to complete the journey to relatives in Andytown.

Next day, Sunday, I made a mid-morning start. The city centre streets were largely deserted, buses and taxis still not evident. I began the four-mile trudge up the Falls Road to my aunt's house in Andytown. I soon confirmed why there were no buses from a few burnt-out, mangled remains on the side of the road. I was carrying a big cardboard suitcase full of clothes, clearly heavy. I passed milling, angry crowds on street corners. No one had slept. Debris from the previous night's rioting littered the road and side streets. And this was six days on from the introduction of internment! The smell of cordite and burning hung in the air. I passed patrols of British soldiers, and armoured cars. One man, shirtless and boiling with intent, stood out from a group at a street corner and offered a patrol a 'fair go'. Others gathered by him, raging but impotent. I walked on, as if channel-surfing, to the next corner face-off, all the way up that road burdened with the suitcase. Nobody paid me the slightest notice. All were too centred in their very particular focus of fear and rage to give me any heed. It was too much for me to take in – a bewildering blur of impressions. That was my introduction.

I was on the fastest learning curve of my life to date. I would go out with cousins, about my own age, and with older family members, for now it would be potentially dangerous to go anywhere on my own, as I would find out. I sensed a tension underlying the often-encountered good-natured manners of friends of theirs to whom I was introduced. With them I was the cousin from England. I would accompany them to several bars and clubs in west Belfast: the Glenowen, the Green Briar, the Hunting Lodge (then in what seemed the countryside), and to Kelly's Cellars and the Heather Lounge in the town. My English accent must have jarred but I was shown courtesy. I had always been able to drop the English for the Belfast brogue with ease, when relatives from there visited Norwich or when I stayed with an aunt whose own Irish accent had remained strong despite decades in London. But I was loth now to go native, sensing this might be misinterpreted as trying too hard to fit in and might be judged suspiciously.

There was a club adjacent to Milltown Cemetery. After several visits I thought my face would have been noted and that therefore it would be okay to go there alone. One Sunday I was having a drink upstairs when someone started asking me questions about which football team I supported. I had nothing to hide, but in an attempt to sound local I professed a somewhat over-egged but recklessly underinformed devotion to Celtic. Small talk held its perils, as my ignorance of the latest result was to prove. The toilets were downstairs. On reaching the bottom of the steps, I was grabbed by four guys and hustled outside and into a car in a manner I felt could easily draw attention. By their aggression, I think they really believed they had hold of a Brit spy. One who held me in an armlock had heavy beery breath. There was a Brit fortified observation post or sangar in the bus depot facing the main cemetery gate. I was concerned not to do anything that might get these guys lifted, and expressed my concern. The whole foolish business was resolved once my identity was checked out with relatives woken up for the purpose. A half-baked English accent was a dangerous handicap and I was determined from that moment to lose it quickly, and perhaps from then on even reluctant to speak about being brought up in England, 'the mother of all our sorrows'.

In contrast to the many families who left the North at this period, mine decided to return. To this day, this is not an entirely explicable decision. This was in November 1971. My parents had four younger children: Geraldine (aged eight then), Malachy (seven), and five-year-old twins Sandra and Colin. Sean and Susan had both flown the nest but were to visit separately soon after. The family had never seemed closer. I heard from Mum subsequently that Dad had made the decision to return to Belfast with the family after an aunt had expressed concern to Mum that I was heading for serious trouble. The aunt in question did think me a bit wild. But was it enough to justify Dad selling up in Norwich? I had shown no inclination to become involved in the violence. But Dad took the concern seriously enough to up stakes and leave, bringing my younger brothers and sisters in tow. Apart from short spells staying in the family home in Norwich and occasional visits to see them, I had had little contact since leaving home before my fifteenth birthday. Suddenly I was included in the family. It crossed my mind at the time that Dad too had returned because of a pressing need to see for himself at close hand events in his native city. And Mum also may have been possessed by a similar desire.

Through a relative from the Market who had for years lived near Tates Avenue, they rented a house in Lower Broadway in the Village, a Protestant area soon to become a loyalist stronghold. This would never have been a wise option but at that time was particularly hazardous. And I was supposed to be the rash one in the family! Our neighbours, from minimal contact, seemed good but thought we were Protestant. We all rapidly grasped the peril. Dad drilled the young ones with the need for vigilance, impressing upon them the necessity of not revealing their identifiably Catholic names. At night we kept quiet while local vigilantes, the precursors to the Ulster Defence Association (UDA), would parade in the street, wearing blue construction helmets and carrying baseball bats. This was a pattern repeated in other loyalist areas. Within days we organised a moonlight flit to a nationalist area where flats were available: Unity Flats – Dad's old home district of Carrick Hill, now a notorious interface, which helped to explain the availability of accommodation. It was still only December. McGurk's Bar, in which fifteen people had been killed in a loyalist no-warning bomb attack only days beforehand, was less than a quarter of a mile from Unity. We were still far safer there, in a nationalist frontline, than in the Village.

And so, in December 1971, we moved into an upper-floor maisonette in Unity Walk, a small nationalist enclave at the base of the Shankill Road, the Protestant heartland, and seemed to represent a huge thorn in its sense of entitlement. Dad had lived at 10 Tyrone Street in the old district, as mentioned. On holidays to Belfast I remember visiting Joss there with Dad, so I felt a strong connection with the place. Because of its location, the people of the district had a long history of having to defend themselves against sectarian attack. The sense of dispossession and displacement was etched into their being. From the late 1960s, Unity Flats had gained international media attention as a flashpoint area that had seen hand-to-hand fighting and gunplay from invading loyalist mobs, the RUC and B Specials. One local man, Patrick Corry, was savagely beaten by the RUC and later died, an issue of festering anger among many of the older residents, to whom state killings in the 1920s were still a living memory. Despite the area's scary repute, I felt safe there. Stepping outside its confines posed real danger, however. Loyalist gangs could circle our areas and kill with apparent impunity. The loyalist organisations were regarded by most Irish nationalists as an adjunct of official British state coercion and terrorism.

There were many incidents in the relatively short period we lived there. I remember hearing a commotion below us and going out onto the walkway to see what was happening. A Brit patrol were assaulting a young guy who was holding on to a rail, his feet in the air, while being struck with rifle butts. He was shoeless and his shirt had been torn off in the struggle. Suddenly women swarmed the scene. In the melee the lad got free and disappeared bare-footed round a corner, presumably to fight another day. The courage of those women was staggering. Absolutely fearless. So was the lad who got away.

Being so close to the city centre, the main target of the IRA's commercial bombing campaign, our windows would shudder every time a bomb exploded. We occupied 'the Casbah', easily corralled every marching season behind giant hoardings to spare passing Orangemen from our 'alien' scrutiny. The city centre was *their* city centre. Kids from the flats would rush to the scene of an explosion, knowing that merchandise from the targeted premises would litter the streets. When the Co-Op was bombed in May 1972, destroying what had been a flagship department store (the damage was estimated at £4 million), the Tavern Bar (facing the bottom of the Shankill but only accessible from within the Flats) became a bazaar as merchandise recovered from the scene was openly offered for sale. The IRA put a stop to the practice (I presume to take a stand against profiteering). Meanwhile, bomb-damage sales became routine economic activity in the heavily targeted city centre.

The district also suffered from bomb attacks by loyalists. The worst incident of which the family had direct experience was when a 100-pound car bomb detonated beside the Carrick Hill Community Club, a shebeen facing the front of the Flats, killing a local man, Danny McErlean, and shattering inwards all the windows in Unity Walk. Ours was opposite the seat of the explosion but although the damage was quite extensive, none of the family or our neighbours were seriously injured by the blast, other than a few cuts and bruises. My sister Geraldine was by far the luckiest. She was across the road from the club, going door to door to collect money for the local parish newsletter. She recalled a flash of light before being blown through a doorway of one of the flats below ours. Picking herself up, she found her shoes outside, on the spot where she had stood at the moment of the blast.

On another occasion, a car was abandoned in nearby waste ground, in the boot of which was the body of James Howell, shot dead – the brother of a man who within three years would be teaching me *Gaeilge* in Long

Kesh, Ted Howell. And on yet another occasion of horror, one of several specifically intended to hurt and to terrorise the Flats, a young nationalist was riddled with bullets from a passing car, again the work of loyalists. I saw the blood on the kerbside that morning, after the victim was removed, congealed as thickly as you find in a slaughterhouse. The Venice Cafe, close by, was twice shot up, causing multiple casualties each time. I doubt if an accurate tally of the numerous incidents within and in the vicinity of the Flats is possible to collate. Only a portion of them were reported. The tension was constant. At Easter, the children of the district were evacuated to Dublin, where they were put up in the homes of sympathisers. My sister Sandra, then six, has since spoken of how traumatic she found that experience, split up from the others between sponsoring families. Unity Flats was in siege mode, expecting the worst.

In the spring there had been a release of internees, part of a negotiation off page between the IRA and the Heath government that would soon secure a short-lived truce. Suddenly there were many new faces (new, that is, to me) around the district, some whose names became quickly familiar, such was the buzz generated by their presence. This had a galvanising impact. Defence activity mushroomed to meet the threat of loyalism. There was never a more pressing need. Loyalism, easily equatable with fascism, was asserting itself in shows of strength. An estimated twenty thousand members of the UDA openly marched past the Flats en route to a rally, where they were addressed by the hard-line former Ulster Unionist politician William Craig, now leader of the short-lived Vanguard movement, who threatened to exterminate 'the enemies of Ulster'. Frontline republican areas in response had to organise to meet a clear existential threat. I realised that in the small backstreets and homes surrounding, weapons and explosives were secreted. To this day I do not know the full extent of the preparations for defence. More knowledgeable heads were planning for the worst. It was difficult to penetrate this culture of secrecy, one bred of necessity given the history of repression.

The local community had the additional concern of the in-tandem threat posed by the Orange marching season, particularly during the early hours of the Twelfth (12 July) in 1972, when Unity Flats was on standby while seemingly hundreds of drums or makeshift shields were beaten in unison just a half mile away, reminiscent of a scene from the film *Zulu*.

This time the women as well as the children of the district had been earlier bussed out of the area to temporary shelter, again in various locations south of the border, such was the worry for their safety. Mum and the kids slept in a huge dormitory of a private school in Cork, nearly three hundred miles away to the south-west. Meanwhile, the IRA and local men organised in readiness for any possible encroachment or further incident. Unity Flats, now depleted of its most vulnerable, held firm and waited, a scenario played out in many similar flashpoints.

Unity consisted of little more than three hundred residences. The Brits manned a sangar at the corner of the district, from which they would monitor all comings and goings of locals and visitors. Another post situated on top of the nearby Central Library, supplied by a shuttle service of helicopters, also had a vantage over approaches to the district. There was constant patrolling, two 'duck squads' of squaddies (in loose file formation) each covering the entirety of this small complex of corridors and blocks. We were hemmed in between two barracks: the RUC in Brown Square to the south of the district and the British Army in Glenravel Street Barracks to our north. And Girdwood Army Barracks was only a half mile further away. It is difficult to imagine a more concentrated occupation.

The Brits were simply hated. Incredible to hear that at first they were seen as saviours by some residents, who made them tea and sandwiches and some of whom as a consequence were held unfairly with suspicion. A few local girls 'went with' Brits, judged as acts of betrayal against their own communities. We were in the territory of taboo. They were marked with the accusative 'soldier lovers'. Some in other districts had their heads shaved, or were tarred and feathered, punishments redolent of those post-war images of paraded French collaborators.

Volunteer Louis Scullion was shot dead by the Marine commandos in the early hours of 14 July 1972. I was in bed when I heard the shooting. Four shots, close by in the estate. But you were always hearing shooting so I tried to get back to sleep. It wasn't until first light that morning that I heard Louis had been killed. Louis had in recent months become a friend. I knew him to be a decent, caring man. Easy to like. No side doors to his nature. I went down to the spot beside 'Unity ramp', a pedestrian entry-point to the area, where Louis had lain, in sight of the sangar. It was in the square close to the shops. There was blood on the ground. Four pockmarks on a backyard wall testified to that night's incident. I was able to determine the likely path of one of the bullets as it drilled through Louis before gouging a lump out of the red brick. Nearby I picked up a molten casing, which I later handed to a Sinn Fein worker, Gerry McKeown, who was well placed to raise awareness of the lack of an investigation. There had been no inspection of the scene. No forensic examination. Later that morning a large duck patrol of Marine commandos, upwards of a dozen, trooped past the spot. They had come over from the New Lodge to gloat. One of them turned and with exaggerated movements spat on the spot, which at this time the local people had turned into a wee shrine with a holy picture and flowers. One woman cursed them. I was in some kind of impotent, paralysing rage. Too stunned, no one reacted. Powerless in the moment. But I vowed, not in words, that Louis's death would be avenged. The moment required dignity in the ugly face of blatant inhumanity. There would be time to express outrage. Not in words.

The news reports faithfully issued the Brits' version of what had happened: a gunman had been shot dead. No weapon was found, but we were led to suppose that a weapon had been spirited away by others. Much later I learned one account of what was believed to have actually happened. Although Louis was a volunteer, he was off duty that night. He was returning home after a late drink in the Mandeville when shot. The story goes that the Brits had misidentified him as another volunteer, one 'on the run'. No attempt to apprehend a fugitive. This was shoot on sight.

I attended Louis's and other funerals, and witnessed the cortèges of the bereaved as they carried coffins past the Flats, replacing them in the hearses before crossing the flashpoint at Peter's Hill, where there was the likelihood of loyalist protesters, particularly when the funeral was of an IRA volunteer. That year, 1972, was the worst in terms of the numbers killed and injured. Crowds would line the routes; hundreds, often thousands, would follow the processions. I shall never forget the haunting, deeply moving sound of women singing 'Faith of Our Fathers' as a coffin would be carried past.

To this day I find it amazing that two Brits were shot dead in Unity, an area difficult to operate in and easily sealed off. There were several shootings. After a Royal Marine was killed by a sniper, the same regiment that had killed Louis Scullion about a fortnight before, graffiti appeared

on a gable end: '39 RM' – it was the Fortieth's tour and the '40' was crossed
out. Crass now, but at the time chiming with local sentiment.

For months now, I had concluded that the Brits were our oppressors
and that the IRA were our legitimate defenders. Derry's Bloody Sunday,
when thirteen civilians were murdered by the Brits at an anti-internment
march, confirmed the conclusion. News of the death toll mounted during
the course of that fateful climactic day. I was in the Felons Club late that
night when the first buses returned from Derry. Two young girls were
ushered onto the stage to talk. They were in tears. Quaking in shock. Fury
is the only word I can summon to convey the feeling in the hall among
all who heard their testimony. But after my own anger had cooled sufficiently, I still held back, questioning whether I had the necessary strength.
Was I capable of killing? Of withstanding torture? Stories abounded of
torture inflicted on men from the district. One man was alleged to have
endured electric shocks. Another, drugged. Standing at the ramp one day
with some of the lads, a guy, about thirty, slightly older than us, passed
by. He looked troubled, withdrawn, twitchy. One of the lads whispered
to me, 'That's – –! He hasn't been the same since Holywood [Barracks].'
I was soaking this up. I was nowhere near the state of mind to volunteer.
I still had this vague aspiration to be somehow creative, to paint, perhaps
to write about these experiences. But I hadn't the focus to use what I
was a witness to for that purpose. Maybe one day when all the gallivant-
ing was out of my system. But neither had I made that huge crossing of
overcoming my own self-doubts about being up to the task. I agreed with
what the IRA stood for. I knew that they had the backing of the district;
that they were needed.

It took some time and soul-searching before I managed to summon
sufficient belief in my own capacity to suffer such abuse that I could in
full conscience volunteer. Even then I supposed my contribution would be
short-lived; that I might do enough to perhaps prove myself in terms of
some sketchy notion of loyalty to kith and kin. One episode earlier in that
most dangerous year helped force the issue for me.

4

Joining G Company

In early 1972 I was 'lifted' at about one in the morning with a dozen or so other patrons during a Brit raid on the Mandeville social club, a local shebeen, the same club Louis Scullion was to exit some four months later to be shot dead by the Marine commandos. The raid was simply a trawl, netting a largely inebriated company of mostly middle-aged men. None seemed likely volunteer material (nor, indeed, likely to possess much to volunteer), and despite being the youngest of the catch, I include myself. The surveillance and information-gathering operation, in effect a mass screening, unleashed in the occupied North was one of the biggest assaults on a civilian population ever launched by Britain's military elite. I had wrestled with the idea of joining the IRA, having by now reached the obvious conclusion because of my experiences living in Unity Flats that armed struggle against the Brits was justified, but I still questioned whether I was up to the task. Perhaps my role could be confined to contributing to the defence of the area, an onerous task in itself because of the volatility of the location? In the space of only a couple of years, I had developed from a pacifist who identified with the Martin Luther King line and who thought all war, all violence, was morally wrong and counterproductive, to seeing that people sometimes had no other choice but to defend themselves. I do believe there is a distinction to be drawn between the violence of the oppressor and the violence of the oppressed. We, our communities, were powerless and had suffered much through the forced, undemocratic imposition of partition. Violence was a regrettable but necessary response to the greater violence inflicted on us.

We were brought to Girdwood Army Barracks, which then enclosed the main interrogation centre for north Belfast. The raid was probably occasioned by the changeover of regiments. Parachute Regiment out, Royal Fusiliers in. I suppose the Fusiliers were sending a message as the new boys at the start of their 'tour of duty', just as the departing Paras had felt it necessary to bust a few heads as a parting gesture (as in turn the Royal Marine commandos would up the ante). In the back of the Saracen, (or 'pig', as an armoured personnel carrier was better known), en route to Girdwood Army Barracks, I was forced down on the floor under the boots of the squaddies, who proceeded to stamp on my hands, fortunately in the way of my head.

Upon arrival, the dozen or so lifted were made to sit separately in a row of wood-partitioned cubicles. Uniformed RUC assisted military personnel in running the operation. Barked orders encouraged us to stare ahead at a white perforated-tile wall. If anyone moved, or talked, or nodded off, he would be assaulted with a punch or slap to the back of his head. We couldn't look round but felt the malevolent attention of the RUC at our backs. When one of us deviated from the application of their apparently totally arbitrary directives, a cry of pain would carry down the line. I was kept like that for most of thirty-six hours. With so little stimulus, my focus was on the immediacy of the tiles, about three feet in front. For years afterwards I could have told anyone who might care to listen how many holes were in each tile.

I was questioned only once, late the following evening, by a bearded man with a polished English accent, quite civil, even avuncular in a brown corduroy jacket, a pipe smoker, who admitted that my arrest was a mistake. Indicating a wall heater, he assured me that the heater gave an illusion of heat, not its actuality. I had sought no such assurance and surmised he must be referencing rumours, which he was clearly keen to scotch, of some form of heat torture. Despite realising that I wasn't 'connected', he nevertheless told me that I couldn't be released until the morning. A Kafkaesque moment. The bureaucratic grind of empire. I was returned to the cubicle to suffer and to witness further abuse before being released around one p.m. The reality of blunt power had been revealed to me as a direct mirror of my own lack of consequence to him and his masters; its true reach, all the way back to, I pictured, a briefing room off some corridor linking a khaki-clad type with a grey civil servant, where the order of business was 'What to do with Paddy?' We simply had no rights. The veil was lifted. Later I would hear of General Frank Kitson and in time would endure the attentions of other interrogators, people trained to inflict pain, who appeared to relish their work. It was encoded in power gestures, like the thick cigar, that trapping of bullying authority. It would later emerge, from documents released after the thirty-year rule (the informal name given to the restricted release of politically sensitive government documents), that the decision to use torture had been signed off by Prime Minister Heath and Defence Secretary Lord Carrington shortly after the Conservatives came to power, and prior to the introduction of internment.*

The RUC seemed even more aggressive than the Brits, as if on a personal crusade. We were made to feel like dirt. They cursed, they shoved. They hated. It was too easy to return the sentiment. With the Brits, at least, it came short and sharp. The whole experience left me shocked, causing me to question what might have happened had I known anything. And my experience of ill treatment was in no manner comparable to the excesses of brutality suffered and endured by many others. Over the next two weeks of brooding over my wounds (my knuckles were scabbed and bruised from the attention of army boots, causing a girlfriend to suppose I had put up a fight), anger asserted itself, pushing self-doubt aside. I couldn't let it go. Any lingering qualms were dispelled. I made a firm decision to join the IRA.

Initially I had been attracted to the Official IRA, identifying with their avowed Marxism. The Provisional IRA (or Provos, as popularly or notoriously known) were regularly portrayed by the Officials as 'green nationalists' and sectarian bigots.

At first, of course, I had no direct knowledge and few points of reference to contradict this view. The IRA had split into the two factions soon after its perceived failure to adequately defend nationalist areas of the North in August 1969. The Officials were strong in the Market – a definite pull on my sense of allegiance to the old district. But from what I had begun to witness of the realities of small nationalist communities like Unity Flats, the New Lodge, etc., where British Army occupation and oppression were so evident and where loyalist bombings and shootings directed at nationalists were an almost daily occurrence, I by now judged the Officials woefully out of touch, though I carried no baggage of the ill feeling towards them which I grew to realise was widely held in the Flats. And there was talk that they would soon call a ceasefire.

---

*The Torture Files, RTÉ Investigation Unit Broadcast 4 June, 2014.

Just a few months before, I would have wondered, who were the IRA? How would I know them? What were their demands? Images from film and literature portrayed them as men in trench coats, a distinctive look from the 1920s up till the early 1950s, belonging to an older generation, personified in *Odd Man Out*. A later film, *The Quiet Man*, gave them a gentrified air. I had seen old photos of republicans marching at Easter in Belfast. The reality, I now understood, was totally at variance with the media projection of them as monsters and psychopaths; as a phenomenon external to the communities, parasitical; a scourge. I had come to realise that the IRA *were* the community – of the people and for the people, their response to oppression and fear of the state. It took me a while to grasp this because much of the IRA's activity was, of course, covert. In guarded conversations in bars you would hear talk of 'the Boys', and perhaps less guardedly, 'the Ra' (the media, of course, talked of 'mad bombers' and 'men of violence'). Typically, you might see a group of five or six young lads, their ages ranging from sixteen to twenty, who I soon figured out to be part of the local Provo unit, scooting about the place or hanging out at the Tavern watching football or *Top of the Pops*, say, while interested girls hovered. It all seemed very innocent. While the identity of the Boys may have been an open secret, their activity was subterranean. Beneath the district's surface calm (or what passed for calm in that troubled time) lay a hidden mesh of loyalties and resources: safe houses and arms dumps; wise heads, whispered advice and intelligence; billets and meals; transport. To this day I admire the discretion of our neighbours and of the people of the Flats, a pattern extending throughout beleaguered communities.

Older family men of the district, many of whom had joined the Provo's auxiliary wing, would stand at the ramp at the entrance to Unity Flats, which acted as a sentry post as it afforded a view of the dangerous approach from Millfield, where many a poor innocent identifiable as a nationalist simply for being there had been viciously beaten, or abducted and savagely killed by loyalists. The Brits were a mere fifty yards away behind the sandbags of their sangar, their weapons trained on us, rubbishing their claim to being impartial defenders of the community. The 'Auxies' were a reassuring presence, particularly during some of the most fraught moments of the summer of 1972. Their duties and commitment also clearly extended beyond the nightly patrolling and barricade-manning. For example, when clothing was donated from supporters in the USA, it was the Auxies who organised its distribution. This for me represented a community working in unison during hard times against a powerful enemy.

I gradually gained the trust of a few of the local lads, now deeply impressed at how savvy and streetwise many were. With so few opportunities for employment, for social mobility, nationalist districts seemed hothouses for many very smart people who ploughed their intelligence into the struggle. Some were as young as fifteen and sixteen, many of whom, as I would learn, had acquired an astonishing level of operational experience. Bombs would be planted morning, noon and night, town centre opening hours being no barrier to targeting. The effectiveness of the IRA's commercial bombing campaign in Belfast was such that in response a 'ring of steel' was erected to protect the main shopping area, with vehicles and shoppers being searched before entering its commercial centre.

I finally broached my interest in joining to a guy not yet twenty but who I felt was tight-lipped and whom I believed could pass my application on to the right people. Soon after, a senior republican from the battalion area motioned me aside and told me that I could join, subject to a probationary period during which I was not to arouse suspicion of my interest and to put my eyes and ears to work. I believed I had inherited a healthy sense of discretion from Joss.

When Stormont (the devolved parliament of the partitioned North) was prorogued by the Heath government in March, the event was celebrated in the districts as the smashing of the Orange state. A key Provo objective had been achieved, clarifying the battle lines: we were locked in conflict more directly with the British state. Westminster had averted its eyes from the conduct of Stormont since its inception. Stormont was clearly a failed political entity. Perhaps the way was being cleared for a negotiated settlement. I received the news with mixed feelings. The war might soon be over before I had a chance to fire a shot in anger. There was no more telling proof of my naivety back then. Britain would, nevertheless, persist in presenting its role as a peace keeper or honest broker between Catholics and Protestants.

I joined G Company of the Provo's Third Battalion, Belfast Brigade. In each nationalist area of the city, a company unit was formed. Belfast was designated a brigade area, answerable to a Southern-based leadership. The city's topography allowed for three battalions. The Third covered the north of the city – Unity, the Lodge, Newington, Bawnmore, Ardoyne, the Bone (Marrowbone) – plus the Market and the Short Strand to the south and east. This was the set-up until a major restructuring in the later 1970s into cells – and of at least equal importance, overall leadership of the conflict in the North would thereafter be vested in a Northern command.

My first instruction was received in the Avenue Bar, or the Ave, then a local hub, bombed and shot up by loyalists on several occasions. Standing at the corner of the bar, a lad from the Flats, about my own age, who had become a mate and who I thought I knew well, having been on shared dates with two girls from the New Lodge, whispered an order to me. I was to report to a certain address within the Flats at a specified time for a meeting. I hadn't figured him for a volunteer. While I would have had my ideas about who was and who was not active, I was surprised to now learn the identity of some of my fellow volunteers.

The meeting place turned out to be a box bedroom in one of the 'chocolate blocks' – small, three-storeyed blocks in the centre of the estate. The purpose of the meeting was a gun lecture (GL). Two other lads were already there – these I knew – all crowding the box bedroom. Also familiar to me was the training officer (TO), a local with a fierce reputation, one of the first to be interned, who was authoritative. Shortly after, a young member of the gCailíní (a republican equivalent to the Girl Scouts) brought the weapons in: an M1 carbine and an old Webley revolver. On top of a sheet on a single bed in what must have been a child's room, we were shown how to strip, reassemble, load and maintain each. Which we did in turn, naming each part. A memory test. But we were to learn that the basic characteristics of every weapon were much the same. We were also taught how to complete the task blindfolded. The logic being that we might have to clear a jammed weapon at night. On completion, there was a reversal of the process: firstly, the weapons were removed by the same girl, who had waited downstairs rather than risk the attention of leaving and then having to return for the weapons; next, the TO left; then us, one at a time.

I was quickly given my first position of authority or, rather, area of responsibility: company intelligence officer (IO). I flinch at the memory of how embarrassingly naive I was. I was told to report to Ardoyne, where I would receive further orders. I got on a bus that dropped me off near Flax Street on the Protestant side of the Crumlin Road. A stone landed close by

from Butler Street on the other side, from the Catholic side. No one going
to or coming from Ardoyne got the bus. I had to cross the road, then enter
the district while local kids tested my nerve with stones and abuse. I might
have been injured if a couple of women in their doorways hadn't bawled
at them to desist. They may have thought I was 'simple'. I continued on to
the corner of Etna Drive, as instructed. I must have stuck out like a crash
beacon. That was my introduction to Ardoyne. 'Ardoyne for orders' was to
become a catchphrase among us: the seat of the Third Battalion staff.

I found myself again on the wrong side of the Crumlin Road in early
1973. Lifted by the Marine commandos and brought to Glenravel Street
Barracks, I thought myself about to be released after the customary intimidation when instead I was forced into the back of a civilian car by military
intelligence operatives and driven to Silvio Street, in a loyalist stronghold,
where they stopped. This was an attempt to either test or turn me. They
threatened to hand me over to the leader of the Orange Volunteer Force
(the first time I had ever heard tell of them), who they claimed lived in
the house opposite. I was nearly sick with fear but clammed up, reasoning
that they couldn't get away with this (surely?). They seemed amused, next
driving me to the Shankill Road, where I was told to get out. I was in
sight of a bus queue of, I assumed, shipyard workers, who regarded me
as I crossed the road, turning towards town as if I owned the place. As I
approached Brown Square Barracks and in sight of Unity Flats, the same
car pulled up. I was again lifted and driven back up the Shankill, but this
time told to get out in the middle of Agnes Street. 'Here's a Fenian,' they
shouted to women in a doorway. I ran for my life and reached the Crumlin
Road just as the same car drove by. I could see them laughing. I didn't
stop running until entering the Mater Hospital's A&E Department, where
I stayed for two hours, terrified to step outside of its sanctuary, before
gaining composure. I know of other republicans who fared much worse.
The tales that women in doorways could tell!

Months after volunteering, as a sort of bureaucratic sweep-up, I was
sworn in, along with about eight others, in a house in the adjacent C
Company area of the New Lodge. This was army administration on the
hoof. Befitting a guerrilla movement, I guess. The Lodge, with its long
terraced streets, supposedly the longest in the city, and its high-rise flats,
was natural cover and a major battleground. You could see for more than

a hundred yards ahead from many vantages, allowing more scope to move about securely, unlike in Unity, where you couldn't move from one block or square to another without giving it careful thought and if necessary sending a scout ahead. A scout could mean a Fianna or gCailíní member or, say, the twelve-year-old son or daughter of the home you were presently using for a staff meeting. Everyone was involved. Because there was no one else.

In a further example of how active/chaotic those times were, within weeks I was moved over to the position of company engineering officer (EO). The position (I won't say 'rank', which denotes hierarchy, and in the culture of the IRA, authority meant 'first among equals') had suddenly become vacant, as was common, and there was no one else to do the job. Or rather, in the estimation of the officer commanding (OC), the only other volunteer available 'couldn't be trusted with a box of matches'. There was arguably a greater turnover of EOs than of any other role. Bomb skills were crucial in the campaign, in terms of both military and commercial targeting. The Brits gave a priority to removing EOs. The high rate of premature explosions also caused a fear of explosives among some volunteers. In that light, I accepted the job with some misgivings. A crash course was called for.

Within a day or two, I was attending an engineering (explosives) lecture in a back kitchen in Ardoyne when we were interrupted by two guys known to the battalion EO, who was giving the lecture. They needed the room and then proceeded to construct a nail bomb in front of us. When they departed, we continued with the lecture. Within minutes we heard two blasts from a nearby street. There seemed no expectation or concern that we might be raided. The lecture continued and concluded as planned. The Brits, it seemed, were reluctant to rush into any situation in Ardoyne. Can you imagine how immediate and effective this action struck me? The vastly more powerful Brit war machine now looked vulnerable. Heady stuff.

At a quite early stage in my involvement as a volunteer I understood how tight our districts were, and how crucial the support, on many levels, of the people. It came as a shock to discover that this applied closer than I had imagined. One morning, after sleeping at Mum and Dad's, I left the bedroom to cross the landing to the bathroom. I was stopped short by the sight of eleven rifles of varied calibre leaning upright against the landing wall: carbines, Armalites; a Garand. Evidently in transit. Nothing to do with me. I had no idea that they had agreed to store weapons. Nor of how many passed through the maisonette. Years later, talking with an old comrade who had been the quartermaster (QM) in 1972, I learned of their contribution and of the high esteem in which they were held. Mum died aged eighty-seven – some forty-five years after those days. Strange to think that at her cremation service in England, the funeral director cited the British monarchs under whose sovereignty she had lived her life. Most of the family were born and raised in England and had largely loosened or lost ties to Ireland, except for the unhappy but brief childhood memories of my younger siblings. Mum's grandchildren had no idea. How could they. She was part of that generation that took it to the grave, as had her father and uncles.

In early 1973 Dad returned to England to get work. This was to be the last time I would see him for many years. I was becoming increasingly involved, and consequently saw little of the family. As earlier described, Dad's move to Belfast had come as a jolt. But he had quickly established himself and, using trade union contacts, found employment in the shipyard. I subsequently learned that he had received a death threat after it was discovered he was a Catholic. As a child of ten, on Mum's bidding, Geraldine accompanied Dad to the shipyard to collect his due wages. A truly desperate risk. He had calculated on the decency of one man, a supervisor, who minded her while Dad entered the closed office. She remembers men approaching her angrily until told to get back to their work. Then Dad left, holding her hand, while men followed, swearing and shouting 'Fenian'. Once it was plain that he couldn't work, it was inevitable that he would return to England. Within nine months, Mum and the kids had joined him there. I am sure Dad's decision was the correct one.

Decades later, I talked with Mum. She recounted some of her memories of those days in Unity. Her account of coping along with the young ones during Dad's absence while he was back in England was harrowing. I had no idea. The Flats, as I have tried to describe, was a war zone. It was also the children's playground. Among many incidents, they were badly shaken by a loyalist bomb attack on the Tavern Bar. Mum had gone there to use the phone to call Dad when the device, planted outside, exploded, but most of the force was directed away from the exterior wall. One brother developed a speech impediment, due it was believed to the accumulative trauma of what he had witnessed. Back in England, his teacher drew Mum's attention to one of his drawings, which depicted angry faces on boys fighting. They had escaped the context but still carried the scars.

Further promotion entailed that I had to go on the run. The Brits would catch up with me. At the very least, my internment was assured. I had to carry on; to pass on the flame. I moved around a lot within the Third Battalion area, which was extensive. Few areas were safe. I would sometimes billet in other battalion areas, where the Brit presence wasn't quite as in your face as in, say, the New Lodge. It never entered my head to leave Belfast, to cross the border. If anything, I had become more committed to the struggle. It was a privilege to get the level of contact with and insight into our base support afforded from constantly having to move from district to district. I relished the insights gleaned from conversations in supporters' homes. They were risking much and likely all. Considering the natural security concern not to say or know too much (for the less you and they knew, the less to tell), it is deeply surprising how much conversation there was. You were often the stranger in a family home in which, quite naturally, your commitment was under scrutiny, because sheltering a fugitive placed a household under enormous risk. Despite a natural reticence to ask questions, people deserved to be reassured that their own commitment wasn't being abused, taken for granted. It was a rare event to be staying in a house without books. All it took was to refer to a title on a shelf. There was trust and security in knowledge and the sharing of a love of reading.

I also recall with much poignancy the piety of people. One woman would always stand by and bless us with holy water from a small wall font by the front door before we left her home to go on operations. I have heard others recount similar experiences. One day, I unthinkingly walked into a scullery and interrupted a mother and her daughter on their knees saying the rosary, a daily practice for many Catholics, perhaps especially in grief. If local people, with so little, could risk their families' welfare – risk everything – in support of us, how could I have walked away?

The sheer extent of the media coverage of the conflict, with incidents hitting headlines all over the world, made many locations household names: Ardoyne, the Bone, the Falls, Short Strand, Andytown, and the Ballymurphy Estate, which we called the Murph. And Unity Flats, of course. These attained mythical status in the imagination of people abroad. Places to be feared. So, when English visitors actually saw how small, how similar and ordinary our areas were, and although maybe not as British as Finchley (to resort to an ignorant comparison), resembling many districts I had known across the water, the usual reaction was often one of disbelief. How could an army hide in such a small environment? It was as if the street-level scale of life during the years of struggle acted to morph us into a shape better evolved to survive the attention of our enemies. Whatever the opposition and anger felt at the political level, it was at the coalface working-class ghettoes that the most direct suffering had occurred and why there was a continual base of support to enable the struggle to be advanced. The Brits never seemed to grasp that their oppressive tactics guaranteed resistance.

I was a quick learner. I had to be. It didn't take me long to acquire the current level of proficiency in bomb-making and to become familiarised with the requirements of the job and of the areas in which we operated. But competence and resources were always stretched, leaving the IRA as ever reliant on local people, at times acting on their own initiative to extend needed support. I remember one day making my way from Ardilea Street in the Bone to Ardoyne, the two districts then connected by a dark lane, little more than a passageway, beside the brickyard. Before I reached the lane, a woman came out of a house to warn that there was a patrol of Paras out of sight ahead, waiting for me specifically; she had been listening in on their radio communications and heard them saying I was approaching. I don't know for how long I had been in their sights, nor indeed how long this woman, who was unknown to me, had been watching out for my welfare, but her action in warning me meant that I was free for another while to carry on. Scanning Brit radio frequencies to intercept their communications was a common activity in every district. More than curiosity, this was resistance. Our eyes and ears. Within a couple of weeks, if not days, however, my involvement on the ground was to come to an abrupt end.

5
Capture and the Lazy K

I was captured – scooped, as we would have put it – in the New Lodge around noon on Sunday, 10 June 1973, the place and day perhaps not coincidental. It was the annual commemoration of the birth of Wolfe Tone, the founding father of Irish republicanism. Thousands, young and old, from nationalist areas throughout the occupied six counties had that morning boarded buses bound for Bodenstown near Dublin to attend the event. Two years into the IRA's campaign, the occasion provided an opportunity to stand together, to be counted, to recommit to Irish republican ideals and, understandably, enjoy a day far and away from the pressing ubiquity of the conflict. The relief at having exited a war zone once across the border would have been palpable, rendering the mood festive, as I can attest from my attendance the year previous.

The New Lodge looked deserted, even for a Sunday, quieter than at any time during my recent familiarity with the area. Had the Brits seen this exodus as an opportunity to focus attention on those who remained? An urban guerrilla army needs a busy environment in which to function (Mao's 'fish in the sea'). Some ill-intended strategist from Thiepval Barracks (British Army HQ in Lisburn) may have reasoned that the pool was shallower, offering fish out of water. I felt a chill while walking up one of the long streets in the heart of the Lodge, missing the natural cover of what passed for ordinary and habitual in the daily grind of the district.

In consequence of this appreciable depletion in our support base on the day, the safe house I needed to enter was locked, the family southbound and not due back until late. I hadn't planned to be in the district, for we (the republican we) had foreseen difficulties in maintaining the usual lines of contact. Earlier at the battalion call house, located in another company area, I had been briefed to sort out a logistical issue – although operations had been virtually suspended for the day, amounting to an undeclared ceasefire, gear had to be inspected and relocated in readiness for tomorrow, another day.

I knew where to get a spare key, but this involved crossing Lepper Street and thus risking being spotted from the Brit sangar on top of one of seven tower blocks that dominated the streets below. As recently as February, four local men had been shot dead by Royal Marine commandos from the top of the flats (in what is believed to have been the first reported use of night sights during the conflict); two others were killed by undercover Brits shooting from a passing car shortly before. Only three of the six had been IRA volunteers, none of whom had been operating when killed. The New Lodge was always dangerous, but we knew our areas: the blind spots within which to move and operate; where and when to anticipate patrols; whose homes were open to us; the margins of risk. The obverse was that our enemies were never slow to capitalise on an opportunity.

Looking back, therefore, over that day nearly a half century ago, I feel my capture wasn't down to mere chance, to being in the wrong place at the wrong time. The mobile squad summoned to intercept me were working from a planned brief. I had evaded capture several times in recent days and weeks. The area was central to so much activity of the Third Battalion, given its ready access to the town and to major arterial routes, that with some certainty the Brits had only to cast the net and wait.

I remember looking up an empty Spamount Street. Normally, a scout would check ahead for the presence of patrols in adjacent streets. When the moment came, I was on my own. A squad of Paras suddenly turned the corner a few strides ahead of me, entering the district from Duncairn Gardens, what now would be termed an interface, marking the border of the adjacent loyalist area of Tiger's Bay. Too late to turn a corner or to run through any open door, or jump over a yard wall and away, I had no choice but to brazen it out, kidding myself (not them) that this was just a routine check, the proffered ID (false, of course) receiving only a cursory glance. No questions asked, and after an equally perfunctory rubdown I was led away, back along the short route they had emerged from a moment ago. The local Girdwood-based Marines took no apparent part. The Paras maintained a workmanlike, disinterested silence as I was brought into Duncairn Gardens to a waiting Saracen. A jeering crowd from the nearby loyalist streets, alerted by the sight of a lurking snatch squad, had gathered at the flashpoint intersection at Edlingham Street, wondering what was afoot. I found myself once more in the back of a pig, although the Paras remained silent throughout the short journey. A serious riot kicked off in the New Lodge, instigated not only by my arrest but that of others, suggesting there were still a considerable number of locals who had not boarded the buses to Dublin and who piled onto the streets on this otherwise quiet Sunday to express their anger at the intrusion. With only the feeblest grasp of the bigger picture, and still clinging to an unrealistic hope of release, I failed to see that one half of the dire binary prophesy stressed to all volunteers had come to pass – 'prison or a hole in the ground'.

I was taken to nearby Glenravel Street Barracks, to the 'Black Box'. I was no stranger to the barracks. Hardly a male in those parts hadn't sampled the hospitality within its warren of poorly lit corridors, which reeked of sweaty boots and fatigues, gun metal, mess rations and urine. 'You're going for your tea,' the Brits would smirk – their euphemism for what was later identified as the mass screening of the nationalist male population, a technique for gathering information about indigenous rebels developed in previous attempts to suppress insurgencies in Kenya, Aden and wherever the colonial writ extended. Not that my understanding of these matters went much beyond the rudimentary. My level of political awareness then was quite shallow: of the Left but underinformed. I had come to embrace a species of cultural nationalism like an abandoned child. The pull to belong is powerful in times of crisis. Someone later remarked, 'Pat's *nearly* political.' But I had been reared in a Labour home, where the *Daily Herald* and the *New Statesman* were at hand, and naturally gravitated leftward. In the Black Box, I couldn't be further from home.

The whole of the New Lodge and Unity Flats area knew of the Black Box. Every Brit-occupied nationalist district had its equivalent, designed to intimidate, for fear was integral to the entire process of repression. Its reputation preceded it. That is how fear is projected. Yet it was merely a roofless Portakabin-type structure somewhere within the shambles of the base. Black paint created a menacing ambience and, it was mooted, helped to camouflage the blood on the walls. Although from whom? Amnesty International were unlikely to have gained entry for inspection. Disorder reigned. Duck squads would be coming in off patrol or exiting into Clifton Street towards Unity Flats or the Lodge – doors to be booted in, cars to be stopped and searched, 'civvy bastards' to be harassed. I never heard of anyone actually getting a cup of tea. And here I was again. I can now only vaguely recall a lot of shouting and a few slaps (my impression was of busy, cigar-smoking, heavy-set thugs in civvies who enjoyed their work and who had created their own happy working environment). Head down to weather the storm. After the statutory four hours in the tender care of the Marines and of military intelligence, I was then handed over to the military police, the redcaps, and driven in what now is termed a Snatch Land Rover to Castlereagh, the main RUC interrogation centre.

At Castlereagh, as a handover gesture, one of the escort hit me purpose-fully in the lower back with a baton, a well-practiced induction ritual. The reception process there also involved a physical examination by a British Army medic. He had a form to fill. Several marks and abrasions were noted with crosses on an outline diagram of the human body, this dutiful recording of injuries perhaps offering a quantifiable insight into the colonial project for future researchers. No one was paying any heed now. However, the medic did come across as concerned. Hard to tell whether genuine or a well-practiced deceit. Examining my back, he remarked on the bruise from the baton, and when he touched the spot I buckled at the knees. He knew I would. 'You've been duffed up, lad.' With the medical completed (without even an offer of an aspirin), I was formally now in the hands of RUC Special Branch, and although questioned repeatedly during the next three days I was not assaulted further. I learned later that Cas-tlereagh had been full during my spell there, due largely to the detention of many loyalists following an outbreak of shootings between loyalists and the British Army in east Belfast. I also discovered that several of my own comrades had been lifted in separate raids, thus stretching the normal interrogatory case load, and lending credence to the suspicion that the Brits had taken advantage of our reduced activity, given the day, to mount a major search-and-arrest operation, allegedly netting almost the entire Third Battalion staff and one brigade officer.

On the Wednesday I was served with a 'detention order', the Brits refusing to name it for what the international community clearly recognised and condemned as internment. There was no evidence against me. I had revealed nothing and was therefore destined for detention without trial in Long Kesh, a former RAF base, now the notorious internment camp (which also held those sentenced and 'enjoying' special category status, gained a year previously after a protracted hunger strike led by Billy McKee and conferring political status). To the rest of the world I was now an internee, in the proud family tradition of Grandad Joss. Some fifty years separated our identical predicaments. As I waited in a grey, pukey cell for dispatchment to Long Kesh, I reflected that he had been interned aged twenty-one and released some twenty months later. I was twenty-two by two weeks. In 1973, less than two years since the introduction of internment, it had been reckoned that the time an internee was held averaged nine months. I foolishly mused that this pattern might continue. I could be out by Christmas!

A young RUC man, about my age, asked me why had I been arrested. I didn't know, a case of mistaken identity. Clearly. It happened all the time. He seemed uncomfortable about his duty there. Castlereagh had a reputation that may not have sat easy with him. Not proper policing. Although there had never really been proper policing in those parts. Then he said, meant kindly, 'Well, I hope it's cleared up, but if you're lying to me, I hope you burn in hell.' Hell was real for him. After a further wait I was put handcuffed into the back of a small, quite nondescript white bus, little more than a transit van with windows, with two other detainees, both nationalists whom I didn't know and therefore didn't trust (although both turned out to be sound), and driven to Long Kesh, where I was to remain for the next two and a half years. Its current population was some five hundred. During its existence, it held about two thousand internees, ninety-five per cent of whom were Irish nationalists.

And so, with some clarity even to this day, I can recall being escorted, along with the two others, from the interrogation centre on a circuitous route through a parallel universe of leafy, and I presumed Protestant, suburbs beyond our battleground districts to the camp's location, nine miles south-west of Belfast. I was sure of the distance because it came to mind that I had been on an anti-internment march to the Kesh on Christmas Day 1971, which was halted by the Brits at Kennedy Way on the then-outskirts of Belfast and banned from continuing. I was therefore spared the full slog there and back. However, this journey was palpably one-way. Three screws (prison officers) only, including the driver, accompanied us, deflating any notion of our supposed danger to the public. One, no older than me, was quite pleasant, as were the day and the twisting drive through hedge-lined backroads. I sensed it was his first day on the job. A fresh start for us both.

Suddenly the van approached acres of grey corrugated fences, checkpoints, watchtowers and all the trappings of security. Thrust out of my reverie, I tried to soak in as much as I could of what I could discern, looking for but failing to spot any perimeter weakness that one day I might exploit. Long Kesh seemed sheathed within a military cocoon. I marvelled at how Blue Kelly could have escaped from here some six months previously (unaware that he was one of those lifted at around the same time as me).

My very first feeling upon arrival at the camp was relief. A huge, almost liberating, paradoxical sense of it. Out on the streets, on the hop, I had been under enormous stress, more than I had any previous comprehension of. I didn't feel it at the time, from simply having to get on with what had to be endured or done. I had been stretched to my limit, for nothing previous in my life could have prepared me for the constant pressures. With comrades being arrested, having to go on the run or being killed, there was a continual and at times rapid turnover in personnel on the ground. This was how I found myself catapulted into a position of responsibility so far out of my comfort zone. Enormous power was frequently placed on young men and women who had to fill up vacant positions. For the organisation had to carry forward. Some were extremely young. I recall that an OC of one district was barely sixteen. This was by no means unusual, given the attrition rate. The derisive title 'boy general' was often applied in these instances. I think back with awe at the strength and commitment of some of those young lads. At twenty-one I found myself similarly thrust into a role above my experience and ability, and wondered how I might have coped with the responsibility at their age. A tough breed. I was determined to do my best. As ever, I found strength in thoughts of Joss. I swore never to let his name and my family down, nor my allegiance to the cause. After a mere six weeks in a position of authority, during which it was necessary for me to go on the run for the sake of some level of continuity (for being lifted would have been a disruption to the needed work on the ground), my turn came to endure Castlereagh. I had come through its testing three days, honour intact. Now, washed up from the conflict, I experienced sheer relief finding myself marooned on this unknown shore. I felt lighter with the possibilities of a new chapter. In reality, I had been transferred to another war front.

The escort brought us to a reception area, where we were placed into separate cubicles. We were individually mug-shot. More paperwork. The next three days were spent in the hospital compound, possibly to mend, but more likely to ascertain which cage we would be allocated, except that this wasn't in the gift of the camp authorities but of the two major republican groupings who controlled their respective cages. You were required to nominate a compound (which the internees knew as cages), double-talk for declaring which faction you wished to be housed with: Provos, Officials, nonaligned. I chose Cage Five, the only Provo cage with vacancies. Only Provos need apply! I later mused on the irony that this decision in effect could have been taken as an admission of membership of a proscribed organisation and, if judged so in court, might have resulted in a five-year sentence. However, not everyone in the designated Provo cages was a member, some choosing to be located near a relative, say, or to neighbourhood friends.

Harry Burns was the cage OC: mid-twenties, intelligent, approachable, naturally in charge; a very impressive figure. On the outside I had believed our best leaders were here. Harry seemed to confirm the notion. There were many mature, more experienced guys in the cage and throughout the camp. The press talked scathingly of 'older, sinister figures'. We laughed at that, deriding any suggestion that we needed to be ordered about, incapable of thinking for ourselves. The world was primed by media and pulpit to believe we were monsters, violent by training and nature. The reality never acknowledged was that we were all just local people: sons, fathers, uncles, brothers; a few grandads. In compensation for the lack of freedom I could learn much, and there was much to learn. Was there a better opportunity of getting a sense of the broad republican family – rural/urban, North/South, Left/Right, youth versus experience?

Cage Five, or Compound Five in systemese, baked in the summer heat of 1973. Long Kesh had a nickname to match the weather – the Lazy K. There were a lot of very young guys – sixteen- and seventeen-year-olds – with uncontainable energy levels, full of mischief. Water fights became a favoured distraction from the stresses of incarceration, the younger at heart joining in. All were targeted, none spared a soaking. Morale soared in the fine weather. Written accounts from ex-internees invariably focus on the camaraderie of life during those years, on the pranks and capers. A number of wistful memoirs of the Kesh have been published by former internees that include anecdotage detailing the hazing rituals perpetrated on men new to the cages, of which the best-known account, perhaps, is Bobby Devlin's *An Interlude with Seagulls.** These tales, although expressing the truth of the comradeship common to the period, perhaps tend also, I think it fair to say, to mask how tough conditions could be. But the bad times were easily shelved to the back of our collective consciousness because of the way being propped up together as comrades in those shared circumstances lifted all our spirits.

The honeymoon ended for me with a rattle of batons on the outside of the corrugated shell of the hut. I had heard about the Brit raids – to expect them about every four weeks. One was due. At staggered days, cages in turn would suffer the disruption and violence of a raid by a British Army search detail of perhaps fifty, with more on standby, kitted with shields, visored helmets and batons, along with sniffer dogs and their handlers. The raids usually began around five or six a.m. and might last several hours. Typically, we would be rudely awakened by the hut door being thrust open while batons were drawn with a thunderous clatter along the aforementioned corrugated fabric. Each hut held about thirty internees. The search party would take up position in the centre aisle between our beds. The Brit in charge would scream 'hands off cocks, on with socks'. Their own barrack-room reveille that they seemed pleased to share. We were searched individually then ordered out to the gym hut (empty of all except for a punchbag, say), at times having to run the gauntlet of snapping dogs, batons and verbal abuse. Inevitably there would be resistance, which would result in men being thrown up against the wire fence of the cage, assaulted further and forced to maintain stress positions – standing with legs spread, arms stretched out against the cage wall to support their bodyweight. At the end of the raid, which typically took up a whole morning, the Brits

---

*Bobby Devlin, *An Interlude with Seagulls: Memories of a Long Kesh Internee* (London: Information on Ireland, 1985).

would leave, and the screws would resume security duties at the gate. We were left to clean up the mess of our overturned huts. Property would be destroyed or missing. Artwork such as wooden harps, Celtic crosses, plaques, pen-drawn hankies disappeared, taken as trophies, we presumed. Bedding would be soiled by paw prints or urine, whether from the dogs or their handlers. Quite a frightening experience the first time.

I am unaware of any research into the numbers affected by the brutality of these raids. The following is just my calculation to give a sense of the extent. At full capacity, there were eight cages in the internees' end of the camp. Multiply that by two – a nominal average of the unfortunate men picked for a beating – by twelve for the months of the year, then by four for the years 1971–75, and you get a figure of 768 for the brutality meted out. But this must be an understatement. It would have been an easier research task to ascertain the small number who hadn't been at the receiving end. There were raids in which nearly everyone was subjected to rough handling. Many of our activities were planned in anticipation of the boot on the door. Craftwork intensified before family visits planned in expectation of the next raid, and in the immediate wake of a raid, new projects started. (Not least in the field of brewing! A constant preoccupation for some, whose ingenuity factored in risk of lost product.)

Within those first few weeks, the most recent of us to be scooped – a fresh intake of recruits along with many who had been previously interned but freed in the truce manoeuvrings of the previous year – were transferred to the newly refurbished Cage Six, which had been the remand cage for the 'sentenced end' of the camp; that is, holding those sentenced but having special category status. I found myself reunited with many volunteers I had got to know outside. Spirits were high in the cages, despite the obvious setback to the organisation on the ground back in Belfast and all the resultant churning over of command. And the war outside continued in our absence.

Physically, Six was little different from any of the other cages. Three of the four Nissen huts accommodated the seventy of us, or rather two and a half did, for beside the canteen cum wash house, one of the huts was divided between a gym and what was called in every cage the 'half-hut', usually accommodating older guys. Hard to imagine a worse plight than being a married man fretting over all the attendant familial anxieties while stuck in a hut full of teenagers crawling up the walls. Cage Six boasted a large yard, six laps for a mile. Seven laps per mile was the more usual circuit. I would pound the concrete in prison-issue boots. Trainers were unheard-of luxuries (I was nearly thirty before first owning a pair). The main cage recreation, however, was *bowlin'* (pronounced as in *fowl*, not *foal*) – walking, that is, whether alone or in groups, around the inside perimeter of the cage, and always, for some reason lost to me, anticlockwise. Every one of us must have put in several miles every day. The best time to think, to muse, to daydream, perchance to plan an escape.

Lads from all over the North and several from the South found themselves in comradely but involuntary proximity. From Belfast and Derry and Dublin, and many too from rural areas, all jostlingly cramped together. There was even a Yank in our hut, a former Green Beret. I got on particularly well with the 'Derry ones' (or *wans*, as they said it), who impressed me as being open and friendly. Easy-going. In contrast, Belfast lads seemed the more hard-bitten; more inclined to stick with others from their immediate company or battalion areas. To be thought parochial was a put-down, for we were all together in this struggle, but the old district loyalties and animosities were strong: Ardoyne versus the New Lodge; the Market versus the Strand; Ardoyne vis-à-vis the Bone. Belfast was a loose string of ghettoes (and quite apart from that other demarcation of our districts from Protestant/loyalist areas). Perhaps that's unfairly reductive, for there were always exceptions to the crude stereotypes. And the movement was a melting pot. In truth, there was little typical about the average internee. Each would have stood out in any normal society. We had our singers and instrumentalists, boxers and athletes, wits, craftsmen, poets and artists. The spread of different backgrounds and experiences offered a brilliant insight into the thinking and structure of the movement throughout Ireland. Nowhere was the failure of partition more evident. And I had grown up in England (and therefore was much in need of a learning curve).

Age, as mentioned, was another divider. At twenty-two when lifted, I was older than my average fellow internee, many of whom were teenagers, and quite a few were younger than seventeen. An apparent Brit policy change introduced in 1974 led to many more fifteen-year-olds being interned. Up till then, you might hear of arrests following a raid on some shebeen or club. Now, I half expected to read one day that a local unit had been lifted while watching Pan's People. It increasingly seemed that there were fewer old heads out there to carry on the fight. Later it grew apparent that there was a cynical Brit policy of bolstering the numbers as bargaining chips in the rundown of internment: the higher the number of internees, the longer any release programme could be dragged out, never mind the increased pressures on our families and communities.

I felt underprivileged by my formative years in England, disadvantaged; at times I felt somewhat alienated from the other lads, many of whom had grown up together, attended the same schools, dances, came from the same districts, often joining the movement at the same time. I was a rarity in having been brought up across the water, self-conscious of the difference. A friend shared something his mother, an old-school republican, had passed to him: never trust anyone you haven't known all your life. A hard outlook shaped in hard times. I was the outsider, despite having formed close friendships, tested on the streets, and was inclined, if not exactly a loner, to keep myself much to myself. While I was on 'the out', people grew to trust me because I proved my worth as a volunteer; in the Kesh I often felt I was back at square one, again having to establish trust. The fact that I had no apparent family outside to support me with food parcels, even letters, must also have raised eyebrows (Mum finally departing with the kids to join Dad in England in September 1973).

The Kesh that summer was a distrustful environment, the infiltration of our ranks by state agents and informers a matter of continual concern. And never unwarranted. The Brits were past and present masters at counterinsurgency. All freedom movements have to guard against state penetration. Outside, you sensed endless speculation and huddled whisperings in pokey bars and street corners, querying this one or that one's soundness. The debilitating impact of such a whispering frenzy isn't fully appreciable unless you've lived through it. Now it was happening here, in the cages. Part of the psychic fabric that imprisoned us mentally. I began to suspect anyone who initiated such talk. Was *I* suspect? Did they suspect that I suspected *them*? An instance – it was in Cage Two after 'the Burning' (of which more later): I caught one of the countrymen, a gangly, pinched, dirty-bearded Tyrone fellow, staring at me. Several times. He didn't try to conceal that he was doing so. He looked quite mad. Trying to psych me out? Well, none of us looked our best after sleeping rough for a month, a consequence of having destroyed our huts. Bowlin' round the yard one day, Anrai, who at the time was the camp IO, discreetly indicated 'yer man': 'He thinks you're a tout.'

'Why?'

'Because you keep yourself to yourself; that you must have something to hide.' I had been reported by a Secret Squirrel, one of the eyes and ears of our internal security. A valuable lesson. I fitted the bill! Or *a* bill. Discretion in the eyes of the Squirrels wasn't necessarily a measure of soundness. Touts may not be in your face, inquisitive, nosey.

I had tried not to court curiosity; to remain ever vigilant while keeping my own council. There were lads with us, sharing the same restricted huts and cages, who were either known or suspected of having broke during interrogation in Castlereagh. Until they were checked from outside (for all accounts had to be verified through our intelligence network), the staff policy was to insist that all cleared volunteers must feign ignorance about any suspicions to the suspect's face. We therefore had people in our midst whom we knew had broke and who possibly were turned by the Special Branch. The sense of betrayal was incredibly difficult to manage, destructive of any tolerance of weakness. But we were under orders. Depending on the degree of severity of his betrayal, when a volunteer was confirmed as having broke, he might be ostracised and then ordered to leave the cage. He would then transfer to Cage Eight, which also held men who for various reasons might not want association with the republican movement.

To this day I regret one encounter with a former comrade who was known to have broke, for he had declared this upon arrival. I had the greatest admiration and respect for this man, a legendary figure due to his leadership and operational abilities. How could he have broke? But, of course, anyone can. But him! The sense of betrayal was so extreme that all vestige of empathy was thoughtlessly lost in the moment of meeting him face to face. When he greeted me, I could see the shame in his eyes. He wasn't a man to make excuses or to hide what he had done. He deserved that I should have asked 'Why?' What had happened? Instead, I snubbed him. You can argue plausibly of the necessity in war to steel your senses against weakness. I had no words then to comprehend this conflicted mental state: I experienced a bewildering diminishment. I felt shame, as

I do to this day. He was, after all, a victim – and had come clean. The encroachment of that vileness of the dirty war inflicted by the British seemed magnified within our closed space. My way of coping with the resultant toxicity was to say little and, as Dad had often had to counsel, keep my nose clean.

As already indicated, many of the internees were well-known names and some were heroic figures, associated with leadership roles or famous deeds and escapes. In July we heard the news reported that senior Belfast republican figures had been arrested. Those arrested could be detained in Castlereagh for three days, as we all had. If true, this was a major coup for the Brits and a considerable setback for the struggle. Another swoop later in the year would give rise to rumours that many of the replacement staff had been lifted. The struggle dragged on. But there was a buzz about the camp as we anticipated the arrival of this round-up – unless they faced charges.

I wondered how these alleged leaders would conduct themselves and whether their presence might lead to an increased militarism within the cages, which I believed was needed; a corrective to the seeming lack of direction that typified for me the culture in the camp. There seemed to be precious little of what you might term military discipline. In contrast, the sentenced end, comprising cages holding convicted republicans, seemed to be run in a more traditionally militarised fashion. Maybe the overall level of disorder would improve in time through the direction and experience of men whom the media had cast as major players, plotters, planners, organisers and schemers. This was my thinking after the first months.

All those lifted came into Six, among them Brendan Hughes, Paul Marlowe and Gerry Adams. Gerry Adams, an almost mythical figure given what was reported in the news about him and his arrest, was suddenly here among us, and as quickly disappeared into the half-hut. Gerry A (pronounced *ah*), as we all soon came to know him, had long straggly hair, a beard and looked incongruous in T-shirt and bell-bottoms, hardly fitting the media build-up of a terrorist top dog. More an art student or a hippy. These, of course, were positive attributes for me, this failed art student and product of the 1960s. He couldn't have been more than twenty-four.

Gerry A didn't really surface for several weeks. You might get a rare sighting of him heading for the wash-house. Others lifted at the same time walked around the yard, some stripped to the waist in the July sun. All showed the signs of vicious beatings. One man displayed on his torso the worst bruising that I had ever witnessed, then and to date, literally black and purple, joined up all over. There was talk that he had held the rank of brigade QM. If true, you could well imagine how the Special Branch would have gone to town on him. It later emerged that small hammers had been used to beat them. Rumours swirled that Adams was also severely marked.

Perceptible changes did follow, but not really in terms of the type of militancy practiced in the sentenced end. In Six there was an increasing emphasis on discussion: in meetings, lectures. Gerry A and others close to him, perhaps by example more than camp policy, were at the centre of this welcome change. A Sinn Fein *cumann* was formed in the cage, which I readily joined. Beforehand, it was easier to feel yourself cut off from developments outside; now they were more the subject of debate. This development was in itself a unifying force, causing us to think more in terms of *we* rather than *I*; emphasising the collective rather than the individual.

I soon settled into a routine: lectures, exercise, reading, learning Irish. There were many very bright, extraordinarily gifted and clever minds at hand. What an opportunity to learn. I had never in my life before made any real effort to study, though always a reader. Education previously had been a means to a selfish end: the O-levels obtained with a minimum of effort during my approved school days, the only measurable benefit of which at the time was being released two weeks earlier than due in order to enrol at art school. Sufficient justification for me then. Then I wearied easily, prey to any fleeting distraction. But now, for the first time in my life, I learned I had the capacity to focus, and I wanted to know so much. I read anything I could lay my hands on. And there were books at hand in each hut, every cage. History, politics. The most sought-after read was General Frank Kitson's *Low Intensity Operations*, his 1971 formulaic condensation of lessons from imperial outposts, well-thumbed by the time I got hold of it. We simply wanted to understand what our enemy was about.

Fiction was more plentiful. I couldn't have envisaged back then that a discarded Jack Higgins novel, its jacket blurb purporting to offer insight into the Troubles, would one day motivate me to study for a doctorate on how the conflict had been grossly misrepresented in fiction.

I began to attend Irish classes in Six, an interest which flowed effortlessly from a new love of traditional Irish music. There were always a few *Gaeilgeoirs* (Irish speakers) around. I took my *Fáinne Airgid* (the silver ring denoting achievement at beginners' level). Later, in Cage Twenty-two, a group of us were so committed to promoting the language that we were for a few weeks able to establish a *Gaeltacht* hut, wherein only Gaelic would be spoken. I taught a *rang* (class) myself for a few months. That was the essence of the Kesh as a place of learning: you passed on what you knew. Some of the lads who attended my *rang* still to this day refer to me as *múinteoir*, the Irish for teacher. Sad to say, but despite gaining an O-level in Irish while in the Kesh (and later gaining the *Fáinne Óir* for fluency), I have only a *cúpla focal* now.

A lot of time was taken up throughout the camp with doing artwork for the Green Cross, the organisation tasked to support the dependents of captured republicans. Some men made wooden harps and Celtic crosses; others did drawings on hankies using coloured felt pens. Wooden plaques were very popular. Much prized by our families and support bases. Hardly a day of the week went by without you being asked to add your signature in black felt pen to the back of one, plus name your district. The subjects were invariably political – for example, highlighting issues of injustice or supporting the republican area of the artist. I did my share of these but soon tired of the rote sameness, having completed dozens with depictions of barbed wire, flags and guns. Then around September 1973, I received a Mass card for Louis Scullion (by then murdered a little over fourteen months), containing a thumbnail photo of him. Louis, who had been a friend for such a short while before his killing. I had a basic talent for sketching but had little utilised it since my one term at art school. In pencil I copied this blurred likeness on paper, trying to add some detail from memory, then tried the same depiction using black biro on a linen hanky. I developed this technique, using fine cross-hatching, to the point of achieving a photographic likeness but with slightly more depth. The word got around and soon I was being 'commissioned' to do portraits from photos sent in, usually of a dead volunteer or of a loved one killed. The original likeness was often an *In Memoriam* card. I was kept busy.

There was a hunger for answers among us and, as stated, a level of enquiry I hadn't till then experienced. There was, of course, the full range of training peculiar to a guerrilla army in captivity: GLs, ambush tactics, bomb circuitry, etc. And quite a bit of marching. The IRA had designated Long Kesh as the Fourth Battalion of the Belfast Brigade for organisational, line-of-command utility. The expanded level of army activity coincided with the growing knowledge that one day we would be released, back to the struggle. Individually and collectively we had to prepare for that eventuality. Some of us went further in our preparations. While in Six, a group under the leadership of Tommy (Todler) Tolan, one of the most inspiring guys I have ever met, took part in a more structured programme of training and instruction. I eagerly volunteered for this development. About fifteen of us functioned as a group within a half-hut, all our activities separate from the rest of our comrades: rising earlier for physical training and a run; preparing food and eating as a group; lectures back to back; and finishing with a political/topical discussion before lights out at ten. For our pains we were lightly mocked as 'super-Provos' by some of the other lads. This experiment lasted for only a month, but this was by far the most meaningful and instructive period I had in the cages. I grew surer about myself and of my future commitment.

My remaining time in the Kesh was shaped and energised by that experience of comradeship and purpose in Todler's initiative. But there was still the general atmosphere of enquiry to engage with. We would attend lectures on Irish history, and on the justification for the armed struggle. We learned about the importance of categorising our enemies. The word *enemy*, we learned, was too readily applied to our opponents and critics, not merely those who would kill us; a distinction easily lost in times of war, when apparently little difference marked those who presented a direct threat and others whose opposition was political or critical. This was a crucial corrective in those polarising times, especially as our enemies conspired to whip up sectarian tensions. While it may be justifiable to counter violence with violence, lies should be challenged by the truth; their *truth* by our truth. Thus began my appreciation of what later would be termed the 'battle of the narratives'. Much of the matter of these discussions had formed and informed our thinking as volunteers outside, but the pressing grind of the war left us little room to think with greater clarity. 'Them or us' had too often been the logic of those days. We also attended lectures about the reasons for the 1970 split – about how the political direction and analysis of the pre-split IRA had rendered it incapable of defending nationalist areas against loyalist mobs. The term *Provisional* was frowned upon, we learned, now that the movement was constitutionally established. We were volunteers of *Óglaigh na hÉireann* (variously translatable as 'soldiers', 'warriors' or 'volunteers of Ireland').

The knowledge shared from within the pool of talent among us was supplemented by outside lecturers. During the latter months of 1973, a scheme began which allowed academics and writers into the camp. In Six, lectures took place weekly in a Portakabin beside the canteen. I remember hearing Miriam Daly from Queens University explain to about ten of us squeezed together therein that to understand the past – events and people – one should judge them first in the light of their day, not ours. I thought that a mighty insight. Miriam was to be murdered by collusive forces in 1980. Another lecturer who impressed was the writer and playwright Stewart Parker, who later gained some fame for his play *Spokesong* (inspired by a bicycle repair shop in Cromac Square, near to where I was born). He taught us creative writing. This encouraged me to have a go at writing poetry, failing to have been sufficiently inspired by the genius of Seamus Heaney. Mercifully, my wretched scribblings are long lost. Writing, prose and fiction, became a personalised routine for many. Which vaguely brings to mind a conversation about poetry I had with Gerry A, in which he shared a political poem he'd written, epic in scale, that for me seemed very clever in terms of structure and subject. There was no doubt in my mind that one day he would pen something extraordinary and definitive about the struggle.

Adams undoubtedly saw further than any of us politically. I recall one of his lectures particularly. He asked: 'Do any of you think this war will be over soon?' This met with a blank response around the hut. 'Five years? Twenty?' No takers. By this stage, certainly, I was disabused of any notion that I would be home (wherever that might be) by Christmas. However, in the swell of events there seemed little scope to question the likely duration of the conflict. We were all too close to the forest floor to perceive the view afforded from the canopy. Adams had foreseen the future course of the struggle more keenly than any of us in that hut, or indeed within the republican movement. A marker was being set. We had to get real. He understood that our greatest weakness must be turned into our greatest strength. As a movement we were woefully inadequate in terms of the political organisation capable of effectively building the political pressure for reunification. This reality had to set our future course of action. From the here and now, one can discern the trajectory of the movement's development back to those debates in the cages.

While some were looking to a more radical future course for the movement, others kept true to an earlier, more traditional outlook. This became evident to me following a lecture given by an academic from Queen's University, whose name I've forgotten, although I enjoyed his thought-provoking, very informative visits. The lecture was on the history of radical political philosophy, at the end of which all who attended, and it was well attended, were each given a single A4 sheet of notes and suggestions for further reading: Babeuf, Marx, Connolly, etc. Discussions on the lecture continued among us back in our huts, or while bowlin' round the yard. A discussion I was involved in was interrupted when the cage adjutant (second in command) entered the hut and ordered us to hand over the lecture notes on the stated basis that it was communist literature and thereby contravened then IRA general orders. The order in question, number four, that forbid volunteers from membership of the Communist Party, was more in tune with the political climate of the 1930s.* The sheets were handed over to the adjutant without demur. I was shocked, but I also complied when asked in turn. I was following the lead of others, although I had doubts about the action that cut into me, which on the surface seemed nonsensical, for there was a considerable amount of reading matter on socialism and political history and theory readily available to us throughout the camp. There was still a bit of the anarchist in me. I reined in my disapproval. The authority and discipline of the IRA were of overriding importance.

I was interned in Long Kesh from June 1973 until November 1975. During that time I was held in Cages Five, Six, Two, Twenty-two and, finally, Three. The hardest part of internment was the not knowing when you would be released. Without a release date, the day-to-day pressures of

---

*J. Bowyer Bell, *The Secret Army* (Poolbeg, 1997), p. 246.

incarceration mounted, making it more difficult to settle into a routine. Our release was at the discretion of some faceless Direct Rule politician. In consequence, a lot of guys were wrecks, suffering from the Big D (depression), tuning in to every news broadcast for *scéal* (loosely meaning 'information') about any political breakthrough that might herald early releases. It was nigh impossible for many to think deeply about the future while the exigencies of our daily reality, both inside and outside, vied for our immediate attention. These were dangerous times. We were not immune from machinations of the external world. Rumours about political progress were rife, if unfounded. In fact, in what many internees regarded as the absence of effective leadership, the movement outside appeared to have been fooled into negotiating a truce in the belief that the British were contemplating a withdrawal strategy. Merlyn Rees, the Labour Direct Rule secretary of state, revealed the truth of the matter in a letter to Harold Wilson in which he is cited as admitting that the British negotiators 'set out to con them and ... did'.* The struggle for the Republic, as we would have classified it, was never so perilously close to defeat. With hindsight it is clear that the movement was not then capable of negotiating from a position of strength. The best that could be said of the truce is that it bought time for regrouping and reorganising.

To add weight to this perception of the movement's then lack of the necessary strength, at an earlier point, an order came from the camp staff for us to attend what were known as the Brown tribunals, a British initiative designed to put a judicial gloss over internment to allay international criticism. Now, each internee would receive a detention order with a list of allegations, none of which would stand up in a normal court. If the three-man tribunal found in favour, the internee would be released. Evidence from British operatives and informers was allowed and given anonymously. The rationale behind our decision to attend this process was that some men might be released, because men were in dire need outside, due to the scale of attrition. I was one of the first to attend the proceedings, much against my own judgement. My instinct would have been to boycott

*Tim Pat Coogan, *The IRA* (Palgrave Macmillan, 2002), p. 643, citing Sinn Fein, *Setting the Record Straight: A Record of Communications between Sinn Fein and the British Government* (1994), p. 28.

the humiliating sham. But although I voiced my opposition to attending, an order was an order. My detention order came with the list of allegations: that I was the Third Battalion EO, responsible for directing acts of terror, etc. The list included one specific allegation: that I had conspired with others in the killing of a Royal Marine in the New Lodge (about sixty men faced the same allegation). Evidence from an RUC branchman was given, as allowed, from behind a screen. It mattered not a jot that I had had no part in that operation. The whole procedure was a farce. Further evidence, if it were needed, appears in the fact that many men were alleged to have carried out the bombing in December 1971 of McGurk's Bar, in which fifteen customers and staff were killed, an outrage we all knew had been perpetrated by loyalists (the British Army file on the bombing is closed until 2056, spurring the suspicion that British intelligence's Military Reaction Force had some hand in it*). Whether the policy of attending the tribunals made a difference to the struggle in terms of the release of men who otherwise would not have been released is a matter of conjecture. I tend to think not.

Of course, we were never immune from the politics on the ground outside. More than at any other time, the North was on the brink of civil war. We followed the unfolding of the loyalist Ulster Workers' Council strike in May 1974 in opposition to power-sharing and a Council of Ireland under the Sunningdale Agreement of December 1973. The Labour government capitulated to the violence of the loyalists and the power-sharing Assembly was collapsed. We were concerned for the safety of our districts and of our families. The movement outside prepared for a doomsday situation. We also made plans. One scenario envisaged the takeover of Long Kesh by the Ulster Defence Regiment (formed to replace the B Specials, a hated sectarian militia dissolved in 1970). We feared what later would be called ethnic cleansing. Contingencies were actively debated and planned. Conditions in both ends of the Kesh were never good, but they had deteriorated to such an extent that throughout much of 1974 the camp was on the verge of being burned down. There had been near calls. Then it happened.

The order to burn the camp came from the sentenced end. They appeared to be in the driving seat. It was mid-October. There was dissent from the

_____

*Irish News, 11 January 2018.

decision among the internees, with some arguing that we shouldn't. I was playing chess with a Derryman before lock-up at ten. The game was interrupted when a member of the battalion staff, another Derryman, field-promoted my chess opponent to cage OC. My opponent's first duty was to implement the order. Within a matter of minutes, contingencies were in full swing. I managed to gather a few personal items – photos, books, a pen – then joined in, with some enthusiasm, the allotted task of setting the huts alight. The sky was already lit up with the flames from the sentenced end. Our cages were soon ablaze in tandem. The screws all withdrew. We cut our way out of our respective cages and mustered in Cage Four. Gas canisters were dropped on us. CR gas was used, a carcinogenic. According to the CR Gas Research Group, scores of former republican POWs have since died or are suffering from cancer and respiratory illnesses because of exposure to the toxin that night.* Rubber bullets were also fired. John Joe McGirl, a Leitrim man in his sixties, had his cheekbone smashed by one. There was a fear that the Brits would take advantage of the chaos to kill Adams. In the end the sentenced POWs got the worst of the ensuing brutality as the Brits in their hundreds took back control.

We imagined that first night that the prison authorities would have to come up with an alternative location: the cages were clearly destroyed. Uninhabitable. Perhaps we would be moved to the Crum, or into a commandeered military hangar? Some saw opportunities for escape. We in fact spent the next six weeks practically under the stars, save for makeshift shelter provided by the burnt remains of the huts. The intact outer fencing in each cage was judged secure enough to allow for this. The screws took a back seat. The Brits were very much in control. This did not stop us seizing on the opportunity for escapes. Every internment cage had a tunnel on the go, disguised by the rubble of the old huts. We hadn't the logistical concern of how to secrete the dug-up soil. It was a race to tunnel to the perimeter, then a mass escape. I was in Cage Two, the low location of which meant that we tunnelled deeper into the water table. Our tunnel collapsed. Cage Five's tunnel was best situated and reached beyond the perimeter three weeks after the burning. Tragically, Volunteer Hugh Coney was shot dead by a Brit sentry while emerging from the tunnel. Three others escaped

---

*Jim McCann, *And the Gates Flew Open* (Glandore Publishers, 2019), p. 73.

but were caught next day on the outskirts of Belfast. Hugh, or George as we knew him, was from Coalisland, Tyrone. He had been in Cage Six originally, where one night a group of us had chatted about favourite weapons, comparing the merits of the Armalite over the M1 carbine, say. George was asked to cite his weapon of choice: 'Two hundred yards of bell wire.' We all laughed at that. Great man.

In early December, we were shifted from our makeshift shanties to hastily constructed wooden huts in other cages. Conditions improved. Negotiations outside had resulted in a truce. Internment was to be ended. Over the following months, hundreds of internees were released, in batches of six, twice weekly. My time came in November 1975. By then, about a hundred men remained behind the wire. I left the Kesh with as little as I had entered with in material terms – as was customary, I didn't take the few books and art materials I had managed to gather. But I left a stronger person, more determined, better informed and with a clearer vision of what I could now contribute to the cause. The last group of men were released on 5 December. While this policy was being implemented, a wall was being constructed outside of the cages, in sight, which later became the perimeter of what became known as the H-Blocks. Voiced forebodings about the longevity of the conflict were justified. In accordance with the recommendations of the Gardiner Committee's 1975 report, special category status would end on 1 March 1976. The British state signalled its determination to criminalise the republican struggle. Within three years, the Blocks were full.

6

Back to War

'If there must be trouble, let it be in my day, that my child may have peace.'
— Thomas Paine, 1737–1809

On the morning of 7 November 1975, I was woke by a comrade assigned to orderly duties that week in Cage Three, in effect our daily point of contact with the screws over parcels, letters, visits. For months now individuals had been summoned to the gate on Mondays and Fridays to be told they were to be released. Each release brought my moment closer. Now I was wanted at the gate. It was a Friday.

A screw ushered me into the wee hut beside the gate. Inside, a governor, with whom I was often offhand because of his presumption of authority over me, gladly informed me to pack my bags. I was going home. To Belfast anyway, for I had no fixed abode and would have to rely at least initially on the support of friends. The last of the remaining internees, about a hundred men, were released over the next four weeks — I won't say freed, for we returned to our Brit-occupied districts. My two and a half years interned in the Kesh were the equivalent of five years as a sentenced prisoner under the fifty per cent remission scheme then operative, which made prisoners eligible for release from halfway through their sentence. A Green Cross transit van collected the eight of us released that day (among them Whitey Bradley, a fellow G Company comrade, who was to die tragically) for the nine-mile journey to central Belfast. I can now barely recall the drive away from the camp other than that I didn't look back. In stark contrast, never before had I been so fixed of purpose as I faced into the future. No longer in over my head, I knew exactly what I wanted to do. I intended to volunteer to operate in England, to be part of the strategy of taking the war across the water. I was never more focused, determined, committed, more sure of my own mind and responsibilities. I recognised the same determination in other comrades. Any misgivings about the parlous state of the movement soon faded as we upped our engagement in the conflict.

In the contemporary context of fundamentalism, the term *radicalisation* is much bandied about, and often used to obscure rather than enlighten. My state of mind then, however, had nothing to do with indoctrination, the organised straitjacketing of thought, but was a result of the paradoxical freedom allowed within the huts and cages to talk, listen, argue, engage and, vitally for me, to read. We were not reduced to the laboured poring-over of the one canonical text. The choice was as wide as our circumstances of confinement allowed. I took a very cold appraisal of what was needed in terms of the struggle and of how I could best contribute. In reaching a decision, I looked at my contribution to date, of my active days prior to capture two and a half years before. I had learned much of value as an internee. But those formative years in England were also part of an armoury of experience that couldn't be discounted. Many of the guys had never been out of Belfast, let alone abroad. This gave me an edge. Nothing was clearer to me than where the IRA could maximise its impact, pound for pound. England was where I could most effectively contribute to the struggle. If the conclusions reached were extreme, so was the context. Once I had decided, it was a matter of waiting for the moment when I would be in touch with the right people. This was not a decision to entrust to the normal channels. In the meanwhile, I would do whatever was required at the local level. Within an hour of my return to the New Lodge, therefore, I reported back for active duty.

Although on ceasefire, the Provos, in my view, were in the throes of an ill-judged feud with the Sticks (the Official IRA). My first duties involved being on standby to defend the district from further attacks. Thankfully I never had to fire a shot. Feuding with other republicans with whom we were supposedly at ideological loggerheads was at its barest a distraction from engaging with the real enemy, and sometimes engineered or facilitated by that enemy in the spirit of divide and rule, and a matter of deep aversion for me. I was to lose two friends, one of them Tommy Tolan, in another feud barely eight months later, both killed within hours of each other, hammering home the utter futility.

Much had changed (and not just the inflationary jump in the cost of a pint since 1973–18p to 35p!). Before I was interned, all doors seemed open, literally. Not only in the districts I had become most familiar with – Unity Flats, the New Lodge area, Newington, Ardoyne and the Market. In an emergency (for example, to avoid a Brit foot patrol), I had then felt free to enter any home with the certainty of receiving help. This had been true of all nationalist areas without exception, whether in the narrow red-brick terraces of the Market and Falls or in the relatively newer estates of Andytown and the Murph. But during the two and a half years that had elapsed, the mood had changed. People were scared. Of loyalist sectarian killer gangs; of state forces. Some were scared of us. This was due to a mixture of fear about Brit reprisals, of collusion, of feuding among republicans, and, particularly sad to admit, because of grievances arising from abuses of power by a few individual republicans. With most of us either incarcerated or on the run, the movement seemed to drift perilously close to defeat. Supporters who had known me before my internment complained about individual members who had abused their power. They felt that the ranks had miraculously swelled during the ceasefire, allowing many 'undesirables' to become involved who otherwise would never have raised their heads above the parapet or, indeed, have been accepted. There was always a solid core of activists holding the line, however; and there is merit in the view that the ceasefire allowed the movement to regroup and reorganise.

There was also a new social phenomenon – the hoods. Over 1972–3, tartan gangs, gangs of loyalist football supporters, terrorised the city centre. It seemed they now had a nationalist equivalent, the hoods, although their area of sway and pillage was less the city centre than their own nationalist districts. They hated us, hated republicans. Why in little more than two years had this level of grievance and disaffection been allowed to fester, emanating from teens in particular? It made for a more difficult environment in which to operate. Many doors previously open were now closed.

Attitudes had hardened towards the IRA. War weariness had settled in; criticism from pulpit and editorial had become more vociferous. A constant diet of doctored news had also turned off many across the border in the South. In Britain, the public were denied the truth and instead fed a rancid diet of lies about the conflict. Emergency legislation was used to cow the Irish community in Britain. Our critics, North and South, by and large were removed from the realities of the struggle. Easier to be critical when geographically distant from the area of conflict. We had critics within our areas too.

Of course, there were many instances of people in our districts who opposed our armed struggle or politics (or the perceived lack of political organisation or policies). One example is that of the Women for Peace of 1976, who in response to a particular tragedy organised and marched to pressurise for an end to the IRA's campaign. Their message was 'peace now', which republicans interpreted as 'peace at any price'. Our support base sought 'peace with justice'. In hindsight, I perceive the Women for Peace to have been well-meaning in many instances, but anti-republican, and feeding on war weariness to defeat our struggle. Back then I was contemptuous of the Peace People (as they later renamed themselves).

My intention to be part of the England campaign had to wait while I was drawn inexorably into the struggle in Belfast, in the confusion and mess of the time. We all were. I have only a sketchy recall of the mid-1970s there, when I was most involved after release. In order to be reacquainted with those memories I would have to wade through the coverage of that period as reported by the local press: the *Irish News*, the *Newsletter* and the *Belfast Telegraph*. But I am aware from being on the ground during those days that much of what was happening in the districts went unreported.

Initially, I operated within the old brigade structure; before, that is, the IRA's more effective reorganisation into cells. In theory, cell members would not know the identity of other cells' members. Cells would have specific functions; for example, a cell might be dedicated to gathering intelligence. But it was under the older structure of brigade, battalion and company that the IRA went back to war in earnest after the truce petered out at the start of 1976. I was quickly assigned a role in a brigade active service unit (ASU). Promotion followed. 1976 was a busy year.

A typical day for me would begin with an early start. The Brits raided early. It was best to be up before them. I would light a fire in the hearth, ears tuned to the street, then sit close while making a list of what was to be done that day – meetings to attend, places to be. Once I had that clarified in my head, I would burn the list, or sooner if there was a crash at the door. Once the district had woke – the few who had jobs would head out; kids would be running errands to the corner shops – house raids would be less likely because of the decreased element of surprise. I could relax a bit.

Another use of the hearth – no matter how familiar I was with timing circuitry, I *always* drew out a diagram of the particular device required before its use. Again, this helped to sharpen your thinking. The timing mechanisms and the safety routines might be simple, but in the stress of an operation and of the unexpected, it was best to have mentally rehearsed. You could never be too familiar with bomb-making, for you wouldn't get a second chance if something went wrong (Brendan Behan had employed a Gaelic euphemism for dynamite: '*bas gan sagairt*' – 'death without a priest').

It took me two months to make contact with someone who I could trust to discreetly pass on to the right source my request to operate in England. The opportunity arose at a training camp in the 'South' – in Donegal, the most northerly county on the island of Ireland. I had known better than to broadcast my intentions through the usual channels. The least who knew of my intentions, the better. Only those whom I judged needed to know. Now all I could do was wait, for the logistics involved in organising out of the country posed huge difficulties. However, after the recent capture in London of an ASU (dubbed the 'Balcombe Street gang' by the media), I hoped that my application might now receive due attention.

In the meanwhile, I was active in the North. I would be stopped and questioned by Brit foot patrols or at road blocks nearly every day. Sometimes more than once. I was in and out of Castlereagh, the Special Branch interrogation centre, 'like a yo-yo', as a former branchman was to claim decades later in a television documentary. On occasions I'd get beaten, if only a few slaps. At other times I would be arrested under Special Powers legislation and practically ignored, spending forty-eight hours or more in the holding centre, then released. The idea, we suspected, was to disrupt imminent operations, as you couldn't send volunteers out on ops while someone with logistical knowledge was in custody. Arms and explosives dumps might also have to be moved as a precaution. Perhaps the intention was to lift someone to see what stirred. It became increasingly essential to avoid the disruption of arrest, never mind the beatings.

The dynamic of a Special Branch interrogation was often very different from that held by the Criminal Investigation Department. I don't mean because of the amount of brutality that might be sanctioned. A burglar, say, if not caught red-handed, might try to assert innocence, perhaps offer an alibi or reasonable mitigation. IRA volunteers, suspects and supporters, however, understood that in the mind of the state they were already guilty. There was little point or dignity in trying to persuade a Special Branch zealot otherwise. Better to say as little as possible, and preferably nothing. That, in fact, was the directive given to volunteers. The Branch knew in many instances who were responsible from the body of intelligence accumulated. They knew fine well when they were being lied to. I never had to pretend innocence. I only had to keep schtum. To say nothing, or to repeat the mantra, 'No comment.' They were the enemy. You were in their hands. They knew what you were at. You would have the last say on the streets. But you had to get back on the streets.

Oddly, it occurs to me, I have little recollection of having been asked many direct questions during any period of detention about my activities – whether I planted a device at such and such, etc. However, I do recall one – I think half-baked – attempt to recruit me as an informer. While being escorted back to the holding unit after an interrogation, I was halted in a corridor and one of the branchmen offered me £25,000 to work with them. In a mischievous mood, I replied: 'What about £50,000?' I was unceremoniously shoved back into a cell. Either I wasn't worth the suggested amount or they hadn't taken me seriously.

While I was totally immersed in the day-to-day conduct of the armed struggle, which on the ground left little space for reflection and analysis, the publication in 1976 of Michael Farrell's *Northern Ireland: The Orange State** proved for many of us an empowering moment, encapsulating our thinking and understanding of the neocolonial history of the North. During internment, I had striven to understand the historical context. I was certainly more politically aware from that experience. But we all sought a more definitive explanation of the underlying logic of state violence and oppression. Farrell's book was the first serious, detailed historical analysis of the bloody imposition of partition. I think I read it overnight in someone's spare room, although skimming the historical stuff to attentively grasp insights into the more recent developments that we all had some direct knowledge of or opinion about, such as the failure of the civil rights campaign. In truth, I found little space to read in the madness of those years.

---

*Michael Farrell, *Northern Ireland: The Orange State* (Pluto Press, 1976).

On 18 June 1976, I was lifted along with four others from a house in Spring-field Avenue. After sealing off the surrounding streets, the Brit raiding party came through the front and back doors simultaneously. Our hands were tied behind us with plastic binds, the first time I'd ever seen them used (although I have read that they were in use at least as far back as the mid-1973 period). In Castlereagh I was beaten by the branchman who seemed to have been in charge of the house raid. He singled me out for attention. He was a tallish, gaunt-faced but athletic-looking man of about thirty, with a short reddish beard. He slapped me about. In a later session, he was more restrained in the presence of someone who I took to be in charge. In a bit of gameplay, I upbraided him for his earlier manner ('Oh, you weren't so civil when you were knocking me about the room!'), at which he apologised. He had no qualms about tacitly admitting the *supposed* breach in procedure in front of his boss. It was a farce. Brutality was at the centre of Castlereagh's remit. All of us detained were released after three days. Soon after, the Reverend Ian Paisley expressed outrage in the House of Commons, demanding to know why men caught at what he claimed under parliamentary privilege to be a Belfast Brigade staff meeting had not been charged.

I was to encounter the same branchman in Castlereagh about nine months later. By then Roy Mason had replaced Merlyn Rees as secretary of state. Mason threatened to 'squeeze the IRA like toothpaste'. Statisti-cally, in terms of the rate of bombing and shooting incidents, 1976 was the second most active year (1972 being the first). The gloves were off, as I immediately sensed within minutes of arrival at Castlereagh. 'Red Beard' and his colleague beat me for over two hours. Neither seemed overly concerned to get information from me, more to soften me up for further interrogation. No more good guy/bad guy mind games. I felt concussed from the constant slaps to my head and punches to my stomach. In the final moments, Red Beard spat in my face and forced me against a wall. The session ended after he put a gun to the back of my head, threaten-ing that one day soon I would be walking up the road when I would be abducted and never seen again. Abductions were a constant source of anxiety on the streets, given that the loyalist Shankill Butchers were at the height of their sectarian butchery, logistically assisted, we believed, by state forces. I was then questioned for about two hours by another team, who seemed disappointed that the earlier session hadn't loosened my tongue.

When being released around midnight, after the statutory three days, I was warned by a uniformed RUC man: 'We've a surprise for you.' More mind games! But I was released from Castlereagh without further ado, and got into a taxi hired by my girlfriend, Eileen, who was in the car with some friends of ours. On reaching the junction with May Street in the city centre, the taxi was rammed from the side by a heavy open jeep. The car was a write-off; the driver and some of the passengers suffered various injuries – one had a broken arm, others bruised, all badly shaken. We were kept by the Brits at the scene of the 'accident', despite the injuries. An 'off-duty' RUC man had followed in a car. He stopped at the scene and offered to testify that the Brits were at fault, which seemed to bring matters to an end, and we were eventually allowed to go after they'd kept us there for close to an hour. I was convinced that the 'surprise' intended for me was my re-arrest. Had they gone too far, not expecting the casualties? Hard to figure. How would it play in the press if a crash victim was lifted? It was a scary wait. At this time, there was a spate of murder attempts on alleged key IRA figures in Belfast.

During this period of my involvement with the Belfast structure, my freedom of movement was severely restricted – and, therefore, my ability to work effectively. The sophistication of Brit surveillance technology and techniques was paranoia-inducing. Car journeys would entail careful vigilance of the traffic behind and an equal attention given to the manoeu-vrings of the ever-present 'eye in the sky' – surveillance helicopters had the means to monitor not only traffic movement but also movement of people on the ground (at times it was difficult to convince comrades that we were being followed by a helicopter). Typically, at this point I would be stopped by Brit patrols at least once a day; often twice or three times. I was a red light. This was known, of course, to others around me. I recall a meeting one day with Brian Keenan, who was the adjutant general (number two in the command hierarchy and in an absolutely frontline position) and the Belfast Brigade vice OC. Brian said he wanted to stand me down from my position in Belfast on account of the heat. In fact, he argued that this was overdue. I somehow suppressed my glee: now was my chance to operate in England. The vice OC said, 'We need him.' In a sense, that is how bad the situation was. And so I continued in my position despite being, I believed, quite a serious security liability.

Occasionally my role required me to cross the border. I took risks, cutting corners on security. I recall one trip when I was stopped on the way back at a checkpoint outside Newry. I was in the passenger seat. The driver was a friend. There was an amount of sensitive documentation and money secreted behind a door panel in his car that we had agreed to take North as a last-minute favour. It was a stupid risk. Not a significant loss if discovered but sufficient to guarantee a prison sentence. The Paras at the start of a new tour of duty were manning the roadblock. A squaddie checked my ID. I wasn't using false papers. I was too known to ever get away with a subterfuge. After a short delay, he returned to the car to say that his boss wanted a word with me. I had to leave the car and join the local commander of the Paras. We stood in the middle of the roadblock, out of earshot of everyone. He got straight to the point. He couldn't 'give a fuck' about what I or the IRA got up to in Belfast. This was his 'turf' and he threatened to 'deal with' me should I return there. I was then told to 'piss off' back to the car. We proceeded on our journey without a vehicle search. There were similar incidents.

There were also moments that I cherish as instances of a common decency so easily lost in the fog of conflict. Some small consideration. A simple courtesy or kindness that shows the humanity in us all – all combatants. I'll relate one.

I was scooped in Andytown by the Marines and brought in the back of a Saracen to Fort Monagh, one of a series of huge military installations built from 1972 throughout the occupied districts as part of Operation Motorman. I was facing four hours there, then transfer to Castlereagh. The desk sergeant, a morose type, unleashed this vomit of invective at me: 'Facking Irish, everyone facking picking on you facking Irish bastards . . .' He continued at some length in this vein while I was required to empty my pockets. A 10p coin dropped to the wooden floor, rolled and settled at the boot of one of the squaddies. Perhaps foolishly, he picked it up and went to hand it back to me. 'Don't you facking dare … these bastards have us running after them . . .' Surprisingly, I was released. The same young Marine (younger I think than me – I was twenty-five) escorted me to a small gate in the huge corrugated outer wall. He said, 'Sorry about all that.' I think we both agreed that it had been 'uncalled for'. 'Take care,' I said. I hate to think that anything would have happened to him.

Soon after this, I had to go on the run. While still in the North, I believe I represented a potential danger really to anyone I came in contact with because of my high profile. My nerves were bad. I couldn't sleep. I remember being in a house up in the Antrim Glens. I was reading through a recent issue of *Republican News* when my eye caught a memoriam notice. It was for Joey Surgenor, Frank Fitzsimmons and Paul Marlowe, three comrades who had been blown to bits in October 1976 by the bomb they were arming while targeting the army base within the grounds of the Ormeau Road gasworks. A giant gasometer exploded and lit up Belfast like a halogen lamp. It had only been a year ago but I had forgotten the anniversary. I started to cry uncontrollably. The first and only time as an adult. How was it possible to forget such a loss? But that's what you did. Attritional amnesia. You had to accrete protective layers in order to get on with it.

During the havoc of these mere few years of my involvement in the movement to date, I somehow managed to get married to Eileen. I was in disguise entering the church for the ceremony. We had a son. Life was going on for all of us. But having a son caused a massive change in my outlook in terms of my commitment to the struggle. I had left Long Kesh under no illusion about what the future might hold in store for me, and for every one of us: as ever, a return to a prison cell, a life on the run or a hole in the ground. But that didn't seem to dent the drive I felt to do all in my power to further the struggle. Now, though, I had my son's future to think of. There was a new urgency in my desire to be as effective as possible. Meeting Maire and Jimmy Drumm came to mind. I had been interned at the same time as their son, Seamus. Maire, vice president of Sinn Fein, was shot dead in her hospital bed by loyalists in October 1976. I recall not being able to get my head around the fact that Jimmy had spent a total of fifteen years incarcerated (thirteen of them in various periods as an internee) for his involvement going back to the 1930s. This was six years into the current campaign (at which point in time Nelson Mandela had been in prison since 1962 – fourteen years). I didn't want my son to grow up to have to face the same set of questions that I had to answer in 1972. To ensure that didn't happen, that we didn't bequeath that choice to this next generation, the struggle had to end with us.

These were days moving from one safe house to another; nights in different beds but still up before the anticipated four a.m. raid. The returns from all this effort, and the risk to those who protected me, did not match the sacrifices made. I was a danger to everyone around me. Finally, the movement wakened up to its parlous state – never defeated, but certainly less than capable of mounting an effective prosecution of the war. We had to get our act together. Behind the scenes, the perceived deficiencies of the traditional hierarchical mode of organisation were supplanted by the supposedly more secure lateral cellular model. The old brigade was stood down. Under the direction of the new structures, a reinvigorated commercial bombing campaign was mounted.

I was now free to pursue a commitment to volunteer for the England campaign. I was told the rationale behind the campaign: to break the bipartisan policies of successive British parliaments, whether of Labour, then in power, or of the Tories. The creation of such a rift in the cosy political establishment's denial of the normal Westminster cat fight, arguably, would capitalise on public disaffection with policy and cause a thorough policy reappraisal, which in turn might pave the way for or encourage an eventual negotiated end to the conflict. A survey conducted by the *Daily Mirror* at this time revealed a majority in its British readership supported a Brit withdrawal, in line with an earlier *Daily Telegraph* (9 December 1975) poll which put the support at sixty-four per cent.

From 1978 onwards, between long bouts of hanging around, waiting for orders, I was involved in some capacity or another with the England campaign. After the relative looseness of the operational environment we had become accustomed to, operating in England was a culture shock. Firstly, more weight was placed on a volunteer's ability to demonstrate a high degree of initiative and to maintain a covert existence. The other volunteers I was to work with were without exception very capable people, all of whom shared a mutual recognition of the strategic importance of the England campaign. No longer could we trust to the sympathies of local people, latent or committed. In England we were on our own, dependent entirely on each other. Our only point of contact with the command structures at home was via phone numbers that had to be memorised. Phone conversations would be conducted in a stilted code, appearing non-sensical or inconsequential to an eavesdropper. This was in a pre–social media era. A missed call and you were possibly left on your own until the next prearranged window of contact. If that were to happen, and it happened to me a couple of times, the consequences would be hugely stressful, even terrifying. I remember an occasion when I would have given an arm for a broom cupboard to hole up in – just to get off the streets. Suddenly you might be facing decades of your life in prison, or worse. The only choice was to keep your nerve and survive. However, for the most part, I adapted well to this atmosphere, so far removed from all the immediacy of trauma and turmoil of our war-torn areas. I cannot now say, however, that my years growing up in England were of much consequence. I even found it difficult to revert back to using an English accent.

Secretary of State Roy Mason might bluster and squeeze all he wanted. The IRA had proved itself resilient and uncontainable. The stakes were still high, and perhaps higher, for with certainty the state would invest some considerable effort to deal with the threat we posed. But it was a totally different environment in which to operate, and one which bolstered my conviction that we would prevail. A conviction never stronger than the day we stood on the top floor of a shopping mall overlooking the rear of the Brighton Centre during the British Labour Party's annual conference and imagined Mason's reaction if he knew how close we were.

7

Burnout

In 1979 I returned to Ireland after active service in England. I was twenty-seven, already wanted in the North and under strict orders from the IRA not to cross the border in case I was arrested for my activities in England. This was a justifiable precaution, for arrests to do with our overseas campaign would have been a strategic setback for us and a propaganda coup for our enemies. The restriction was also justified because many Northern volunteers had found it difficult to cope with the harsh realities of life on the run in the South. For Northerners, it felt like a form of internal exile. The compulsion to head back to family and to the familiar across the border to the North often proved too strong. I found myself marooned in the Free State.

There was, however, no telling when exactly I might be of further use as a volunteer. I had been told only that I featured prominently in future plans. Nothing was specified, but I took that to mean either a future role in the English campaign or involvement in training, of which I did have some experience. However, from my understanding of how slow things happened outside of the North, I would have much time on my hands in the interim. I had not had a proper break since my release from internment three and a half years before. That part of me now seemed a parallel existence, far removed. Now, I had survived the turbulence of those years with a chance at some semblance of normality; a hard realisation to take in. Despite the hint of a future operational role, it did feel like I had been thoughtlessly shunted into a siding.

Eileen had relatives living in Shannon, County Clare, in the south-west, where numerous families from the North had sought refuge, some establishing roots. We had known each other since shortly after my release from internment. For much of that time I was active, out of the house, or away. Eileen had herself been active in the struggle. We married in 1977 while I was on the run. I had had no contact with her at all for eight months prior to my return to Ireland from England. Not even a phone call or a letter. Hard to imagine how any relationship could survive that degree of disruption. And yet when we were reunited in Dublin after my return she agreed to join me in Shannon, but on condition that I would never again be absent for so long. She left her job, sold her house in the New Lodge and with our son moved South in May to begin this new venture of a life together. A huge decision.

Shannon provided opportunities. Although a bit of a backwater, the new town is located between Limerick city and Ennis, the gateway to much of the rolling beauty of County Clare. I quickly adjusted and soon found work in one of the local factories. We applied for social housing, and within a few short months were given the key of a new three-bedroomed house. We were managing, making material progress. On a Friday night we would budget for the week ahead; together buy the week's groceries from the town supermarket. But part of me was in a cloud viewing this other me planning domesticity. The burden of guilt for being free to get on with life began to press heavily, undermining this new dispensation of normality: partner, father, breadwinner. The conflict was ever-present in my head despite the effort I made to integrate with this strange new normality, like being awakened from a bad dream and yet curious as to how it might end.

I was physically removed from the conflict but it raged on obsessively in my head. The plight of imprisoned comrades, particularly of those I knew in the H-Blocks and in Armagh, at times assailed my thoughts. The reports of their conditions were truly horrendous – guaranteeing resistance, by the POWs and by our communities, as the Brits showed their determination to further the criminalisation of our struggle, a direction that began with the phasing out of special status in 1976. Our POWs, in refusing to wear prison garb, becoming known as 'Blanketmen' because they wore blankets instead, were forced to escalate their protest by smearing their cell walls with their faeces to avoid beatings from bigoted screws while leaving their cells during 'slop outs' (the emptying of chamber pots); this became known as the 'dirty protest'. My new existence seemed a betrayal. The ghosts of dead comrades were never far from my thoughts and dreams. The disconnect with what was happening only two hundred miles away to the north was increasingly proving to be intolerable, and would have a consequent impact on the personal.

When I was eventually contacted to do something for the movement, I surprised myself at how easily I jumped at the chance, kidding only me that I could balance both roles: wage earner and activist. I had been living a pretence. They only had to ask. At one point I lost a well-paid factory job through a quite lengthy absence from work because of my renewed republican involvement. Eileen, to her great credit, understood what was going on with me. Our mutual commitment to the cause had been one of the attractions. But the strain on her was enormous. I had broken the promise I gave her never again to be separated for long. The past can't be unravelled. Eileen and our son had to endure the fallout from my choices. Our time together in Shannon lasted a mere ten months. Eileen returned with our son to Belfast in early 1980. It amazes me that she put up with so much for so long.

I was now in a state of purgatory, awaiting further orders. In the North, the pace of action left you with little room for reflection; in the South you were left to stew on the back burner for long periods, with too much time to think. The lack of a clear course of action played on my mind. I was a wreck. Pulled this way and that. Emotionally out of shape, I began drinking heavily. My essential, grounded republicanism was compromised by a crazy, toxic impulse for action. Action was preferable to stasis. Clearly, I was unfit for further service in this state of mental confusion. I sought advice. I asked a comrade what kept him going. Hatred, he said. There are times when hatred is all you have as a resource. But fear can override hatred. Fight or flight. Reality bit. I was of no use as a volunteer. I was burnt out.

I recognised the imperative to just get away as far as possible. The hardest thing, but the necessary thing. I was for all these years of my involvement, since joining in 1972, through internment, the conduct of the armed struggle, through Brit and RUC brutality, through all of this I was sustained by the certainty of the justification of our cause, and of the exhilarating sense of contributing to a collective struggle. We held out against all the frustrations in the hope of making a difference. Now I felt deflated; shrunk to being an individual. Then began the reconstruction of something shattered in me. I took back control. I stopped drinking. I started to save every penny. Slowly I began to fill my skin. All the energy and commitment previously given to the cause was focused now on the personal – a future centred on rebuilding a life together with Eileen and our son. After notifying the movement, I planned ahead, wanting desperately to burn bridges and cut a new trail. To leave Ireland. Just walk away from the past. Once that mental bridge was crossed, a great weight seemed to drop from my shoulders. I hit the ground running. I was winging it. This was a euphoric 'liberation'.

My initial idea was to move to the USA. Eileen might be yet persuaded to join me there, because she still expressed serious doubts about my ability to achieve that dream of a future together while remaining in Ireland. I had to prove how serious I was about leaving. I saved up just enough money for the journey, even charging relatively well-off friends fifty Irish punts for doing a portrait of their sons, the first and only time I made a few bob from a talent for drawing. I hoped that once in New York I might get work through Irish American contacts. I bought a passport, the first legitimate one I had ever owned, and applied for a visa at the American embassy in Dublin.

The visa application room was very similar to a labour exchange (to be distinguished from a latter-day Jobcentre), crowded with people waiting to be called to a reception hatch in earshot of all. When my turn came, the interviewer checked my name on her computer and blurted out, 'Are you aware that there's a warrant for your arrest in London?' I sensed all eyes boring into the back of my head. I said that there must be a mistake, some technical malfunction, and that she should please check again. She went through what seemed the motions of consulting with some line manager before returning to the hatch to agree with me that, yes, it was a mistake. She then stamped my passport with a three-year visitor's visa. Thank you very much. The wisest course was to assume that my card was inadvertently marked (dismissing any notion that I was being deliberately forewarned). I couldn't take the risk on the USA. I was sure to be arrested. And to judge by the fate of other Irish republicans subsequently arrested there, I would have faced many years in prison fighting extradition (Joe Doherty, one of eight republicans who escaped from the Crum in 1981, was to spend nine years in custody in the States before his extradition to the North). What might have been seen as a setback could have been a stroke of luck – if you believed in luck. After seeking advice from a comrade about other options, I decided to move to the Netherlands, which he assured me had a reputation as a liberal, progressive, civil rights-based culture known for protecting political exiles. I would be okay there.

At that time – this was still the summer of 1980 – there was a labour dispute at French ports and the Rosslare to Le Havre ferry was regularly being rerouted to Rotterdam. Another 'stroke of luck', offering me the opportunity of avoiding travel through France, where I might run the risk of detention then extradition to England. Money was still an issue and here was a chance to get to my favoured destination relatively cheaply. However, halfway across the Channel there was an announcement that the ferry would disembark at La Havre as normal. The dispute had been settled. I had to hitch through France and Belgium to Holland but, mercifully, without incident. After that relatively minor second setback, everything seemed to fall into my lap.

Within hours of arriving in Amsterdam I spotted an ad for seasonal work. After a successful interview with a recruitment agency, I had to rush to board a train, my journey ending in the small village of Overloon, in the south of the country, where I worked for a month in a brick factory. The work was temporary, but it was a foot in the door. I stayed in a converted barn with two other workers; the landlord was a very kind man called Jan Vloet. He often invited us into his home for a meal with his wife and two young daughters. I began to learn Dutch with the help of the younger daughter, Daphne, and in turn to improve her English. I started to again take an interest in drawing. I think I did a pencil sketch of one of the girls. So much potential opened up in such a short while away from Ireland. I was in a time and place of what seemed unlimited opportunity.

Determined to keep up the pace of this new life, I took a day off work and went in search of more skilled, lucrative and potentially more secure employment. And before the morning was out, I got a job as a lathe operator in a small engineering plant in Venray, close to the German border. Jan gave me a bicycle to get to the factory, a journey of some seven kilometres. I heard of an apartment available nearby that would be suitable for Eileen and our son. I visited a local bank to open an account. Amazingly I was interviewed by a manager, who offered me a cup of coffee and chatted freely. This Continental courtesy augured well. Things were progressing at a breathless pace. I even contributed to the factory's holiday scheme – money towards a bus outing across the border into what was then West Germany – although conscious of my vulnerability to arrest in that jurisdiction, but I could deal with that when the time came. I felt good about the future. But before I could put these plans into effect, the past caught up with me.

While I was cycling to work on a September morning, a van closed silently behind me in view of the factory gates and knocked me sprawling to the grass verge. Dazed, I craned my neck off the ground only to face the muzzle of a sub-machine gun. I thought I was about to die. Then I thought I was to be rendered across the border into West Germany – all in a split second. Finally the realisation that my kidnappers were not British – in fact, an elite unit of the Dutch police. I was handcuffed and held face down for what seemed like ten minutes before being put in the back of the van that had run me off the road. All of this was witnessed by a group of my bemused workmates before the van sped off to a police station, where I was informed that the British authorities were seeking my extradition. The warrant was for my alleged role in a bombing campaign in England circa 1978–9. In the case papers that were subsequently produced it was revealed that, following a top-level meeting of Interpol chiefs in London, warrants were also issued for my arrest in neighbouring European states, were I to venture into other parts. Many years later I heard that the Dutch police had been watching the converted barn prior to my arrest.

I was held in Maastricht prison, for part of the time on the top or eighth floor, the only other prisoner being, I was told, a Czech spy, who I never saw nor heard. My cell was a virtual eyrie, affording a view from the window out across the Belgian border. I exercised alone for thirty minutes daily in a wire-mesh-covered, walled yard on the roof, only slightly bigger than the cells. My mail was strictly censored. When a copy of Peter Taylor's *Beating the Terrorists?* was withheld, I complained to the governor, who revealed that the British authorities had advised that I shouldn't receive the book. Clearly, they were monitoring all aspects of my detention. Most of my time was spent reading. I must have ploughed through all of the prison library's meagre stock of English-language fiction – typically, A. J. Cronin and W. Somerset Maugham.

I hardly spoke at all during those months. I spent a lot of time in a sort of reverie, revisiting incidents, some still trauma-inducing, causing me to shout out involuntarily. Years later I would identify these outbursts as a symptom of post-traumatic stress. I had no such insight then. The radio was the other voice in my life. In early December I heard the news of John Lennon's murder, the loss magnified, if that is possible, in those conditions of isolation. As a counter to the sadness I felt, within weeks the BBC reported that Gerry Tuite had escaped from Brixton while on remand. I let out a triumphant whoop which summoned two screws to the Judas hole, genuinely concerned for my state of mind. I was merely ecstatic that another comrade had beaten the system.

Now facing extradition and the likelihood of a long sentence in an English prison, I identified with the hundreds of POWs incarcerated in the H-Blocks, Armagh, Portlaoise and numerous other locations. I was an Irish republican POW, whatever the Brits thought or the Dutch authorities did at their bidding. That time spent alone in the eyrie caused me to reflect hard about things. I had put all my energy into trying to leave the past behind and to build a future distanced from the conflict. An enthusiasm matched only by the energy I had put into the struggle. Even now, again in a cell and my future again uncertain, I believed absolutely, as I still do to this day, that the armed struggle was our only option. But I also questioned many of our practices. Incarceration afforded the opportunity for reflection.

Terrible things had happened. We had killed innocent civilians. One thinks of Birmingham; of La Mon. It was not good enough to hide behind the fact that neither outcome was intended, or that the inadequacy of the warnings in too many instances had led to horrifying slaughter; this wasn't a case of being assailed with doubts about the conduct of the armed struggle while a prisoner far removed from the actual conflict. Rather, it was a recognition that we had to do more to prevent such tragic circumstances from recurring. The movement had tried to learn from its mistakes. And to introduce improved safety procedures in response. I was involved in the early drive to implement the new thinking.

Standardisation of timing mechanisms had been gradually introduced from 1974. Up till then, the EOs were required to build their own devices, typically using clocks or watches as time switches in simple circuits. Too much had been left to the skill of the individual bomb-maker. One consequence was that Brit bomb-disposal operatives were often able to identify the maker or designer from the characteristics of the circuitry and components, what was known in forensic terms as the 'bomber's signature'. In addition, it was more difficult to train volunteers about how to arm devices when there was such a wide variance in the making. From the mid-1970s, timing units would be made on a centralised production-line basis. I knew of a senior EO who was dismissed from the position for failure to implement the development. Standardisation was taken extremely seriously. 'Box timers' – the Brits called them TPUs (time power units) – became the norm. The circuitry was not only safer for being secured in a light wooden box but was simply armed by removal of a dowel peg which acted as a switch. Previously, there had been instances when a device consisted of little more than a detonator wired to a clock, sitting on top of an explosive charge in a plastic shopping bag. Volunteers had lost their lives carrying or transporting such crude, unstable devices. Those days are far behind but I can still shudder at the recollection.

One conclusion I came to then was that we hadn't given sufficient attention to our warning procedures. They had evolved in the course of the campaign but Birmingham proved our failure in this regard. More attention was paid to the 'run-back', how to return to base successfully. If at least the same attention had been given to warning procedures, there would have been far fewer civilian casualties.

The armed struggle was the right and inevitable course we had to follow given our lack of resources. We went to war because we were weak, that is, politically powerless. We lacked choices. Our enemy had vastly greater resources and therefore more options but *chose* violence. It had always done so. It was in the nature of the imperial beast. The Brits and their collusive henchmen *deliberately* targeted civilians as part of a terror strategy. Much evidence has come to light in subsequent years to support the republican understanding of the British occupation, building on the movement's analysis of Kitson's terrorist policies. Research is casting new light onto British colonialism. And you don't have to go back to Amritsar, the slave trade or to the Opium Wars. Or how the Black and Tans were posted to Palestine after their defeat by the IRA. In the decade before being sent to the North, the Brits were brutalising nations – in Kenya (1952–60), where Frank Kitson ran 'counter-gangs', a strategy he introduced to the North in the early 1970s; in Brunei (1962–66), where Harry Tuzo had served before his posting to Belfast as general officer commanding in 1971; and in Aden (1963–7), where torture tactics were honed and then used against the 'hooded men' in Ballykelly army base just four years later, in 1971.*

In October 1980, seven republican POWs in the H-Blocks began a hunger strike, the culmination of more than three years of protest over brutal conditions and the denial of their rights as political prisoners. I had known three of the seven men from our time in the internment cages. Others joined as the strike progressed, including three woman POWs. When I notified the Maastricht prison governor of my intention to forego food over the approaching Christmas period as a token of my solidarity with the hunger-strikers, the news was received with utter bemusement. These matters, so central to our existence, were unseen and untranslatable at a distance. The strike was ended, however, a week before the planned timing of my gesture. The point is that in that prison cell, some nine hundred kilometres distant from the H-Blocks, I felt entirely at one with every Irish POW. I was not alone. This depth of solidarity could never be apprehended by our gaolers.

However, I found the Maastricht screws to be decent guys. I heard that some of them had registered concern about my conditions in solitary. Whether that led to the subsequent relaxation, I cannot say, but just before Christmas I was transferred to a cell on, if memory serves, the fifth floor, then shortly after to the fourth, the decreased security at each stage increasing my hopes of a positive outcome to the upcoming extradition hearing in Den Bosch.

Now out of solitary, I found my fellow inmates to be a mixed bunch. The full range of local Dutch villainy; a few conscientious objectors to Dutch military conscription; some South Moluccans and Surinamese, recent immigrants from the former Dutch colonies. There was also a women's wing, mostly immigrants – shoplifters and prostitutes. I attended a Christian religious service to get out of the cell. I was sat at the back of the chapel, kept separate. All necks in front turned to the balcony above as the women prisoners were escorted in to an unholy cacophony of wolf whistles.

Finally, my day in court. I was represented at the hearing in Den Bosch by a leading Dutch civil rights barrister, Willem Van Bennekom, who took on my case pro bono because of its political dimension. I was also very ably assisted throughout the period by a court-appointed lawyer who, I

---

*The Legacy of Colonialism–http://www.patfinucanecentre.org.

regret to admit, I didn't trust at first but later came to respect and to like (the looming prospect of being sent to England to face a heavy sentence can make you see agendas everywhere). Fourteen offences were listed in the warrant, eleven of them relating to a conspiracy to cause explosions, including bomb attacks on a gasometer near to the Blackwall Tunnel, London, and at the Canvey Island oil refinery. There was then (is there now?) no concept of conspiracy in Dutch law and therefore it was not an extraditable offence. That howler aside, thanks to the efforts of my legal team and vocal support by Dutch sympathisers in the court's public gallery, I successfully contested the remaining allegations and was provisionally released in January 1981, pending a later considered decision, which was duly delivered in my favour. I had spent four months in Maastricht, three of them in solitary.

The Dutch press gave my extradition case and release a lot of coverage, my first experience of such attention. In fact, the last (and first) time I had been referred to in print was after my capture and subsequent internment some seven years previously, and amounted to a two-line piece in the *Irish News* to the effect that a leading Provo, unnamed, had been lifted. Back then, everyone lifted was accused of being a leading Provo.

The media attention led to the very welcome help of new Dutch friends, some of whom were in the Irlande Komite, a political support group in the Netherlands. Through a network of contacts among political activists, I was able to stay in several Amsterdam squats for some weeks and found work in Haarlem. They also came up with the funds to allow Eileen, with our son, to visit me in Amsterdam. I took the evening off work to meet them at Schiphol. At this point I still harboured hope that Holland offered a future for us together.

As a condition of my release from Maastricht, I was required to report to the Immigration Office in Amsterdam, a dark Gothic pile of misery situated by one of the outer canals. The atmosphere was oppressive. My passport was taken from me brusquely at reception. I was concerned at the implication, witnessing the authority's contempt for 'stateless others' being processed for deportation, held in a barred pen within the building. The dismal, dehumanising experience was unsettling. I feared returning there alone the next day as required for my passport. Willem Van Bennekom readily agreed to accompany me. In his presence, the immigration officers could not have been more civil. My passport was returned to me. Once outside, I mentioned to Willem the difference in manner from yesterday. He told me that the thing to remember was that the same building and bureaucracy had collaborated in the Nazi transportation of the Jewish population of the Netherlands. Had Anne Frank passed through that building, or similar?

I returned to my squat one afternoon to be told by a friend that two English journalists, purporting to be from the *Daily Mail*, had asked about me and that they were parked across the street from the building. I checked this out from the angle afforded by a top-floor window and confirmed that there were two men sitting in a car looking up at the building, aware that I had just entered. There was no back way out of the building. I was convinced that the two were either police or spooks. My friend and I came up with a plan. The squatter movement, or *kraakers*, was widespread in Amsterdam. She rang the local *kraakers* cafe, a meeting place for the many forced to squat because of the acute shortage of accommodation nationally. Within minutes about half a dozen of her friends arrived at the front below and immediately surrounded the car. One of them, who I later got to meet, a muralist, was six feet tall in her bare feet, except that she went everywhere on roller skates. The added height was further augmented by a blue punk haircut a la Grace Jones. All told, she added up to an almost seven-foot intimidatory presence. She and her friends proceeded to jump on the bonnet and successfully distracted the two occupants while I left by the front door and disappeared into another squat nearby (that night we all celebrated at a punk event in the Paradiso). A report of the incident appeared in the *Daily Mail* claiming that two of its reporters had tracked me down to the squat in order to interview me. However, in 1986, it was admitted in the press that the two had in fact been members of British intelligence. Later media hype had me in the Netherlands to set up IRA cells, derisible when you consider that I was there working openly in the country under my own passport. In fact, I am sure that a routine passport check had flagged my name up to the security authorities. I had assumed this would be the case when opting for the Netherlands. A recently published book claims that I had 'fled to Holland' to evade arrest for an alleged letter-bomb campaign in 1979. The spin continues.

We can be slow to recognise even with perfect hindsight what are the essential turning points in our lives – those critical moments that signal massively different outcomes should one path be taken instead of another. My arrest in Venray that day had crashed my dreams of a normal life. I look back now and realise what I then did not grasp: that my Dutch experiences amounted to such a pivotal moment, given the impact on people dear to me. I've wondered since how my life, and the lives of those close to me, might have differed had I felt able to stay on in the Netherlands. I could think of no viable alternative to my returning to Dublin.

I can be accused of naivety for thinking that I could walk away from the struggle with impunity; that the Brits would not pursue me abroad. I was certainly naive to think that I could move to the USA. However, I had sought knowledgeable advice before the move to the European mainland. Due to the incident with the 'press', and the earlier experience with the immigration police, I anticipated that the British would make another extradition attempt or, worse, abduct me and then take me across the border into Germany, where the authorities were more likely to accede to an extradition request. There was also the fear that I might end up floating in one of Amsterdam's canals. I was suspicious of my own shadow. I decided to return to Ireland. It was a reluctant choice. I did not know what lay ahead for me, but I knew not to return by air, lest the plane might make an unscheduled landing in England. This was not a paranoid moment. I had been in contact with the Belfast solicitor Paddy McGrory, who strongly advised me against returning to Dublin by air from Amsterdam. He argued the possibility of the plane being diverted to London, where I would again face the prospect of twenty years' incarceration. Friends returning to Ireland helped me out, at some risk to themselves. I travelled back with them by road through France, aware that there might still be a warrant out for me there. My friends approached the ferry at Le Havre separately from me. Their vehicle was pulled over for a rigorous search and ID check. I boarded and disembarked on foot without any hitch.

8
Recommitment

I set foot back in Dublin at the end of February 1981. I had been in the Netherlands about seven months, four of which, as described in chapter seven, were spent in Maastricht prison. An old comrade was to jest, 'That'll knock the travellin' out o' yeh' – I had billeted with him in Cavan prior to heading abroad, sure then I wouldn't be seeing him again for many years, if ever, so convinced was I that my days in the movement were over. Leaving seemed permanent in that moment. Now, I was back at the starting line.

I called on another old comrade who I had often billeted with, Frankie Rafferty. Fuzz, as he had been known since the internment days, had a flat in Ballymun, a concrete high-rise wilderness on the edge of Dublin's north side, close to the airport, where many from the North had settled after seeking refuge during the course of the conflict. And yet another old comrade, Frank Mulholland, was staying with him, but room was made for me without a second's thought. Both were on the run from the North. Big Fra had been a comrade during my early involvement in Unity Flats. Fuzz would later do time in England for planning to blow up electricity substations. Both were ex-internees. Both are dead now. Such brilliant, capable guys, who in different circumstances would have prospered.

The immediate thing on my mind then was to get back with Eileen. She had agreed to another try at making a go of it, but first I had to get a place for us. Jesus – what I had put that woman through! I saw no prospect of being able to live or to find work in any part of the country other than in Dublin. My recent experiences in the Netherlands, and the impact on me of the reportage of the dirty protest and now the impending hunger strike, had shaken me out of any notion that I could walk away from the conflict. I had to find some compromise between starting anew with Eileen and my renewed commitment to the struggle. I would soon be thirty. The future, personally and politically, looked uncertain. Had it ever been otherwise!

Within a week of my return from Amsterdam, I received word that yet another old comrade, from the Kesh, Ted Howell, wanted to see me about working for the movement in Dublin. That would suit me fine because Dublin offered the best chance of also finding a more permanent role. I was to meet him at the offices of *An Phoblacht/Republican News* (*AP/RN*), the movement's weekly newspaper, in 44 Parnell Square. The building also housed the national headquarters of Sinn Fein. I wasn't sure what role Ted might have in mind for me. Ted had taught me Gaelic in the Kesh. He worked in Sinn Fein's Foreign Affairs Department – maintaining and developing the movement's international links. Perhaps to help with *IRIS*, the department's monthly journal? Whatever was on offer, I would give it a go until something more permanent turned up.

I hardly had my foot in the door and had exchanged greetings and the catch-up when I was tasked to go through a pile of communications (comms) from the H-Blocks – smuggled-out messages, minutely hand-written on toilet paper and wrapped in clingfilm. I knew many of the authors personally. Their intention was to raise awareness about the looming second hunger strike, announced to start within days. In an initiative to inform the world of their (and our) struggle against criminalisation, our POWs had come up with the idea of writing directly to celebrities in the drama, art and literary spheres, one of a raft of initiatives, putting the case for building support for better conditions in the H-Blocks that would amount to political status. There were several dozen comms to carefully unwrap, check out and forward appropriately. One comm was addressed to Brigitte Bardot. It was written by a great friend of mine. I laughed. Rather too loudly, for it drew a rebuke from a leading Sinn Feiner, who didn't know me and who thought levity inappropriate under the circumstances. I could as easily have cried. I pictured my comrade in a cold cell, its four walls smeared in his own faeces, wrapped only in a prison blanket, yet having the spirit to compose an appeal to the world-famous French film star. I don't know what you call that – incongruous? Surreal? An inspired, and inspiring, heartfelt plea, certainly. Other comrades from those still quite recent dark days in Belfast and in Long Kesh during internment had penned similarly poignant appeals for support. Locked up in appalling conditions, they were steadfast in their refusal to be criminalised. I was again part of a common struggle.

I began working in Number 44 – odd jobs, nothing definitive. Then I was introduced to Danny Devenny, a former POW from the Short Strand, who was in charge of the 'paste-up' (art) department (and later would gain renown as a political muralist). Danny had contributed artwork for *Republican News* even while held in the sentenced end of the Kesh for a bank robbery during which he was shot. He had heard that I could draw. I was put to work immediately and continued working there, off and on, for the next three years, during which he became a close friend. The introduction to this new role coincided with the beginning of the second hunger strike.

Eileen and our son joined me in Dublin where, after staying with Fuzz, we squatted in a Ballymun flat, a fast-track to getting a permanent offer of council accommodation. We made our application to the council and soon after moved into an allocated flat, also in Ballymun. We enrolled our son in the local Gaelic-speaking school. Life was a struggle in terms of money but we managed. Soon after, Eileen also began working for *AP/RN*, as a typesetter.

Overshadowing all our lives was the hunger strike. Bobby Sands began his fast on 1 March. It was a terrible time. The worst throughout the length and breadth of the island. I was in no doubt that the Brits would let Bobby die, but that widely held but – by tacit understanding – unspoken belief caused none of us to stop in our efforts to try to raise awareness and save him. We did fear that the disputed conclusion to the previous hunger strike (which had been called off before Christmas to save one of the strikers who was close to death, in the mistaken belief that concessions would follow) would now impede efforts to again raise international support. And, of course, no one was more conscious of this than Bobby Sands. That was the terrible inevitability of his sacrifice. The movement's task was to convince opinion at home and internationally of the commitment of Bobby and the others who would join him on hunger strike. The world is a hard judge and it was watching his and our collective resolve. Our efforts to increase awareness took on the fervour of near spiritual commitment over the course of the support campaign. This consciousness mirrored what was happening in every district and townland and suburb and village and further afield. In the particular but, I do believe, essential purview of the art department, we all worked tirelessly in support of the campaign, to publicise the horrific unfolding of our history in the making. That also involved the publication of the movement's political weekly. The intensity of the constant effort required kept me grounded, for working in such a creative environment was a new, challenging experience. I had to focus to keep up with the task. There was so much support activity going on, both in Ireland and abroad, that we laboured virtually around the clock (two- and three-day shifts were common) to produce all the posters and leaflets for all national and local Sinn Fein demonstrations, protest actions, meetings and other initiatives. The urgency of the workload made it a strangely fulfilling, exhilarating time, requiring maximum effort all round, during which we all could only hope or pray that we might make a difference. Each of Bobby's sixty-six days on hunger strike seemed to mark our every waking moment.

The sad demise of the independent nationalist MP for Fermanagh and South Tyrone, Frank McManus, led to the inspired nomination of Bobby Sands for the seat, generating hope which was to propel the momentum for change. We did not dare despair. In the bi-election of 9 April, Bobby was duly elected. In a subsequent election to the Dáil in June, two other hunger strikers, Kieran Doherty and Paddy Agnew, nominated on an anti-H-Block ticket, won seats.

Bobby's election heralded a huge leap in the development of Sinn Fein as a political force. The republican movement, and no longer just its leadership, woke up to the need to enter electoral politics and to harness the support of republican constituencies to further our political objectives. Traditionally, republicans were deeply suspicious of the constitutional path to change. I certainly was. We were sick of the system and wanted to smash it. I held a very narrow view of politics, regarding (and despising) politicians as sell-out merchants. But now, in order to save Bobby and the other comrades who joined him on the hunger strike, there was a huge shift in political consciousness occurring throughout the movement and country. We wanted to show the world this quantifiable support for our prisoners and, by the clearest extension, our cause. Our communities, in their dignified thousands on the streets, in their resilience to and defiance in the face of state repression, in their determination to be counted electorally, expressed our collective support for and faith in the judgement of Sinn Fein. It was an empowering moment for which we had scarce previous experience. A reality-changer. A moment of epiphany. Prior to the 1981 hunger strike I would have been deeply opposed to electoral politics, believing that violence was the only recourse to move the British. I was now a convert to the potential offered by Sinn Fein's political development and successes. These developments offered a viable addition to (and, in the long term, an alternative to) armed struggle. We had much further to go along that path but that year was a watershed.

To illustrate the changing dynamic, I remember a conversation with a sixth-form student, a son of the owner of a billet I was holed up in for a week. We would talk when he came home from school. He knew my score, of course, and his brother was a Blanketman. He wanted to join the IRA. I had had these conversations at times with other young prospective volunteers. Now it seemed the issue needn't solely be about the suitability of the potential recruit for the rigours of life in the movement. We had reached a point when other options were now viable. This was a bright young man. I told him that the nature of the conflict had progressed to the stage now when more than just the bomb and the bullet were needed to advance our cause. The future in increasing measure lay in the lap of educators, lawyers, communicators, community activists, political representatives.

The rapidly emerging spirit of a new political reality, within the movement and among our supporters, was not in the least matched by the British, who regarded our political development as a threat. The British political establishment was hell-bent on a military solution, despite the advice of its generals, who by 1979 had realised that the IRA could not be defeated. Brigadier General James Glover, whose secret report on the IRA's capacity, *Future Terrorist Trends*, was intercepted by the IRA in 1979, argued that we could not be defeated (a claim he repeated ten years later in a Peter Taylor documentary). Glover was *the* senior army officer involved with intelligence work in the North. This should have prompted a rethink but, deplorably, in 1979, Thatcher had trumpeted that Airey Neave was her choice as secretary of state for Northern Ireland and that he would pursue a very hard line. Neave was assassinated by the Irish National Liberation Army (INLA), but his successor, Humphrey Atkins, by continuing with a hard-line counter-insurgency policy, demonstrated the British government's tragic dearth of political vision and foresight. Protest was batoned and shot off the streets. Official RUC figures show that nearly thirty thousand plastic bullets were fired in the North during this period in an attempt to quell the upsurge in street protests.

Ten comrades died on hunger strike in a prolonged nightmare we couldn't waken from until, in October, individual relatives used their prerogative to ask the prison authorities to intervene to save the remaining hunger strikers once they slipped into unconsciousness. These were heart-rending choices.

Without the hunger strikers' sacrifices I now have no doubt that the movement would in time have built politically, but the deaths of Bobby and our other comrades acted as a catalyst for change. The longer I am here to think back over that awfully dark period, the more I revere their memory.

While working on *An Phoblacht*, once the hunger strike had ended, I volunteered once again for active service. My sense of recommitment to the struggle had been rekindled by the hunger strike campaign and the British government's intransigent response to the POWs' just demands. The best usage of my effort and experience now was again on active duty in England.

Plans for a return to England were well advanced when, shortly after the end of the hunger strike, on 25 November 1981, fate (if I were to allow it credence) intervened. I was shot twice in the right leg in the foyer of Number 44. I heard what sounded like a firework cracking on the ground in front of me, unaware that I had been shot. A surgeon later explained that the heat of the bullet had cauterised nerve endings. Danny Devenny was also shot. I'm certain neither of us was an intended target and that the lone gunman was merely covering his escape once spotted acting suspiciously by Danny, who shouted a warning. However, the gunman wouldn't have known (although it was a matter for conjecture at the time) that his action effectively scuppered an imminent IRA operation across the water. A certain comrade had said, 'We'll give these bastards a Christmas they'll never forget.' The Ulster Freedom Fighters – a UDA flag of convenience – claimed the shooting. There was a suspicion that the intended target was a prominent republican, perhaps Joe Cahill, a legendary figure within the movement going back to 1942 when he was sentenced to death, later reprieved, for his role in the killing of an RUC man, for which Tom Williams was hanged. I greatly admired Joe, who died in 2004.

Anyway, at the end of 1981, instead of active service in England, I found myself in the Richmond Hospital, Dublin, with a police guard in the corridor outside the ward, supposedly for my protection. They seemed more interested in checking my visitors. I was in hospital for ten days. One bullet had passed through my lower right leg, chipping a bone before exiting. The other bullet had lodged close to an artery behind the right knee. The surgeons decided to wait a week before operating to remove the bullet, to allow some healing of the wound. The operation was successful. Gunshot wounds were then quite novel in the South, and the surgical team seemed very rightly pleased with their efforts on my behalf. I was advised that arthritis might be a future issue (which has been borne out). A period on crutches followed. Plans were on hold. The next time I met my certain comrade, I enquired why there had been no operation in England as mooted over Christmas. 'You were it,' he said.

Years later (in 2004, in fact – the year Joe Cahill died), a young guy revealed to me that it was his father who had shot me, adding that he had claimed, 'I shot one of the good guys.' This seemed a genuine acknowledgement of regret by his father who, whatever the reasons for his opposition to the movement, bore me no personal ill will. He had acted as an agent of the state, as a henchman, but perhaps had rationalised that all republicans were not bad, that there were grievances that generated the movement's resistance. He might be judged as just another protagonist in the conflict going over the past, taking stock of events.

In 1982, Gerry Tuite, who had escaped from Brixton Prison in 1979 while I was being held in Maastricht (as mentioned in the previous chapter), became the first republican to be sentenced under the Dublin government's recently enacted extra-jurisdiction treaty, introduced to avoid the politically sensitive usage of extradition, meaning that one could be tried and sentenced in the South for actions committed in the North, in Britain or elsewhere. Gerry had faced very similar charges, relating to the same bombing campaign, to those that I had successfully challenged in the Netherlands. I sought professional legal opinion and was advised that my arrest was not only highly likely but imminent. It was time to go underground again. You can imagine the impact that had on Eileen. Another extended period of little or scarce contact.

At some point Eileen moved back North, although she continued to work for the paper and travelled down every week to do so. We eventually agreed to a divorce and obtained a decree nisi (legal permission to divorce). We both recognised it was for the best. My life was too chaotic.

But towards the end of that year I was stopped by Dublin Special Branch and surprisingly released after an identity check. They knew fine well who I was. Years later I learned that the Irish authorities in conjunction with their British counterparts had decided not to use the new legislation to charge me, believing it better to let me run, so to speak, reasoning that I was sure to return to England, where if picked up I would receive a far greater prison sentence than under the extra-jurisdiction process.

In fact, I was nearly captured in Blackpool, Lancashire, some months later. The IRA had been lured into a trap. An agent provocateur had approached the movement in Ireland with a plan to target British Army personnel from Weeton Camp, a huge transit and training facility near Preston. Realising the trap, I and a fellow comrade managed to evade a massive police surveillance operation and then a nationwide manhunt before escaping from England and returning to Ireland.

There was a suspicion at home that we had panicked. No one could credit that we had narrowly escaped a trap. The person who had set us up had the nerve to maintain contact with the movement in Dublin and was persuasive enough to convince people that we had no cause to abandon the operation. It appeared my operational days were over. I remember saying as much to a comrade, who agreed. This was in the late summer of 1983. From then on it looked as if my contribution would be confined to logistical support. I did what I could, when I could. It should be noted, however, that there was no endless queue of recruits for the England campaign. There was also a series of setbacks resulting in the arrest of several key operators. Within a year I was to return to active service in England.

9

Nineteen Eighty-Four

At 2:54 a.m. on Friday, 12 October 1984, a bomb exploded at the Grand Hotel, Brighton, killing four people and injuring thirty-four others. One of the injured died five weeks later. I planted the bomb. I did so as a volunteer in an IRA active service unit committed to the continuing, long-term strategy of taking the war to England.

The Grand was booked out with prominent Conservatives, including the prime minister, Margaret Thatcher, and government ministers attending their party conference, held in the adjacent conference hall where, six years previously, we had overlooked the back of the building – and wondered what was possible, as had others independently, all intent on furthering the England campaign by targeting those we considered most culpable for terrorism in Ireland.

The Brighton operation was *more* than a revenge attack for the hunger strikers' deaths, and the deaths of those killed by the British state as part of its terror strategy. The British military and their political masters were in pursuance of strategic 'containment'; that is, they were happy to settle for decades of bombs in Belfast, remote from the domestic political agenda. Apart from the occasional banner headline coverage of some particularly spectacular incident, reporting of the conflict was increasingly confined to fewer and fewer uncontextualised column inches, and to third- and fourth-item status in the attention pecking order of the media. Brighton was a wake-up call to Britain's political establishment, the architects of repression in Ireland. As long as their predatory, selfish, undemocratic hold on the six counties was maintained, the IRA would continue to organise to target England.

There is a saying, going back to the Fenian bombing campaign in England in the late 1800s, that one bomb in London is worth a hundred in Ireland. In the contemporary context, the truth was probably closer to one in a thousand. After some fourteen years of conflict, the death of a

British squaddie might merit a Page Two single paragraph in a newspaper, if that. Only major incidents in Ireland gained front-page exposure. By the early 1980s over two thousand people had been killed. The figures of security force personnel killed and injured up to and including 1984 reveal that 196 RUC and Reserve personnel were killed, 4,857 injured; 384 British soldiers killed, 3,774 injured; 147 Ulster Defence Regiment members killed, 294 injured. In the same period 30,264 shooting incidents were recorded and 7,990 explosions, while 3,623 bombs were defused. The figures do not include deaths and injuries of prison officers.* For some in the British political and military establishment, this was an 'acceptable level of violence'. The British government's containment strategy, by attempting to limit the theatre of war within the Northern six counties, and therefore as much out of sight as achievable, hoped to ensure that it remained largely off the front pages and television screens of the British public and, crucially, that the cosy cross-party consensus would continue. Despite earlier IRA operations in England and on the European mainland, the containment strategy was largely effective. The scale and audacity of the Brighton operation – targeting the Tory elite, their financial backers, and party officers – signalled a new, more ruthless progression. As long as Britain continued its military oppression in Ireland the IRA would relentlessly pursue its counter-strategy of taking the war to them.

As declared from the outset, I won't talk about the operational side of the Grand Hotel bombing, of how the IRA planned and carried out the attack. Suffice it to say, many were involved in the planning and logistical backup, few of them known to me, but of those I did know, all came from the poorest districts, north and south of the island. A detail I will share, however, is to confirm the IRA's statement after the bombing that the charge consisted of 100 pounds of gelignite, and not the 30 pounds of Semtex estimated by the British authorities and unquestioningly repeated by numerous journalists and writers ever since. In fact, about 105 pounds of gelignite were used. At the time my preference would have undoubtedly been to plant at least a similar amount of more powerful plastic explosive like Semtex to effect the maximum impact. Even a lesser charge of Semtex

---

*Statistics from Sidney Elliott and W. D. Flackes, *Northern Ireland: A Political Directory 1968–1999* (Blackstaff Press, 1998).

TOP LEFT: My maternal great-grandmother, Mary Donegan *née* Smyth, holding my uncle Seamus (aged six months), and my Aunt May (aged five). Castlewellan, County Down, 1925.

TOP RIGHT: My maternal grandmother, Ellen (Lena) Donegan *née* Robinson. Belfast, late 1930s.

BOTTOM: My maternal grandfather, Henry (Harry) Donegan (seated, second from right) in a bar in the Market, Belfast, with Sammy McReynolds, husband of my Aunt Bridget, to his right.

OPPOSITE TOP: My dad, John Magee, righthand centre, with workmates on deck of a ship in Harland and Wolff, Belfast, c.1950. He moved the family to Norwich in 1954.

OPPOSITE BOTTOM: Mum, her twin, Bridget, and their youngest brother, Harry, on the day of their First Communion, c.1938. I believe their father took the photo, outside their home 8 Catherine Street North.

ABOVE: In the back garden of St Vincent's Probation Hostel, Brockley, South London, spring 1967. I was fifteen.

TOP: The aftermath of the 'no warning' loyalist bombing of McGurk's Bar, 4 December 1971, which killed fifteen people. [©An Phoblacht]

BOTTOM: The funeral of victims of the McGurk's Bar attack, passing the site of the explosion. [©An Phoblacht]

TOP: Resistance from republican POWs as the British Army gather to quell the protest. At 11:00 a.m. on the day following the burning a British Army helicopter fired CR gas dibenzoxazepine (ten times stronger than its CS counterpart) down on the prisoners. [©An Phoblacht]

BOTTOM: Aerial view of one of the wrecked cages, following the burning of Long Kesh, 15 October 1974. [©An Phoblacht]

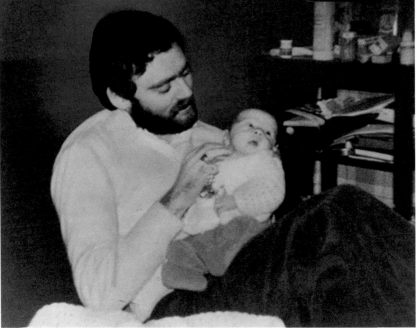

ABOVE: Photo page of fake passport, part of the evidential case file during the Old Bailey trial, 1986.

OPPOSITE TOP: In Hillman St, the New Lodge area of Belfast, while on the run, 1977. I am cutting out the binding for a book.

OPPOSITE BOTTOM: Again in the New Lodge area, early 1978, with baby son.

OPPOSITE: The front of the Grand Hotel, Brighton, after the bomb of 12 October 1984.

TOP: With co-accused Gerry McDonnell in the exercise yard of the special secure unit, Full Sutton Prison, Yorkshire. Photo taken in the months preceding our repatriation to Maghaberry Prison.

BOTTOM: Demonstration *c.*1987 on the Falls Road, Belfast, by relatives of republican POWs held in England, demanding their repatriation. My wife Eileen is on the right, holding a placard with my name.

TOP: Painting a portrait in my cell, Full Sutton Prison, c.1993.

BOTTOM: Gerry Adams, with Cyril Ramaphosa and Mathews Phosa, briefing the press after Sinn Fein's historic endorsement of the Good Friday Agreement, 1998. Cyril and Mathews had earlier visited the H-Blocks, accompanied by prominent Sinn Fein negotiators, in support of the Agreement and in an expression of solidarity between the IRA and the ANC. [©An Phoblacht]

OPPOSITE: Letter from Harvey Thomas, dated 9 December 1998. Harvey Thomas was Margaret Thatcher's press and public relations director in 1984 and was injured by the Brighton bomb.

HARVEY THOMAS C B E. F I P R. F C I J
International Public Relations and Presentation Consultant

Phone: ████ • Fax: ████ • International Code: ████ • E-Mail: ████

December 9, 1998

Mr Patrick McGee
The Maze Prison
Belfast
Northern Ireland

Dear Mr McGee,

This is not an easy letter for me to write – and it has taken me a long time and much Prayer before doing it! It is a personal letter – I cannot speak for others who were injured – or who lost family members in the Grand Hotel in 1984.

I was the Producer of the Conservative Party Conference in Brighton – and the Occupant of Room 729 – immediately above the Room in which the bomb was placed.

As you prepare to leave the Maze Prison, I felt that – as a Christian – I must write personally to say that God forgives each of us, if we repent and put our faith in Jesus Christ. In the Spirit of Christ's teaching, I offer you my <u>own</u> forgiveness!

The Bible urges us to be Reconciled to each Other – as we can be reconciled to God through Christ – and that is my motive in writing to you! I hope that you will receive this letter in the spirit in which it is written. I enclose a copy of "In the Face of Fear" that I published in 1985. I hope you find it interesting.

I pray that as you return to your Family, you will also feel the Spirit of Reconciliation and come to know God's forgiveness.

Sincerely,

Harvey Thomas CBE

ht/m

Patrick Magee
H3 B, Long Kesh

15 December 1998

Mr Harvey Thomas CBE

████████████
████████

Dear Mr Thomas

Thank you for your letter and the copy of *In the Face of Fear*. I have given much thought to both. Your account of being buried in bomb-rubble and of drawing strength from your religious faith, along with thoughts of your wife and the imminent birth of your daughter, is a deeply-moving testimony (all the more poignant because my wife gave birth to our son in recent days).

While I do not share your evangelical views - indeed, I am not a Christian and, beyond a vague notion of a divine purpose to life, I have no religious faith to speak of - I respect the depth of your conviction. I also respect and acknowledge the moral courage of your decision to write offering me your personal forgiveness. As you indicated in your letter, it could not have been an easy journey to arrive at that frame of mind and then decide to contact me.

Your generosity of spirit demands a fuller, more open reply than I am able to offer at the present time. For now, all I feel I can state is that I do believe firmly in the need for reconciliation. I use the word in a political rather than a religious sense. I see reconciliation as an endeavour to be pursued as much as an end, and entails the fullest allowance and respect for difference; and politics when guided by the spirit of reconciliation becomes the art of harmonising diversity. Dialogue is always a crucial first step. As you say in your book, 'at the heart of every failure in the church and in politics is a failure in communications'.

I wish you and your family well. Yours sincerely

Pat Magee

OPPOSITE: My reply to Harvey Thomas, on 15 December 1998.

TOP LEFT: Ella O'Dwyer, my co-accused, on pre-release parole in 1998, selling *An Phoblacht*. [©An Phoblacht]

TOP RIGHT: Martina Anderson MEP with Michel Barnier, former EU chief negotiator on Brexit. Martina, my co-accused, was MEP for Derry from 2012–2020.

BOTTOM: Book-signing at the launch in Belfast of *Gangsters or Guerrillas?: Representations of Irish Republicans in 'Troubles Fiction'* – Beyond the Pale, December 2001.

TOP: Brian Moody's 2003 photo of Jo Berry and me, which still features in The Forgiveness Project's touring exhibition. [©The Forgiveness Project]

BOTTOM: Launch of The Forgiveness Project at the OXO Gallery on London's South Bank. Archbishop Desmond Tutu gave the inaugural address. Also in the photo with Jo Berry and me is the project's founder, Marina Cantacuzino.

TOP: Discussion about the dynamic of my first meeting with Jo Berry at a rehearsal of *The Bomb*, dramatised for Action Transport, Runcorn, in 2006.

BOTTOM: Meeting peace campaigner Robi Damelin in Tel Aviv, Israel, in 2010. Following the death of her son in 2002, shot by a Palestinian sniper, Robi has dedicated her life to the Parents Circle, working for peace with Israeli and Palestinian families who have lost children to war.

TOP: Jo Berry and me speaking to students and academics at a peace conference in Sarajevo in 2014 to mark the centenary of the onset of World War I.

BOTTOM: Group photo of a very inspiring meeting at Queen's University, Belfast between myself, Jo Berry and Veterans for Peace UK, chaired by Claire Hackett, in 2014. The meeting came at the end of the group's visit to various specific locations in the six counties where they had served on tours of duty. The event led to an invitation for me to attend VFP's annual conference in London the following year.

would have been more effective than gelignite in that brutal logic. A smaller amount, also, would have eased the logistics of bringing it into the hotel, which was already in preconference security mode, and would have reduced the difficulties in finally secreting the long-delay charge.

The bomb was placed about three weeks prior to detonation. Much careful consideration was given to the timing. The hotel had been reserved solely for the use of government ministers, National Union of Conservative and Unionist Associations executive members and HQ staff, except for a limited number of lobby correspondents. We wanted to lessen as far as possible the likelihood of injury to hotel staff. The device was timed, therefore, to go off when staff were less likely to be present. But there was simply no guarantee that staff working a late shift in the bar and reception areas would escape the impact of the blast. At the time I would have considered all those attending the conference to be Tory warmongers and therefore legitimate targets. Any civilian casualties would be deeply regrettable, but this was a chance to strike at the heart of a particularly vile British government, whose troops and collusive forces had targeted civilians, tortured prisoners and murdered children on the streets of Belfast and, indeed, throughout the North, and whose abuses of power had gone largely unrecorded by the world's media.

If you had asked me then what the specific objective of the operation was, I couldn't have answered with the insider certainty of a key strategist. I was not privy to the thinking of the leadership. I didn't need to be. The target was an obvious one, requiring little further thought.

I was concerned of course at the likely reaction from the British state, and also about that of the government in Dublin. The obvious expectation was of a security crackdown. Possibly the most far-reaching and violent to date. I had to believe that the leadership had calculated the probable reactions to the operation and would plan accordingly. Any such qualms were heavily outweighed by the wholesale anger among republicans and the wider nationalist community at the deaths of the hunger strikers. Many of us identified too with the plight of the striking British miners and of their communities. Miners' wives came to Dublin to raise funds. They received much solidarity from republicans. In London I had been disturbed at witnessing the existence of cardboard cities of homeless people. The Tories had much to answer for.

Before the bomb went off, I was billeting with sympathisers in Cork. Although aware that I was a volunteer on the run, the people had no inkling of the Brighton operation, or that I was wanted for previous operations in England. I had a certain freedom of movement in Cork, because of the west's pre-eminent status as a tourist Mecca. There were many hotels and guest houses in which to lie low. That would have been more difficult in Dublin, with the capital's heavier concentration of Special Branch.

On the eve of the hour of detonation I had a small transistor radio beside me, tuned to a local off-shore pirate radio station. It was a nerve-wracking wait for confirmation that the bomb had detonated. There were no radio or television stations giving regular, on-the-hour news updates. Reception was poor where I was billeted. After two a.m. all you got was a looped repeat of the syndicated news prior to that hour. And given the extent of phone-tapping, I had to presume a call, even in coded terms, to someone with better access to the latest news was out of the question. Consequently, I didn't hear that the bomb had successfully detonated until the first updated broadcast, at six a.m. The report gave the barest details, confirming that a bomb had exploded and claiming two dead.

Thinking back on that moment (thirty-five years ago, at the time of writing), my immediate emotion was relief. Relief that the device had worked. That will, undoubtedly, strike many as cold and callous – certainly the victims and their relatives. But that initial response was of me as an operator. As the volunteer responsible for planting and arming the device, I carried arguably the heaviest burden for the outcome of the operation. If for technical reasons it hadn't detonated, then the failure would have been down to me. Security at all future events would be reviewed and further tightened. We would have been unlikely to get another opportunity like Brighton, with much of the Tory leadership vulnerable under one roof.

I did not believe that Margaret Thatcher was certain to be killed or injured. Without firm knowledge of what rooms she and her cabinet colleagues would be using, it was impossible to select a location for the device within the hotel to guarantee optimum impact, perhaps with a smaller charge secreted as close as possible to where we might have anticipated Thatcher to be staying. The Grand Hotel presented a massive structure, a huge Victorian pile. To be certain of killing Thatcher, only the use of a high explosive such as plastic or dynamite could ensure success. I only had gelignite to work with, albeit a sizeable amount, because more powerful material was not available to me. My best guess was that she would be in the so-called Napoleon Suite on the second floor overlooking the seafront, a choice that seemed to fit our understanding of her personality. Alternatively, she might choose the top floor. The device was planted on one of the upper floors on the front. My view was that the explosion would directly reach the third floor but that debris and falling masonry just might extend the bomb's effective killing range. In fact, a huge chimney stack collapsed and its rubble plummeted to the basement. But I was sure that the size of the charge would blow out a large portion of the front of the building and that the death toll could well be considerable. The world would be left in no doubt that this was a serious assassination attempt and that we meant business. The black gaping hole in the front of the hotel, which has since become an iconic image of the attack, marked the epicentre.

As the days drew nearer to the moment of detonation, I had to brief a comrade on what I considered the likely physical impact of the explosion, in terms of damage to the building and killing range. He in turn would brief others in order to plan for the likely reaction. In a Dublin bar, on a napkin, I roughly drew an outline of the Grand's frontage. I indicated with a small x where the device was concealed and then drew a circle to show the likely reach of the explosion. In light of the facts when they emerged, my assessment was very accurate.

As we now know, five were killed, and although the bathroom of Thatcher's suite was damaged, she and her husband emerged largely unscathed. The press claimed afterwards that her attention to paperwork in preparation for her final conference address later that day had kept her out of the bathroom where, it has been suggested, there was an increased likelihood she would have fared far worse. There was also a later report that extra joists had been added to her room to enhance sound-proofing and that this had restricted the damage.

Anyway, on the morning of the twelfth, due to some physical anxiety from having had to live with the knowledge that the timer was ticking down towards detonation – and mindful that the device could be uncovered at any time, either through a security check or because of maintenance work – I had got little sleep through the night. Following the first news report, exhaustion took control and I slept for about four hours. When I did eventually waken I went into Cork city and watched the live reports of the rescue operation as it unfolded on a lunchtime cable broadcast in a city-centre pub.

The bar was packed. All eyes were on the televised news reportage. Feigning disinterest, while waiting for my Guinness to settle, I watched, also listening to the reactions of the punters round the bar. Little was said, few wishing to advertise their support or otherwise. Reports from Belfast over the coming days were of widespread jubilation from within nationalist areas.

Margaret Thatcher, addressing her constituents on the following Saturday, said, 'We suffered a tragedy not one of us could have thought would happen in our country,' which conveyed the astounding arrogance of the British political elite, that thought itself beyond the reach of those it oppressed, and its ignorance about the ability and determination of the Irish republican movement to pursue its objectives.

The IRA's statement of admission when released nine hours after the explosion, and repeated later that day, seemed to strike an approving chord among our grass roots. It read: 'Mrs Thatcher will now realise that Britain cannot occupy our country and torture our prisoners and shoot our people in their own streets and get away with it. Today we were unlucky but remember, we only have to be lucky once. You will have to be lucky always. Give Ireland peace and there will be no more war.'

It was only afterwards that I allowed the full enormity of the action to enter my thinking. A good friend told me that I grew very quiet, reflective. I had learned to be quite quiet and introspective, part of the armour you affect to camouflage intent, but I knew he meant more. He picked up something of the thought trail in my head. What struck me forcefully was that this bomb would have profound implications for me directly, deeper than any from my previous involvement. My future, in the immediacy of this track of thought, seemed irretrievably narrowed. It was not that I had naively failed to appreciate there would be repercussions. I had been on the run from the North since 1978 and was already sought by the British for bombs in England and had successfully challenged an attempt at extradition from the Netherlands. For years I had been monitored by Irish Special Branch. I knew therefore that if captured, either in the North or across the water, I faced a hefty sentence. Judged by the outcome of court cases relating to comrades I had worked with, I estimated twenty years. But

Brighton was on a different scale. I expected that the Brits would pull out all the stops in pursuit of those they held responsible. I knew that my name would be in the frame. Special Branch would have me shortlisted as a likely suspect and would eventually move me closer towards the top of the list, if not to the very top, by cross-checking reports of the movements and availability of other suspects. Indeed, after a few months, there was press speculation (in the *Sunday Times*, I believe) that, although not naming me, made it clear to those in the know that I was being sought. It later emerged during my trial that my name was in the ring by the end of October, that is, within three weeks of the bombing. Because of Brighton I would always be looking over my shoulder. They would never forget. Indeed, the British government announced the setting up of a new top-level anti-terrorist committee, TIGER (Terrorist Intelligence Gathering Evaluation and Research). But before and during the operation, and until that moment of relief at its successful completion, to function effectively at all in a situation of protracted stress, one had to focus on the practicalities.

Still in Ireland, by the New Year I became aware of increased surveillance. I spotted four individual cars that kept making appearances around the Ballymun flats, where I was now staying. A close watch was kept on my flat in Shangan Road from cars that would park within school grounds opposite. I would board a bus into central Dublin, about a four-mile journey, and be fully aware that an unmarked car would be behind the bus, sometimes in front, to check whether or not I might get off along the route. I was wary of all who might board. I noted the number plates, makes and colours of suspicious vehicles. I passed on the details up the line. The word I got back was that I had underestimated the scale of the surveillance operation and that eleven cars had been identified routinely checking my movements to and from Ballymun. Who knows, it's conceivable, if paranoid-sounding, that our intelligence people may also have underestimated the scale of attention. Paranoid times. Even if you did spot something suspicious, there was always the possibility that the activity was not Special Branch or British intelligence but drug squad or serious crime related, given the high level of criminal activity associated with the area.

The part that Ballymun and many of its residents played in the struggle has remained largely unacknowledged and therefore unappreciated. The area provided a springboard for many England operations. It was one of the poorest, most deprived areas in the country. This, of course, was in the relatively low-tech 1980s, and there was never a problem for our people to evade surveillance for a few hours or a day, in order for example to prepare for the next tasks. While the few routes to and from the Ballymun estate ensured it was easy to monitor the movements of cars and buses, the vastness of the area made it difficult to keep tabs on anyone entering or leaving on foot. It could take fifty minutes to walk across the estate. There were numerous shortcuts, alleyways, footpaths and playing fields, none of which could be effectively monitored by surveillance teams without drawing attention. But I also realised that once I slipped the net to return to England, there would be no clearer signal that further attacks were being organised. Despite this consideration, England was a big field of haystacks within which to lose a needle and once there we had the element of invisibility and surprise, steering well clear of the Irish community, who were heavily scrutinised and harassed under the Prevention of Terrorism Acts.

The bombing of the Tories at the Grand Hotel broke Britain's strategy of containment. I would argue that it had a more immediate but allied significance within the IRA, besides being a morale booster to comrades and our support base. Prior to Brighton, not everyone was convinced that taking the war to England was our single most effective strategy; nor were many convinced of our capacity to further the strategy. Some argued that we needed to increase the level of operations in the six counties; others believed that gaining de facto control of territory, that is, the creation of so-called Green or liberated zones, was an essential goal. Each had strong advocates and valid arguments. Resources of arms, explosives, personnel and money were always scarce and hotly contended. We had upped the ante. But we had to maintain the momentum. That meant a continuation of the England campaign. Only sustainable, dogged pressure would move the British. I believe that after Brighton, as a direct consequence, the movement were fully won over to the conviction – which beforehand only a rump had held – that we could best further our objectives by a long-term, sustained and sustainable campaign of operations across the water. I and those immediately around me were committed to this strategy. Following that logic, we prepared for the next operation. I gave a personal commitment to remain on active service outside of Ireland. There was nowhere to run, after all.

10

Capture and Trial

And you dare to call me a terrorist
While you look down your gun
When I think of all the deeds that you had done,
You have plundered many nations, divided many lands
You had terrorised their peoples, you ruled with an iron hand
And you brought this reign of terror to my land
−Brian Warfield, 'The Ballad of Joe McDonnell'

Brighton alone, albeit extremely important in terms of the specificity of its targeting – for we were striking at the heart of government – was only one attack in what was envisaged as a long-term campaign. We had to be able to sustain the pressure; prove that as long as Britain maintained its criminal, oppressive hold on the six counties there would be resistance. That meant more bombs in England.

By the spring of 1985 I was again across the water, part of an ASU tasked to mount a series of operations later that same year, subsequently dubbed by the British press as the 'seaside bomb blitz'.

The plan was to detonate sixteen small devices concealed mainly on beaches, and a few planted in seaside hotels, around the English coast, apart from one (the only one actually planted), which was secreted in the Rubens hotel, Buckingham Palace Road, London. The devices would have been set to go off one per day. Each would consist of between three and five pounds of gelignite. There would be warnings given in all cases. The idea behind the operation was to commercially damage the British tourist industry. Basque separatists had previously used this tactic to target the Spanish holiday trade. The complexity of the campaign required meticulous logistical planning.

Our plans were curtailed when I was captured, along with Gerry McDonnell, Martina Anderson, Ella O'Dwyer and Peter Sherry, at a flat in Langside Road, Glasgow, on 22 June 1985. That morning I had set off from my base in London to rendezvous with Peter Sherry in Carlisle. Unfortunately, Peter was the subject of a heavy surveillance operation (led by Ian Phoenix, an RUC Special Branch undercover operative, later killed in the Chinook helicopter crash in the Mull of Kintyre, 1994). I walked into the trap and, in turn, we were followed to Glasgow, where we were arrested with the three named above. Within days, a follow-up search in a basement of a block of flats in James Gray Street, less than a mile away from where we were arrested, would net a considerable haul of explosives, timers and several assault rifles.

A knock at the door interrupted our meal. It seemed that the landlord had come by for the rent. An envelope containing the money was on the mantelpiece in the front room. I opened the door to two burly strangers, immediately realising that they were police. If memory serves, I asked, cooperatively and with an English accent, 'Can I help you?', buying precious seconds but also in hope that they were there making some general enquiry – perhaps in regard to a nearby break-in? A later account claims they were posing as pizza deliverymen, although I had no under-standing of this as I was unceremoniously pulled into the hallway (where a gun was immediately put to my head), momentarily transfixed by the gaping barrel of the revolver pointed at my face. In the flurried second all this took, a full squad emerged as if from nowhere and rushed the flat and arrested the others. I feared there would be a shooting match. There were only two pistols in the flat. It would have been a bloodbath. But to my huge relief no shots came. My shoes were removed and I was handcuffed before being led out of the tenement and across the main road to where waiting arrest vehicles had assembled. En route to whatever lay ahead, I was assailed with thoughts of escape; my imagination was in overdrive, seeking desperate opportunities, weighing up every moment and space for some exploitable weakness, a window to hurl myself through, and out of chaos, the slightest opportunity created to get away. I had known, and lived with the knowledge for years, that if and when captured I faced some twenty years behind bars. I had now to assume that Brighton could be on the interrogatory agenda.

We were held in the main police lock-up in Stewart Street, central Glasgow, for seven days under the provisions of the Prevention of Terrorism

Act of 1974. This was it: the moment for which I had for years mentally prepared. Despite best efforts, one day I knew I was liable to be captured. No matter what, I would be going to jail for a long time. How long might depend on what happened during interrogation over the next week. My only recourse was to say nothing; to utter not a word nor to give any signal. At the end I might conjure up a defence with the lawyers, a strategy in court to perhaps mitigate the worst that the British court system might contrive to inflict.

Before the expected processing due on arrival at the police headquarters, I was suddenly alone for a matter of seconds in the towering presence of one of the arrest party. The others seemed to have disappeared. This was a new technique in my experience – or a variation on the standard practice to intimidate while resolve was judged to be weakest. I was being tested and my response in that moment would determine the shape of subsequent interrogation. I was asked some specific questions, none of which I can now recollect. I stayed silent. In a sense any response from me would be of less significance than an indication or interpretation that I was vulnerable to threat.

Interrogation sessions took place every day for seven days, morning, afternoon and late into the evening. I didn't respond at all to their questions, none of which were specific, and stayed silent throughout all the sessions. I remembered getting slapped or punched in Castlereagh every time I responded to a question with 'No comment.' I wasn't touched at all in Stewart Street. On the third or fourth day I had an extraordinary encounter with one of the interrogation squad which I have often pondered over and to this day cannot really figure out to a satisfactory conclusion. In a break from the standard interrogation procedure, I was brought from a cell to face, for the first time, a lone detective, but in one of the offices, not in an interrogation room, nor in a corridor, although I am certain we were monitored. Any departure from routine is suspicious. This was, for me, a new mind game. The detective stated that he felt out of his depth; that this situation was beyond his experience as a policeman. At face value, he seemed to be marking my card – like he recognised he wasn't dealing with the normal type whose criminal activity he investigated. Was it possible I was being complimented, in however backhanded a manner? He went on to state that there were senior detectives from at least three other constabularies queuing up outside for a chance to question me. He said he thought they would go to extreme measures. He was watching for a reaction from me. He must have gauged that I wasn't showing fear, then toned down the implicit threat of torture to suggest the intended use of truth drugs. He wasn't involved in any further questioning, although I would later see him in attendance during a pretrial hearing at Lambeth Magistrates' Court.

After that incident, which again was the third or fourth day, the teams were changed. I recalled a time in Castlereagh when by the third day I might see how ragged the interrogators looked: five o'clock shadows, bags under their eyes, grubby shirt collars. I wouldn't have washed for three days, so any sign of slippage in their appearance gave me some comfort. Perhaps this might explain why the team at Stewart Street was changed after the third day, rather than any failure to gain information; the replacement squad fared no better.

One week after our capture, the five of us were transported under heavy security to an airport and onto a military transport plane. I saw the others for the first time since being lifted. We didn't speak, mutually realising that our every word and gesture would be carefully scrutinised, but we each got a morale boost from the others' general demeanour. We had all come through. The plane landed at RAF Northolt, from where we were taken along the M4 in a large prison bus to Paddington high security. As the bus turned to enter the building I pressed my right hand up to the window in a sign of victory, hoping that one of the many press photographers there might capture the moment of defiance. One of the tabloids had a front-page photo of a two-fingered gesture from one of us on the bus.

Within a few hours of our arrival at Paddington, minutes before the seven-day detention order ran out, I was charged with 'murder contrary to common law' on five counts: for the deaths of Jeanne Mary Shattock, Eric Geoffrey Taylor, Anthony George Berry, Anne Roberta Wakeham and of Muriel Maclean. I was in turn charged with 'unlawfully and maliciously causing an explosion' and that I had 'deposited an explosive device' at the Grand Hotel, Brighton. Other charges followed in the coming days and weeks.

I was questioned by the Sussex Constabulary chief who was in charge of investigating Brighton. I didn't respond to his list of prepared questions.

He barely suppressed his loathing for what he imagined I represented. He revealed that he had also questioned members of my family. He mentioned my youngest sister, who was then a trainee nurse, stating that unlike me, she was motivated to save lives. I was later to hear from her that he had been bullying, nasty. My mother also confirmed that he had treated all the family roughly. I had deliberately kept far away and out of contact with all my family in England for years precisely in anticipation of such a likelihood. His manner was thuggish, hectoring; used to inspiring fear. Having come through the Castlereagh experience, I was well prepared for bullies.

I later heard more detail about the extent of the investigation triggered by our capture. The Scottish authorities rounded up dozens of republican supporters and left-wing activists – I know because as part of the disclosure of evidence we obtained through our lawyers before the trial, I read a sampling from boxes of statements made at the time, which indicated that the police had used the occasion to gather information on the Left. The press, too, followed their own agenda. Anyone remotely connected to me was approached for a statement, garnering childhood accounts from former schoolmates. An ex-girlfriend who had left Belfast before my internment and had since built a career as a nurse was detained and questioned about me. After that experience, she was contacted by one of the tabloids and offered a five-figure sum for the 'low-down' on us, even though we had broken up in early 1973. She refused. I cannot help reflecting on the unfathomable gulf between her integrity and the tabloid's squalid agenda.

During a preliminary questioning at Paddington, I was told to remove all my clothes. I was handed a pair of blue overalls to put on, which being comically oversized, I immediately discarded. I sat naked with arms folded and said nothing. One of the branchmen summarily ended the session: 'Back to the cell.' His colleague demurred, realising that a policewoman was on duty in the corridor outside. But I was taken past the young constable, who looked, to her credit, uncomfortable at the sight of this naked Irishman marching by her. About twenty minutes later I was given overalls that did fit, by the branchman who wanted to spare the policewoman's blushes.

After a long weekend at Paddington we were brought before a magistrate and then remanded to Brixton Prison. Myself, Gerry MacDonnell and

Peter Sherry stood in the dock handcuffed and, rather than wear the custodial overalls, wrapped either in a towel or blanket cut to make a poncho, in solidarity with every captured republican who had ever resisted criminalisation; a ritual as much as a protest, marking the beginning of a new front in our struggle against the British state, not removal from that struggle. Relatives and friends present in the gallery would know our morale was high.

We were held in the top-security D Wing. Martina Anderson and Ella O'Dwyer were in cells directly above our landing and we were able to shout out to them from our barred windows. Except for an East German, Sonja Schulze, who was facing espionage charges, they were the sole women prisoners in Brixton. The spirits and morale of the women were unshakeable, despite enduring a harsher regime than any male prisoner. They were constantly strip-searched by the female staff assigned to them in the landing above us. They suffered a punitive regime deliberately designed, we believed, to break their spirit. Martina used to sing out through the bars. This became a nightly morale-booster. Remand prisoners from other wings would shout over requests for songs. Security was very tight. D Wing was the top security unit in Brixton, after all, but within months was further strengthened with the construction of an anti-helicopter grill on top of its exercise yard.

During a remand hearing at Lambeth Magistrates' Court, I was issued with a book of photographs of the victims: awful, nightmarish photographs. None of the bodies depicted were identifiable. Each of my co-accused for the seaside bomb blitz also received a copy, despite the fact that none was charged with Brighton, in an attempt, we thought, to prejudice their cases.

We were jointly charged with conspiracy to bomb coastal locations. I was separately charged with placing the device that was defused at the Rubens hotel. I had, as outlined, already been charged with Brighton. After some weeks, additional charges were made against me: for planting and conspiring to plant bombs in England in 1978–9 (the substance of the extradition case in the Netherlands some five years before), and for conspiring in 1983 to bomb Weeton army camp (as mentioned at the end of chapter eight).

I was walking around the yard when I got news of the extra conspiracy charges involving Weeton. You couldn't wipe the smile off my face.

Extraordinary to recount, but it was one of the most liberating days of my life. At the core, all I had was my name. The case papers vindicated me in the eyes of my comrades, proving that the IRA had been fooled by an agent provocateur and that me and a comrade had successfully evaded capture once we realised the trap being set for us. It was a short-lived sense of euphoria, the pressures mounting as the trial date approached.

I received few family visits. Eileen travelled over from Belfast to attend the first remand hearing. We had a short visit afterwards. To this day I regret the outcome. She had a copy of the decree absolute with her, which when signed by me would have finalised the divorce. Eileen asked, 'Should we tear this up?' In a moment of profound weakness I said yes. If instead I had answered no, Eileen would have had the freedom to begin a new life. Her loyalty to me as a captured republican seemed to outweigh her recently found independence. I robbed her of that choice, a decision which eventually would have massive consequences for her mental health. Our son too, of course, would suffer the absence of a father. I had seen him last, with Eileen, in March, before they boarded a train to return to Belfast. He was seven. The next time I would see him in freedom, he would be an adult.

Dad was able to visit me only the once, while I was on remand in Brixton. He had made the journey from Ashford, Kent, the day previous but was refused entrance for the visit because, it was claimed, he hadn't the required identification. Undaunted, he returned the following day. I hadn't seen him in twelve or thirteen years. He was fifty-five but looked older and didn't appear to be in the best of health. He scrutinised my face. 'You're the double of my father,' he said (I had never thought of myself as resembling Joss and, indeed, had always thought I owed more in appearance to the Donegans). 'I can see you're strong enough,' he added, assured in some way that I was up to the tribulations ahead. Our visit lasted twenty minutes, not a second more. That was the last time I saw him, except in dreams. He died in 1995 while I was still in prison.

The trial began in Court Two of the Old Bailey, the high-security court, on 6 May 1986. According to contemporary media reports, police marksmen lined the roof. The trial was to last six weeks. It was an extraordinarily stressful time. Not because of the anticipation of the outcome. From a quite early stage I was reconciled to the near certainty that I would be found guilty, whether of Brighton or of the other charges. The pressure came from having to handle the daily presence in court, where I felt under constant scrutiny. And there were the journeys to and from the Old Bailey in the escorted prison van. We could see freedom flashing by from the van window. That was hard to witness. The routes would be varied but unavoidably we saw central London, on occasions passing the anti-apartheid picket protest outside the South African Embassy in Trafalgar Square.

I pleaded not guilty to all the charges, beyond which I played no further part in the trial. I did not give evidence. To have pleaded guilty would have been to accept that the actions attributed to me were criminal acts. At one time the more usual republican response would have been to refuse to recognise the court's jurisdiction or legitimacy to try us. A more pragmatic approach evolved during the course of the struggle as hundreds of individuals were imprisoned by special courts, after beatings in RUC holding centres such as Castlereagh. My actions were carried out as part of the armed struggle, a justified struggle with much support throughout our communities. I have had moments of doubt since, as I did at the time, whether I should have taken the stand and given a robust political defence of my actions. The prosecutor was Roy Amlot. I was represented in court by Richard Ferguson QC. At the time, there seemed a plausible chance that he might successfully challenge the prosecution's argument; that I should therefore allow him to do so and not distract or complicate the jurors' task with a political speech from the dock. Ferguson, who was a former Ulster Unionist MP, had argued for reform of local government in the six counties and would later join the Alliance Party. He, sadly, died in 2009.

The focus of the prosecution case was on Brighton, despite the fact that none of the others in the dock with me had been charged with Brighton. This clearly was highly prejudicial against the others, and their barristers had unsuccessfully argued for separation of the charges against me for Brighton from the joint charges we faced for the seaside bomb blitz and for the possession of the weapons and explosives found in Glasgow.

The case against me for Brighton was based mainly on forensic evidence, particularly a partial finger and palm print found on a registration card retrieved from the rubble. Usually, such evidence is only admissible when a certain number of fingerprint matches are found, but the standard of admissibility had been lowered – whether for my case or as a recent development, I cannot now say. Ferguson, who had gained a reputation on his knowledge of forensics, questioned the authenticity of the fingerprint evidence and the alleged discovery of part of a timing mechanism in a toilet bowl, an important find because it was claimed to accurately locate the seat of the explosion. The suggestion was that its discovery was all too convenient. Ferguson, who had represented several defendants in IRA cases in England, thought it suspicious that the same team of forensic officers (fingerprint expert, exhibits officer, scene-of-crime officers) were involved in all the cases, which resulted in a string of convictions based largely on their testimony.

I knew to expect that the police would stoop to any lengths to gain convictions against republicans. Two years beforehand, an arms and explosives cache was discovered in Salcey Forest, Northamptonshire. Contained in the haul were box timers similar, it was alleged, to the type found in Glasgow after our arrest. A newspaper article appeared subsequently claiming that my fingerprint was found on one of the boxes in the Salcey haul. I had no involvement at all in this cache, but apparently a warrant was issued for my arrest based on the alleged fingerprint. It was only a matter of the state authorities capturing me and of having a charge of possession at hand. However, despite conspiracy charges being levelled against me going back to 1978, no mention was made of Salcey during the trial. Could it be that the Salcey fingerprint was transferred to the Brighton case? I was sure in my own mind that at the moment of signing the registration card at the reception desk of the Grand I was sufficiently diligent in preventing any direct contact that would have left a print.

Much was also made of police evidence that my prints were identified from records of criminal offences I committed while an adolescent. It was not as if the authorities would have had difficulty in identifying me for lack of my prints. There must have been literally dozens of prints taken in my frequent arrests during the previous twelve years of IRA involvement. To me this amounted to propaganda: the belittling linkage of criminal delinquency and IRA actions. After all, I had successfully challenged an extradition request by the British authorities through Interpol five years previously. Surely that warrant would have required proof of identity such as fingerprint evidence?

Perhaps, though, the ploy was to suggest the effectiveness of normal good police procedure and to hide that the state at an early stage regarded me as a likely suspect for Brighton.

For the most part the prosecution case was countered quite effectively. At least my defence managed to create a measure of doubt about much of the prosecution evidence. At times I would try to gauge the jury's reaction to the case. I judged them to be listening attentively throughout and believed them to be objective. However, at about the fourth week, on a certain morning, their attitude changed dramatically. We entered the box from the cells below and I became conscious that some of the members of the jury were looking up at us in the dock with open hostility, while others wouldn't look at all. Something had happened to change what prior to this had been the jury's general air of impartiality and, further, to sour the atmosphere in the court. We heard it claimed later that evening that a piece of paper had fallen from the visitors' gallery directly above where the jury sat, causing some of them to imagine that an attempt at intimidation had been made. There is absolutely no substance to this. As I said, we actually thought the trial was going quite well. And anyway, even if a slip of paper had fallen, it was only a matter of presenting it and its message to the court usher. No. I have my own theory but no proof to back it up. But I have a clear impression of the look on some of the jurors' faces and no slip of paper could have warranted the venom on display. Perhaps they were shown photographs of the dead victims, truly appalling images, and these caused the change in attitude.

One witness in particular stood out. I was impressed at Donald Maclean's dignity while giving evidence. His wife Muriel was one of the three women killed in the blast. He spoke quietly and simply, without any outward show of bitterness. I know from statements he has made since that he thought me and the others in the dock were animals, but he displayed none of this while speaking from the witness box. After giving his testimony, he unassumingly and quietly walked out of the courtroom, passing the dock without looking in my direction.

After a trial lasting six weeks, Judge Boreham sentenced me on 23 June to multiple life for Brighton. Life times eight, five of which were mandatory for the five people killed. The jury had deliberated for some five hours. I was convinced that I would be found guilty. Apart from a posse of screws, I was on my own in the dock. My co-accused in the seaside bomb blitz remained in the cells, and we would be reunited in the same dock some days later for sentencing for the joint venture. When ordered to stand, I remained seated in the dock and was forced to my feet while Boreham passed sentence. He described me as 'a man of exceptional cruelty and inhumanity'. To an English judge, and perhaps to the British public weaned on ignorance and misinformation about the nature of the conflict and of Irish republicans, this may have seemed a fitting assessment. There was no psychological profiling, witness evidence, nor previous convictions to substantiate Boreham's delivered judgement. But then, he was merely another English dispenser of that classic lack of judgement regarding Irish matters, as much shackled to his worldview as, for example, I would assume, some imperial castrator in Kenya under Pax Britannica.

Boreham recommended that I should serve at least thirty-five years before I could even be considered for parole. My mind seized on the figure. I *was* thirty-five. I would be seventy. Based on me living for as long as the mean average longevity of my grandfathers, I calculated I might have four years of freedom before I died. I held my sight fast to this chink of light.

I declared the obligatory '*Tiocfaidh ár lá*' (Our day will come), adding '*gan dabht ar bith*' (without any doubt), before being led below to begin, if the British state should have its way, the rest of my life in prison. In that moment I connected with every volunteer who ever stood similarly in the dock and passionately proclaimed that victory would be ours one day, as indeed many more would shout defiantly in the moment of sentencing. At least I was not alone in terms of what lay ahead, unlike Kieran Nugent, the first Blanketman, who told his persecutors that they would 'have to nail the uniform' to his back. Previous struggles of Irish prisoners had established some measure of tolerability. I would have comrades to welcome me into whatever prison lay designated.

I did not stand trial for the other charges: the bombs at Canvey Island oil depot; the bombing of the gasometer near Blackwall Tunnel; the conspiracy to bomb Weeton army base. The Crown prosecutor, Roy Amlot QC, in an attempt at levity, I thought, said that in order to spare the public purse, the Crown would not contest the other charges except in the unlikely event of a successful appeal against the Brighton conviction.

Strange as it may seem, I felt a certain relief. I had just endured what at the time seemed to be the most stressful period of my life. Under constant scrutiny of judge, jury, the world's media and a crammed visitors' gallery, the pressure had been intense.

Did I get a fair trial? After the trial, in the lawyers' visiting area, I asked Richard Ferguson whether he thought so. I had put him on the spot. With reluctance, he said no. I am certain that he brought all his considerable energy and skills to bear on my behalf. I cannot fault his efforts. We had been discussing what next. On what grounds should I appeal? But I had meant more. The trial had been political even though we had agreed to fight it in terms of the law, offering a defence and some of us giving evidence. No Irish republican could receive a fair hearing in a British court, even if, as I have stated, the jury were open and objective, as I believe our jury basically were. Had I been tried in the 1970s I would have refused to recognise the court. A fair trial would have entailed a political defence that would have put the British political and military establishments in the dock for their terror in Ireland and for the injustice of partition. I was acutely aware, as were the others in the dock, of what we stood for; that we represented the republican cause, that in effect this was another front in the struggle, and that perceptions about the movement would be here shaped by how we dealt with the pressures of the trial and by our conduct throughout our weeks in the courtroom spotlight.

I don't think I am exaggerating when I claim that there was something in the papers about the Brighton operation every day for many, many months. The tabloid domain had a new demon to roast on a spit: 'the Brighton Bomber'. It also emerged that the British security authorities had concocted their own name for me – 'Chancer'. Their perception, it appears, was that I kept taking chances by repeatedly returning to England to operate. In fact, I considered myself to be ultra-careful, the person least likely to take chances. Other media claims were equally bizarre, for example that I was either Soviet- or Libyan-trained. There was even speculation of direct involvement from Libya. I thought at the time that these stories were designed to lessen the credibility of the IRA as a guerrilla force; one lacking the necessary experience and resolve to carry out this level of operation on its own.

Soon after the trial a television documentary dealt with the Blackpool allegations. In what must have been a huge embarrassment to the security authorities, the programme advanced the thesis that Brighton may not have happened had I been captured in Preston. A ridiculous line. The IRA were not short of potential replacements. The targeting of the Grand Hotel would have happened with or without me.

Another annoying aspect of the media coverage was that the lies and inaccuracies reported were repeated in many references in books dealing with the conflict. For example, in one newspaper report it is claimed I was sentenced to two years for IRA membership. The record will show that I was in fact interned during the period in which it was claimed I was a sentenced prisoner. Another report, I think in the *Express*, claimed that I was heard crying back in my cell after sentencing. Some entrepreneurial screw made a nice few quid from supplying that fabrication. The worst claim, however, the one that rankled, also appeared in the *Daily Express* subsequent to the guilty verdict. The rag asserted that I was responsible for the deaths of three comrades who were killed in a premature explosion during an attack on the British Army base in the grounds of Belfast Gasworks in October 1976. The volunteers, all of whom I had known, were Joey Surgenor, Paul Marlowe and Frank Fitzsimmons. The story illustrated perfectly the nature of many sections of the British press, central agents in the propaganda onslaught.

I recall what was perhaps our last journey from the Old Bailey as the prison wagon and security cortège weaved through the rush-hour traffic of central London, sirens blaring. From the van's window, by some quirk of timing, I spied Roy Amlot QC disappearing unassumingly down the steps of a Tube station, another day in court over. I was about to disappear into the bowels of the system, all the turbulence of the trial now in my wake.

11
Life X 8

Once sentence was handed down, I ceased to be a remand prisoner. The 'privileges' of that designation were summarily removed and I was required to wear prison clothes, a matter of consequence for a political prisoner, conferring as it did the stigma of criminality. No republican imprisoned for the cause of Irish freedom would willingly don prison garb. As mentioned in chapter five, Billy McKee, after a prolonged hunger strike in 1972, had gained special status. Its removal in 1976 led to the 1981 hunger strike. However, republican prisoners held in England, fewer in number, were dispersed and isolated throughout the enemy's penal system. They took the pragmatic decision to wear the uniform rather than risk virtual deep-freeze in solitary confinement for failure to comply, in order to maintain organisational structure. The priority. In Brixton, after sentencing, Eileen visited me before her return home (she had stayed for most of the trial). She was clearly shocked to see me in prison clothing. It was shaming.

Back on D Wing, there was a more risible impact. A young screw took keen delight in reducing my ration of milk from the more adequate measure allowed on remand; my immediate introduction to 'hard time'. This newly imposed temporal order, designed to last the remainder of my years, weighed heavy. Whereas before I had the trial to preoccupy every cellular moment alone, I left the dock to face life times eight (or 'life x 8', as it was recorded in the official notification) – times five for the five people killed at Brighton, and times three for conspiracy to kill. Capture had transported me to a new battlefront, one that generations of Irish republicans had not only to endure but to challenge and survive: the driven attempt by the British state to criminalise or depoliticise our struggle; instead, to treat it as a criminal venture and me and imprisoned republicans as gangsters. Now in the emasculating garb of the lag, in prison-issue striped shirt and oversized jeans, I awaited transfer to some steel and concrete tomb. I recalled the dire career trajectory forewarned when I first volunteered: felon's cell or hole in the ground. Hair-splitting alternatives now loomed: either a high-security dispersal prison or, the more likely expectation, an SSU (special secure unit), whether at Leicester or to either Parkhurst or Albany on the Isle of Wight. I would have put money (had I access) on Parkhurst, which was purpose-built (rather than converted), and mindful too of the additional security provided *ex gratia* by the Solent. Within a few days of sentencing I was taken northward amid elaborate arrangements to a location in the English Midlands.

Upon arrival at the final stop, I was unsure of its precise location, certain only that the cortège had headed north from London, and therefore spared me a ferry crossing. Parkhurst was ruled out. I was escorted, handcuffed, through what I soon determined was the integral visiting block of HMP Leicester's SSU, the cuffs only removed in my allocated cell. As if seen through the wrong end of a telescope, all these years later I seem small in that moment – from van to the lone entry to the unit beyond. My sighting of the first prisoner, however, not only confirmed the location but boosted my morale.

I hadn't seen Brian Keenan since the late 1970s – since, that is, his capture outside of Newry and subsequent removal to England to face trial for conspiracy charges related to the IRA's campaign there. I knew that he was in the Leicester SSU. By this stage, Brian (who died in 2008) was six years into a twenty-year sentence. I held him in highest esteem for his visionary leadership and boundless energy, and viewed the prospect of doing time with him as mitigation for the loss of freedom. Brian was on a visit. I passed by the window of his visiting room (in the SSU's integral visiting facility), where he sat with several members of his family over from Belfast. I managed a smile as I was escorted through a security gate and into the SSU's landing: word would quickly filter home that I had arrived unscathed. The unit would comprise all I would tangibly know of the world until the distant future.

I also knew that the unit held two other Irish republicans of high calibre and reputation, Paul Kavanagh from Belfast and Brendan Dowd from Castlemaine in Kerry, and within minutes was in their company. I was introduced to the unit's other notables: two Londoners each doing twenty-five years for the Brink's-Mat gold bullion robbery, Mick McAvoy and Brian Robinson, and another Londoner, Billy Skingle, serving life for killing a policeman during an armed robbery. Now that I had joined them, the unit was at its full capacity of seven. On that first day I ate the best meal I'd had since my arrest, a year before, the centrepiece of which was an egg, soundly fried for the occasion by Brendan, and the lads allowed me a few days' grace before I was allotted my share of the cleaning duties, an altogether welcome reception after the austerity of the Brixton regime.

The SSUs were designed as escape-proof units, prisons within prisons, within which a small group of, say (as in this case), seven prisoners would spend years together under the continual scrutiny of staff and cameras. A regular staff were assigned to the wing and would be changed every six months. Other members of the same contingent would also survey us through the large window of their duty room, which afforded a full view of the central body of the block and gave the impression that we were the subject of scientific interest.

We were assigned Special Category A status, the highest risk assessment based on a Home Office perception of levels of potential outside support for an escape attempt. The units were designed to hold those who it was feared had the necessary wherewithal to effect an escape. We had no contact with other prisoners and never left the unit, even for visits, for as already mentioned, the unit had its own integral visiting area. The unit also had its own exercise yard, over which was constructed a seemingly top-heavy, slanted grill roof designed to prevent escape by helicopter.

Two such units were established in the 1960s, at HMP Leicester and HMP Durham, because of the embarrassment to the Home Office caused by a number of high-profile escapes, such as those of the Great Train Robber Ronnie Biggs and of the spy George Blake. Leicester had been chosen because it has the highest perimeter walls in the English prison system, and indeed from outside it looks a formidable fortress (although I had to wait years before seeing this for myself).

The unit comprised a closed-off area of cells from what had previously been a second-floor landing. A former inmate (armed robber John McVicker, who had famously escaped from Durham) dubbed it 'the Submarine' and the gateways in as 'airlocks'. I've also read a description of it as an 'electronic tomb'. Criticisms of the units, which deemed them psychologically damaging, led to calls for their closure, and this would have happened had the IRA's bombing campaign in England not commenced in the 1970s.

Over the course of the previous fifteen years, imprisoned republicans in England, like their captured comrades back in Ireland, had campaigned to be treated as political prisoners. Isolated throughout the English prison system, as mentioned above, they had still managed to win concessions and to help improve conditions for all prisoners. We gained from their struggle. Prison work was negotiated to be defined as maintaining the cleanliness of our own lived environment. The unit, our living space, was kept spotless. I soon settled into the remorseless drag of unit time.

At the first opportunity I sought Brian's counsel. While walking round the yard during our then-daily hour's exercise I expressed an interest in education. I had in mind that eventually I might do an Open University degree but kept that grand idea to myself. His best advice was that I should not make any firm plans for at least a year. He knew of many instances of prisoners taking on arduous study loads only later to abandon them under the strain, not of study per se but because of all the pressures facing prisoners while adjusting to heavy time – coping with the life sentence, sparse contact with family, visits, the 'Dear John' and pressures among the lads arising from proximity and the resulting overfamiliarity – and, then, with the screws and administration. It was sound advice. I could spare a year. A year in which to acclimatise to life times eight.

It is beyond my imaginative capacity to convey the bleakness of incarceration in a single chapter. I'd have to concertina countless diaries filled with quotidian drudgery: eight a.m. – slop out; ten a.m. – exercise yard, etc., entered year upon year. Survival meant salvaging space and a semblance of control.

Imprisonment can assume the cloak of grief – grieving for the life you had – and it began for me from that moment the cell door slammed shut behind, leaving me with the fading stamp of the screws' boots, jangling of keys and accompanied whistling. Screws were always whistling, often to wind us up. You're left staring at the four walls, bereft of a horizon, conscious of the creaking of the hot water pipe skirting the outer wall of the cell and to the thousand unidentified sounds emanating from within the closed world that in time I could read like a familiar book, as if I had developed the senses of a trapped hare. The moment is a total rupture from the known. I was stunned with the obvious: this could be all I will know from this moment to, possibly, my last breath. Life up till that moment is over, taken from you. Forfeited, others will argue. Days and weeks merge, you mark two years, three, eight, eleven. At best you achieve a numbed acceptance of the moment and get on with creating something from within to push the ever-encroaching walls back from crushing you. I do not exaggerate – I have seen how it destroys people.

I've somehow managed to block out much of those days. You had to rely on and nurture your own inner resources. I strove to remain informed about the world outside. I read; I followed what I could get of the news in Ireland from Radio Ulster, dependent upon the reception, often having to hold the radio at arm's length to the ceiling for the news at eleven p.m., when the signal was stronger. But even in Belfast you would never have relied on that source alone. My hold on the reality of the progress of the ongoing struggle began to loosen. There was no substitute for being on the spot. After about two years I realised how out of sync I now was with external reality. My singular clarity of purpose now was to survive. This was another front in the struggle. To stand still was to shrink. I grew determined to wring value out of every day; never to waste a moment of what it now meant to be alive. Not a precious second was to be squandered. I also acknowledged the illusory sense of freedom that pertained before my capture and the slamming of the gates: I had been no more self-determining prior to capture. Education would be my liberation.

The first year I read every book within reach pertinent to the political struggle. Supporters sent me in books. The other lads' own interests in politics and history ensured much reading material at hand. I include the non-political prisoners in the SSU, for they were bright guys and interested in current affairs. Much of the thin trickle of academic opinion and research on the Troubles published contemporaneously had escaped my notice, given the distracting reality of the very same Troubles. A labour of catch-up. I also wrestled with the Marxist canon. My son, who in a flash of relative time turned nine, sent me *The Complete Works of James Connolly* (in two volumes, which I still proudly possess). Very little fiction then, as I recall. Additionally, an interest in classical music acquired during years on the run was now more thoroughly explored, to the extent that I very seldom heard any contemporary stuff. I mean, in the world outside, whether you wanted to or not, you would assimilate pop culture. I went nearly a full decade inside without knowing what was number one in the charts. This appreciation of music and hunger to read absorbed my time alone in the cell. Eileen had sent me in a cassette player and small speaker system and I would order cassettes from a classical music club.

I began to sense something one-way and potentially limiting in these efforts. I wasn't a sponge. I needed critical engagement – feedback, structure, direction, goals. I contacted the prison education department at Leicester in August 1987. From that time until the day I was to finally emerge through the prison gates, I was engaged in some level of formal education. I did not begin to study with the Open University until 1989. Leicester was not a designated OU centre, a requirement if academic tutors were to be allowed admittance. Persistent lobbying by the prison teaching staff on my behalf eventually succeeded and Leicester obtained the required status.

The prison experience, however, was to confront me with the limits of my own mental strength. I had learned to roll with the punches; to stay on my feet. However, I was to come close to a nervous breakdown. After less than three years at Leicester I began to suffer severe panic attacks in my cell at night. At about two in the morning I would wake to find my heart racing as if I was about to have a seizure. Typically, I didn't dare move, not even to summon medical assistance via the alarm button over by the door of my cell, for fear that any strain, like shouting for help or raising myself to get off the bed, would cause my heart to explode. Notifying the medic was pointless. My only defence was to control my breathing until the attack subsided. These attacks were regular, sometimes nightly. I had to figure this out alone.

Here's how I reasoned what was physically happening to me: prison rules forbid an inmate from expressing anger, in an environment that guarantees anger. When not expressed, anger is internalised. The antidote, I soon figured out, was to vent poisonous, self-devouring rage. That moment of truth occurred after a confrontation with screws, when I expelled all that brewing emotion. From then, I never experienced another panic attack. A slight case of alopecia barbae also improved (clean-shaven at the time of my capture, I had grown a beard). To survive long-term imprisonment, and I admit this is only my experience, you have to play the long game – analyse and problem-solve; and, if possible, avoid reacting. But on occasions confrontation was absolutely necessary for my physical well-being and even my sanity.

Within the strictures of the external security, the so-called fabric of walls, cameras, grills and, we suspected, hidden microphones, the day-to-day atmosphere of the unit was in many ways better than that pertaining in the rest of the dispersal prison system for Category A prisoners, or what we termed 'normal location'. We prepared our own meals from ingredients supplied by the kitchen, supplemented with items we bought and pooled from the canteen. We had cells to ourselves, unlike in other locations where doubling up was prevalent because of the massive population strain on the system. We still, however, had to slop out in the morning, my routine for almost all of my time held within the English regime.

I was to spend four years at Leicester, then a further four in a new, purpose-built unit in Full Sutton Prison in Yorkshire. Throughout my time in English prisons, relations between prisoners, and between prisoners and staff, were generally good. I usually found head governors to be progressive in terms of trying to work with us to build liberal regimes within the constraints of security and budgets. A few lower-grade governors and some prison warders were bigoted towards IRA prisoners and would find ways to cause problems for us, but the majority acted professionally and I found quite a few to be very decent people. I used to think that to be a screw is a contemptible occupation. Some were contemptible. In time I learned differently, and to treat them as I found them. Many had served in the British Army and joined the prison service on the incentive that their service pension benefits could be transferred over.

I recall the librarian in Leicester, a former Coldstream Guard, who went to some trouble to get the books I ordered, mostly about opera, a subject we would occasionally discuss. Another warder, a former Marine commando, in charge of the prison kitchen, lent me music cassettes, certainly an infringement of security. One was a recording of the Royal Marines Regimental Band, unsolicited. This was some while before an IRA bomb killed ten Royal Marines at their School of Music in Deal, Kent, in 1989. He had left the prison service by then. I would have hated having to face him – a decent guy. Where a warder had a son or other family member doing a duty tour in Ireland, we might have a problem, but I can't really recall any former squaddies who acted less than professionally. That was my experience. Others tell it differently. For the fact is that Irish republicans, and many prisoners wrongly accused of IRA actions, were brutally beaten by police, prison staff and other prisoners. Particularly in the early years of the campaign, during the 1970s. The atrocious treatment of the Birmingham Six and the Guildford Four is well documented. But by the time I was sentenced it seemed all the major battles had been won and that Irish republicans, who were very often to the fore of prison protests, had gained the respect of fellow prisoners and of prison administrations. We benefited in terms of more humane regime conditions from more than a decade of previous struggle for better conditions by Irish republican prisoners.

Of course there were incidents. For what is gained has to be protected. In fact, if things were running smoothly for more than a month or so, you knew to expect a problem to arise or be created by an overzealous search or because of an ill-judged staff decision. The biggest source of possible conflict was over visiting rules and conditions. Visits are sacrosanct, and prisoners will always resist measures that affect the quality of the precious time they spend with family. Many Irish POWs endured dozens of 'lay-downs' (periods of solitary confinement), and were often 'ghosted' (that is, transferred without notice), punitively, under the GOAD (good order and discipline) rule to another prison, regardless of long planned and awaited visit arrangements, causing great stress and inconvenience to their families.

However, there was a corollary: the prison authorities were loth to move anyone out of the units because of the security headache this would cause. The transporting of a Special Category prisoner typically entailed the organisation of a convoy – of prison van and escort of three cars with armed police in front and three behind, sirens blaring, and possibly a helicopter in contact above. And the crossing of each constabulary boundary meant a changeover of escort. Such operations were hugely expensive, hence the reluctance to move any of us out of the units. This understanding we held like a trump card, never to be wastefully shown face up; the suspicion that we held it gave us some leverage when it came to negotiating improvements to conditions, for a protest was likely to entail a move.

I was ghosted only once, to the punishment unit in Frankland Prison in December 1989, consequently losing Christmas visits with Eileen and our son. This resulted from a protest over the refusal of the authorities to improve conditions to a standard recently established in other units. I had written a critique of the unit's regime and handed copies to the governor and to the board of visitors. In their appreciation I was moved from the unit to the punishment block prior to being transferred out on lay-down.

Transfer entailed me being led out through the 'airlock' gates onto the main landing, then down an iron staircase to the ground-floor wing. My legs were shaking from using muscles unexercised in three years (there were no steps in the unit). All prisoners had remained locked up while I was led through two menacing lines of screws, then out to the escort team. It seemed as though the whole prison regime had closed down to facilitate the move. Some point was being made. It was way over the top and typical of the crazy security levels we experienced in the units. I was handcuffed and put in a prison van. The escort joined us outside the prison walls. The windows of the van were tinted, bestowing a warm patina on the fields flowing by, though nature was beyond improvement. It was my first sight of real grass, trees, anything green, except for weeds in the exercise yard, since my reception three years before. The driver and escort were unit regulars. I was their sole prisoner for the ghosting. There was little exchange between us. They were, for the most part, decent enough blokes, and in a mood, I felt, to be generous within security needs. This was a day out for them. A break from their routine also. The Golden Rule: never reveal anything in your look, words, gestures, that might conceivably inform your enemies. I was hard-pressed to disguise my inner turmoil from them, but to have attempted to reciprocate their banter might have revealed much for the official paperwork they were duty-bound to submit on their return to Leicester after depositing me in the hopefully tender custody of god-knew-where. Wakefield? Frankland? The former was a byword for brutality. The escort – three cars in front, three behind – continued on course for both unwelcome destinations, the constabulary changeover of outriders and siren-blaring marked cars occurring north of Manchester.

I had been on the road for some two hours when the cavalcade did a pit stop. Wakefield. The name was enough to send a shiver down the spine. Its block was notorious among prisoners. This was where the most recalcitrant were sent for a beating. On arrival at Wakefield, I was put in a sort of cubicle where four local screws were having a tea break. They were curious about me but asked no questions. Instead they offered me tea. I accepted, deciding to trust their better nature. The tea was hot, strong, in a canteen mug. Maybe they had spat or pissed in it. Or worse. But it seemed palatable and unsullied. The detective in charge of the operation asked me if I needed to use the toilets. I said no, perhaps a little too curtly, for he checked my handcuffs and tightened them, all the while closely studying my face for a reaction. The cuffs were biting but I denied him even a flinch. I could see that the Leicester screws were annoyed for me. He was letting them and me know who was in charge. The implication hung in the air that they had been lax when cuffing me before leaving Leicester. Mercifully, the journey continued further north to Durham, to the more recently built Frankland dispersal prison. When we were on the road I asked one of the screws to loosen them. He saw the weals on my wrists and loosened them a notch or two. As I said, they weren't bad blokes at all.

The block in Frankland Prison forms an L-shape, one spur holding prisoners considered disruptive, the other spur holding paedophiles and rapists – the lowest of the low in the penal caste system. I was put in a cell in the latter spur. Each spur had its own exercise yard, separated by a wire fence. When it came to my first exercise period I was concerned about which yard I would be assigned to, and greatly relieved to be brought down from the spur to that of the 'ordinary decent criminals'. I was first out. About another dozen joined me but kept to themselves until, with five minutes left, a guy with a Scouse accent asked directly but without malice, 'Who ar'ye, mate?' I identified myself as an IRA prisoner, at which point he greeted me warmly and invited others over. All were friendly. I learned from them that upon being unlocked each had been told that an IRA man was down in the yard (nudge, nudge). I got on very well with these men, all of whom had a history of confrontation, often violent, with prison authorities and were consequently unbiddable to the scheming of bigoted screws. Conditions had created their resistance to the system and refusal to be cowed. No well-ordered prison regime would have produced so many misfits and rebels.

However, my six weeks on lay-down in Frankland left a deeply unpleasant scar on my mind that I still recoil from to this day. Orderlies were all sex offenders and while mopping the landing, apparently unsupervised, could look through the cell door spyholes. I would hear conversations echo along the spur outside my cell whenever one of them would encourage some sexual performance from another still locked up. A new take on a peep show. Screws were absent from the spur when this activity was happening and it seemed to be a common occurrence. My cell was opposite the spur's wash house. Each prisoner was allowed to access the wash house singly for half an hour. On one occasion, I heard a sex offender and an orderly noisily performing some sexual act while using the bath.

While there I put my name down for a haircut. A young local woman was contracted to come into the unit once a month to act as barber. I started to talk to her, just a bit of banter. You didn't get to see many women, other than the female screws, whose introduction increasingly became a feature of change within the system. She was quite cold with me. I wondered whether her coldness was due to me being an IRA prisoner but then copped on to her presumption that I was a sex offender because of the location of my cell. That was an awful realisation. That period must rank as the lowest of all my time incarcerated.

I can record, however, one very positive experience, apart that is from conversations with the prisoners on the other spur. While looking out of the wash house window, which overlooked a path leading to the education block, I recognised an old comrade passing by – Joe McKenny, whom I had known from Dublin. Joe had been arrested in 1986 and sentenced to sixteen years. He was sixty years old at the time. The significance of this encounter was that Joe could notify other republican prisoners in Frankland of my presence there. Up to this I had felt vulnerable, lost within the system. From then on I used my wash house visits to communicate with Joe when possible, and with other republicans, such as Eddie Butler from Limerick and John McCann from Dublin. The sight of another comrade was always heartening. At Christmas the lads tried unsuccessfully to negotiate with the governor to let me spend the day with them. It didn't matter that he refused their request. I knew I wasn't alone. Or, rather, I felt less alone. Joe died in 2015. He was a legendary smuggler and used this experience brilliantly as a quartermaster. It was said that he could travel the length and breadth of Ireland without crossing a main road.

In the New Year I decided to take the initiative by putting my name down to see the governor. He suggested that I should write to the Prison Department at the Home Office. I did, outlining the dispute over conditions at Leicester and the mishandling, I argued, of the situation by the administration there. I doubt if it had any bearing, but after some six weeks at Frankland I was returned to the Leicester SSU to find that in the meantime most of the sought improvements in conditions had been made or were earmarked for implementation. That was not the only change. In the course of those six weeks, the world had gone through a seismic shift – the continuing collapse of Stalinism throughout the Soviet empire, capped by the summary execution of the Ceauşescus. A pub sign on the Old Kent Road came to mind: the World Turned Upside Down. Thanks to the radio, I had followed events but had no images to augment the verbal reports (just as in Maastricht in regard to a radio announcement of John Lennon's murder). But back in the Leicester unit I was able to slowly catch up with the news. And major changes continued in the world. I sat in the social room and watched with the other lads as Nelson Mandela was released. I think we all imagined the day of our own release and the reception awaiting us.

We also followed developments in Ireland. Electoral support for Sinn Fein continued its growth spurt, North and South. The four of us in Leicester had earlier played a small but not insignificant part by writing a letter supporting a Sinn Fein motion to end abstentionism to the Dáil, successfully carried at its 1986 Ard Fheis (annual party conference) in Dublin. The IRA also seemed to be better organised, with a sustained increase in operations in England. We recognised that the current level of IRA activity had successfully achieved what we had failed to implement – a sustained campaign. We sensed the imminence of a political breakthrough. Our morale was high.

Unfortunately, after a particularly fraught summer visit, I ended up in confrontation with the screws and administration. I count myself largely to blame. On a visit with Eileen, I told her I couldn't continue with the relationship. This was in 1990 – four years after our decision not to proceed with the divorce. I found it impossible to bear the pressure of separation. I convinced myself that she would be much better off without me. We could still maintain contact, I reasoned, but she should have her freedom. I could not have handled the situation worse. She was in tears. I didn't relent. It was weakness, not strength. It was cruel. I ended up punching walls. I think I was as close to a nervous breakdown as I am ever likely to suffer. Back in the unit, after the visit, my head went into a tailspin. I threatened consequences if I wasn't transferred out of the unit. I had to get out, away from the immediacy of the trauma. This was a simple flight instinct over-riding rationality.

As a result, I was moved to the punishment block in the basement of the prison, where I was held in a bare cell. At night I would be given a mattress. When the cell light was extinguished, in the sliver of light from under the door I could still make out cockroaches swarming into the cell. I would be on my feet all night. In the morning light I would tally the body count of trodden cockroaches on the concrete floor, like crushed peppermints. After a week, and an ignored request to be moved back to the unit, I was transported to the new, purpose-built SSU at Full Sutton in Yorkshire.

The move to Full Sutton was welcome. I settled into a routine of education and physical exercise. While there, I recall only one episode when the normally good relations between us and the prison authorities were strained. This resulted from a bad decision made by an inexperienced junior governor which led to the riot squad or MUFTI (minimum use of force, tactical intervention) being ordered in to do a lockdown and cell search. We barricaded our cells with the few bits of furniture at hand and waited on the MUFTI breaking in. Our efforts were token. The outcome certain. All we could do was register a protest by making the search difficult and perhaps cause the prison authorities to think twice before resorting to violence the next time. It took them all of five seconds to remove the cell door and clamber over my quickly stacked 'barricade'. In the ensuing melee I somehow ended up breakdancing on the ceiling above their helmets and shields. Better there than on the ground. Apart from a few scrapes and bruises, we (that is, me and the other protesting prisoners) came through relatively unscathed.

For all the privations, it was our families who suffered most. A prisoner would usually get one visit per week, but the journey from Ireland imposed a heavy cost burden on the families of Irish republicans. The costs of travel and accommodation, given the long distances involved in order to visit, were prohibitive. Republican prisoners would save up their visits and then combine them, typically, into two periods of 'accumulated visits' lasting three or four days, perhaps, at Christmas and/or during the school summer break. Our families were doing time with us.

Soon after sentencing I had applied to be repatriated to a prison nearer to Eileen in Belfast. The application was made on humanitarian grounds, consistent with EU human rights legislation, the provisions of which for years the Home Office flouted, despite a ruling binding them to ensure that families of prisoners would not suffer unduly from the stresses of separation. Republican prisoners and their families had been campaigning and petitioning for years on the issue. At the time of ending the relationship with Eileen, I had rationalised that at least she would be spared the twice-yearly travel ordeal and the expenses involved.

During the early summer of 1994, the head governor of Full Sutton, who was progressive and responsible for maintaining a quite liberal regime within the unit, surprised me by asking whether I had a view about when transfer might happen. He may have been probing to ascertain how informed we were about the progress of the repatriation campaign, but perhaps also because of concern should we have information about timing that may have assisted a prison-van escape attempt. I had no insights but replied that it could be within two years but maybe sooner. In July 1994, I was notified by the Home Office that I would be transferred to Ireland on a temporary basis subject to logistical concerns. The waiting began. Within weeks, four comrades were repatriated – Martina and Ella (my co-accused), Paul Kavanagh (who had married Martina Anderson while in prison) and Paddy McLaughlin.

On 31 August 1994, I was in the lounge watching television with comrades. It was a momentous day. The IRA had just declared a ceasefire. It seemed that the war was over. We watched the unfolding of events via satellite reception of RTÉ (the Irish television channel), a recent improvement in our conditions. We viewed the scenes of jubilation as a black taxi cavalcade drove through west Belfast sounding horns, with Sinn Fein members waving tricolours. Our own mood was one of stunned elation. After years of feeling cut off and apart from the struggle at home, we felt as if we were there sharing the moment. It had a very tangible import for us too because this would surely represent a significant progression in our campaign for transfer. Political negotiations were bound to follow soon and a future amnesty might be on the cards.

Then to cap it all, and that day was hard to cap, a prison officer entered the room and told me, Gerry McDonnell and Tommy Quigley to 'pack

our bags' (meaning our prison-issue property boxes) because we were to
be transferred to Maghaberry in the morning. Could this development be
part of a deal to mark the ceasefire? The timing did seem too good to be
true, although the process of transferring republican prisoners had begun
several months before. The move, when it was made public, led to many
questions about the timing and caused some political embarrassment.
It was reported that the British prime minister, John Major, ordered an
inquiry about the transfer.

That night, my last in the English prison system, we celebrated with
a sing-song out of our cell windows. The next day we were moved in an
armed cortège to Hull airport, where a private flight returned us handcuffed
to Belfast International. Crazy security precautions all the way. But once
back on Irish soil we were put into a single prison van and brought to
Maghaberry Prison. It felt like I had woken from a lucid nightmare to the
reassuring familiarity of Ulster accents, our first tangible evidence of being
home.

There persisted a nagging doubt among some of us that the ceasefire
might be premature. Had the IRA established a sufficient position of
strength to be effective in subsequent negotiations? As political prisoners we
were all also acutely aware of being, and resented being, political hostages.
The British would hold out the prospect of some form of amnesty to gain
concessions during negotiations from the movement. These doubts were
swamped in the sheer thrill of the return to Ireland. The one certainty
borne throughout those years was that I would never be released from an
English prison short of victory. Being back on Irish soil signalled a huge
step towards freedom.

12

Gate Fever

In the following weeks, about eight of us were repatriated (the Home Office insisted on their term, 'transferred' – always advancing their spin) to Maghaberry, a new prison, west of Lisburn, opened in 1986, the year I was sentenced. Our choice would have been to join our comrades in the H-Blocks of Long Kesh but the Home Office stipulated Maghaberry, which ran a 'conforming regime', meaning that the various republican and loyalist groupings hadn't the virtual control of the wings achieved in the Blocks since and as a consequence of the settling of the prison protests for political status of the 1980s.

Most prisoners in Maghaberry were from a Protestant background, many of them loyalists who had transferred out of the Blocks, falsely lured by the vaunted prospect of earlier and more favourable release opportunities, or because of disaffection with their command structures, or through peculiar fallouts and associative rivalries. There were also a few republicans who for similar or ideological reasons had chosen to move. However, a majority of prisoners were non-political, from both communities or neither, and were popularly identifiable as ODCs (ordinary decent criminals) – robbers, murderers, embezzlers, etc.; then paedophiles and sex offenders. Our near elation at being transferred from the privations of the SSUs to a prison where everyone spoke with an Irish accent was tempered by the knowledge that we would have to constantly watch our own and each other's backs. During my time there, I was always the only republican on the landing; others were in the landing above, or in other 'houses' (separate blocks, that is). Maghaberry represented a potentially explosive mix. Loyalists appeared to me to have been left wrong-footed by the IRA's ceasefire. Tensions eased, however, from 13 October, when the Combined Loyalist Military Command announced its ceasefire and expressed 'abject and true remorse' for all 'innocent victims' (a decade and a day, incidentally, after Brighton).

Some screws were bigoted, on a crusade, whether against 'Taigs' (Catholics) or Fenians (republicans), to the extent they were individually able to distinguish between the two, and who made no effort to disguise their hatred of republicans. There were also some very decent prison officers who always acted professionally. To mention one example – he might not be thankful if I were to identify him – I recall a senior officer who invariably could be relied on to help with the usual routine requests: letters, visits, complaints, etc. It was instructive, therefore, even revelatory, to see televised footage of the same man in the thick of the rioting at the Drumcree standoff in 1995 over opposition to provocative or 'coat-trailing' Orange marches passing along the nationalist Garvaghy Road. He managed to separate his professional mindset from his evidently deeply held political views. And that is to be respected, particularly in the context of the missionary anti-republican zeal of other prison staff members.

As republican prisoners, and perhaps particularly as high-profile republicans, we always had to look over our shoulders. But generally a 'live and let live' spirit prevailed. In my two years in Maghaberry there were few incidents, even when the IRA's ceasefire ended in February 1996 with the bombing of Canary Wharf (the damage reckoned at £86 million). A hairy moment which held the potential for serious violence were it not for the good relations between republicans and loyalists built within the prison over two years of compromise and respect-building.

Loyalists' anxieties deepened at a changing political climate which appeared to them to be more favourable to republicans. Nevertheless, I got on quite well with several of the loyalists and have remained friendly or at least on amicable terms with some of them to this day. It isn't that rare an event to bump into one or other of the former loyalist prisoners in Belfast city centre that I knew from Maghaberry. These encounters have invariably been civil, even friendly.

I spent most of my days in the education block, where the atmosphere was generally good, particularly in what was called the OU room, which as the name suggests was set aside for Open University students. Loyalists and republicans studied together – an oasis of amicable discussion about our respective courses but also on wider themes, including politics. I recall the day that Bill Clinton visited the North, late November 1995. There had been media speculation of a choreographed encounter on the

Falls Road between the American president and Gerry Adams. The two leaders duly met and their handshake was beamed around the world. There was a television set in the OU room, tuned to the live broadcast of an event of clearly historic importance. More were present than usual in the room, mostly loyalists, none of whom appeared interested in the coverage. I showed as little enthusiasm in front of them. Then a slight buzz was detectable as it was picked up that the presidential cavalcade had taken an apparently unscheduled detour onto the Shankill Road. The loyalist lads individually inched their way towards the set. We saw Clinton emerge from his bulletproof limousine for what seemed an impromptu walkabout when he was approached by a couple of clearly excited and welcoming women who had emerged from a nearby store. Basher Bates (notorious to nationalists as a Shankill Butcher) could hardly contain himself: 'Look! That's our Aggie.' Bates's aunt greeted Clinton. The six or seven loyalists who watched this were genuinely moved. Frankly, I found it touching to witness their quite joyful reaction. Most often disparaged in news reportage, they in turn despised the media. Here was a world leader giving their heartland and community respect. It seemed to transcend gesture politics, and for me was instructive as to the potential for cooperation if more of our mutual suspicions and misapprehensions were tackled through dialogue and contact.

Despite some disruption to my studies caused by the transfer and the pressures of coping in a more stressful environment, I graduated from the OU with a BA (honours, first) in October 1994. I majored in politics and modern art. Incidentally, two of the eight firsts from the six-county OU region that year were republican prisoners, the other being Ann Marie McArdle, then held in the women's wing of Maghaberry.

In the light of that success, I immediately wanted to register for a post-graduate degree in politics, but there were no courses available through the OU in the upcoming academic year. I was impatient for a further academic challenge. Then a notice went up detailing an initiative jointly run by the Prison Education Department and the University of Ulster. Postgraduate research degree places were being offered to what the notice termed 'two outstanding OU graduates'. I remembered a discussion I had, as far back as my time in the Leicester SSU, with a teacher who thought that perhaps a book should be written about what I argued was the clear anti-IRA bias in fiction. We had been discussing something current, perhaps *Harry's Game*. The very subject for me! I had read some articles on Troubles-related fiction and believed it deserved a more thorough treatment. I formally applied to the admissions office in October 1995, with a proposal to 'research the contention that Irish Republicanism has been misrepresented in fiction spanning the last twenty-five years, and to attempt an explanation for the perceived political and ideological bias of much of this output' – a hybrid of politics, literary theory and criticism.

I didn't wait for a response to the proposal. Even while drafting it I had begun to check out what material was available in the prison library. I gathered any examples at hand on the wing. Novels by Jack Higgins and Gerald Seymour were plentiful, and thus clearly popular.

I read every turgid example of the genre I could get hold of. I found the prison librarian at Maghaberry particularly helpful. This kept me busy and focused until my release. However, it was to take a full year before my submission was finally accepted (of which more below).

My father died in September 1995. I was called to the duty PO's (principal officer's) office first thing. Never a good sign. I didn't know this PO. My son had rung the prison with the news of Dad's death. I could tell that the PO was scrutinising my demeanour for a reaction. I showed no outward emotion, for he ventured that the news mustn't be a surprise to me. It was the biggest shock of my life. I was stunned. I would never let them know. For the next week, I physically slowed down, coping through rote activity. I applied for compassionate parole to attend Dad's funeral but was turned down on the grounds that 'I would have a strong motive to abscond'. I knew my petition would be refused but I had to try. The refusal ignored the unblemished republican track record of honouring parole. To have granted my request would have conceded that an Irish POW's word was sufficient guarantee of compliance.

My application for compassionate parole had an unexpected spin-off. As a 'transferred' prisoner, I was still subject to Home Office rather than Northern Ireland Office (NIO) responsibility. Up till then both had refused our requests to be moved to the H-Blocks on the basis that such decisions rested with the other. In its argument for denying me parole, however, the HO stated that other matters, for example where we were held, were outside of its remit. On this basis, a judicial review (JR) was taken by Paul Kavanagh and Tommy Quigley, both of whom had been repatriated from England and who together worked effectively to scrutinise legislation that affected POWs. Their JR was successful, the upshot being that in August 1996, I and my fellow repatriates were transferred to join our comrades in the Blocks.

This was a further, hugely significant, step nearer to freedom. On arrival in the Blocks, the feeling of relief was immediate and overpowering. I hadn't appreciated the stress I was under in Maghaberry. Removal from it and then experiencing the heady solidarity of comrades in the Blocks made me count my blessings. I was in H Seven. Reminders of the dark days of the blanket protest were everywhere. I was put in a cell near one of the infamous double cells where, in each spur, many Blanketmen were beaten viciously during body searches. It was still staggering to realise that in 1983, less than two years after the hunger strike, thirty-eight republicans had escaped from Seven, including several old friends and comrades – among them Gerry McDonnell, lifted along with me in Glasgow less than two years after the escape. And there was more to remind me of what progress had been achieved. From the mid-1980s, after withstanding the continuing policy of criminalisation, including the failed policy of forced integration with loyalist prisoners, republicans had gained a measure of self-determination unparalleled since the removal of special status.

Within the Blocks, the POWs had achieved space to organise their own cultural and educational programmes. Our wings became republican communities, influenced by the guiding philosophy of the Brazilian educationalist Paulo Freire's *Pedagogy of the Oppressed*. Sharing was the essence of this unique cultural experiment. Education classes were organised by us, in Gaelic, Spanish, yoga, history – whatever pool of knowledge we possessed at any given time and/or wing. Other inclusive ventures included drama groups, a poetry magazine, history workshops and a quarterly magazine, *An Glór Gafa* (*The Captive Voice*). There were political lectures and discussion groups. We had successfully negotiated the removal of cell locks. We secured our cell doors with bits of string or shoelaces to signal when we wanted privacy. We also cooked and cleaned for ourselves. I settled down to work on my doctorate, anticipating that the moment of freedom was closer because of the prospects of an eventual breakthrough in the political situation, albeit that negotiations were presently stymied by John Major's reliance on the Ulster Unionist leader, David Trimble, to have a working majority in the House of Commons.

Shortly after my transfer to the Blocks, my application to do postgraduate research was eventually accepted after a quite rigorous vetting process involving the visit to the H-Blocks of six academics from the Coleraine campus, including a dean and two heads of departments. I believe the delay was due at least in part to concern that my notoriety might reflect adversely on the university given that the campus was situated in a unionist heartland. Tensions were high because of the ongoing (by now, seemingly annual) standoff at Drumcree, Portadown, where an Orange parade was blocked by the RUC and British Army from marching past the nationalist community of the Garvaghy Road, and of conflict around the Holy Cross school in Ardoyne, Belfast. Any concern could only have been magnified in that the other place awarded went to Ella O'Dwyer, my co-accused for the seaside bomb blitz, then being held in the women's section at Maghaberry.

I was assigned an academic supervisor, Professor Robert Welch, dean of the Faculty of Language and Literature and editor-in-chief of the *Oxford Companion to Irish Literature*, and one of the visiting deans who had interviewed me. Bob, an accomplished author, would visit the Blocks once a month, his tutorials always a pleasure and a privilege. He commented on the scholarly atmosphere in our wings (I thought this generous of him).

Eleven years after Judge Boreham's delivered recommendation that I should do thirty-five years, the Tory home secretary Douglas Hurd notified me of his intention to set a tariff of fifty years – well, he had signed the notification that I had received. Then, after some shuffling of the Cabinet, Hurd was replaced by Michael Howard, who actually set the tariff, and I was informed of his decision that I was never to be released – whole life. Paul Kavanagh and Tommy Quigley also received whole life tariffs. They successfully challenged their tariffs through another JR in the High Court, on the basis that whole life contravened European directives, obliging the Home Office to reconsider. My tariff had also to be looked at afresh. The Home Office complied and finally reset our tariffs at fifty years, thus making me eligible for consideration of release in 2035. The decision both confirmed Howard's vindictiveness and highlighted Tory insincerity in regard to the peace process.

A lesson well learned from England was that when things are going smoothly for any length of time then some issue or some event will surely spring out of nowhere and cause havoc to our sense of well-being. Harmony is ever a temporary illusion in those circumstances.

The IRA in the Blocks did not sit back and await the outplay of the current political negotiations, perhaps one heralding an amnesty. An audacious plan to escape from H Seven by tunnelling was in an advanced preparation when, in February 1997, we were all summoned by the OC within the H-Blocks to the canteen and told to expect an imminent raid. The IRA, with great ingenuity and impressively tight security, had been organising with zeal and stealth, and its efforts if successful would have been a major propaganda coup, except that an unfortunate dog-handler (or, rather, a dog-handler unfortunately) had stumbled into the tunnel, which had collapsed. Disappointment at this turn of events aside, we gave the OC a spontaneous clap of hands. You couldn't dent morale. In the ensuing lockdown of the Blocks and forced move, prisoners were manhandled and abused, including me, by the MUFTI squads, drafted in for the purpose. Compensation claims would later be settled, except for mine (due to outstanding fines imposed as part of my sentence back in 1986). More annoying was the disruption to my doctoral studies because of the loss of research material during the raid. As part of the RUC investigation into the escape attempt, computers and disks were removed, causing considerable disruption to education schedules. Anxious times until the computers were returned months later, but the RUC held on to disks containing research notes on some sixty novels. Tommy Quigley, who was also a doctoral student, fared worse, losing a year's research work. I was able to carry on from old, mostly hand-written notes.

We now found ourselves in H Eight, a clone of Seven and of every other block, but we worked together to put our own stamp on it. Gradually, what passed for normal service was resumed following a period of austerity; in fact, we were to gain more access to the yard while in Eight, which we could thenceforth access at night, as negotiations outside entered a final stage, culminating in the Good Friday Agreement. Tony Blair had become prime minister after the landslide victory of New Labour in May 1997. Immediately the mood changed positively after the prevarications of the Tories under John Major, who were reliant on the support

of David Trimble's Ulster Unionists at Westminster. A Sinn Fein delegation visited us to sound out opinion as to progress and the way forward. I
argued for the restoration of the ceasefire on the basis of Blair's approach
to furthering negotiations, but I also cautioned that he might only have
a two-term opening for progress allowing the peace process to bed down
and hopefully be irreversible. Should the Tories be re-elected at the next
general election, we might expect a reversal in potential gains accrued
from negotiations while Labour was in government.

In October 1997, those repatriated from England gained the same rights
as other prisoners to pre-release parole. As a lifer, I was now entitled to ten
days of home leave each year. The optimism of that time is also borne out
by my decision to get married while still in prison. I had formed a relationship with an American woman who, through correspondence, had been
helping me with some research. We had married in the H-Blocks chapel two
months previously. I took three of my ten days' parole under the scheme on
23 October 1997, twelve years and four months after my capture.

In arguably the most bizarre development to date, in May 1998, most
of the republican POWs, including that is the woman POWs held in
Maghaberry, were gathered together in the main gym of the H-Blocks, a
huge hangar of a space, to be given an update by Gerry Kelly and Siobhán
O'Hanlon, both part of Sinn Fein's negotiating team, on the progress of the
negotiations. They were accompanied by two prominent South Africans:
Cyril Ramaphosa, who was the African National Congress's (ANC's) chief
negotiator during the country's transition from apartheid to democracy
(and, at the time of writing, is the newly elected president of South Africa),
and Mathews Phosa, premier of Mpumalanga (formerly Eastern Transvaal),
who together described their experiences of the South African negotiations to end apartheid. Solidarity was expressed between the ANC and
the republican movement, and comparisons drawn between Robben Island
and the H-Blocks. A small number of screws kept a low-key watch at the
entrances and seemed utterly dumbfounded at this development – surely
unique in the annals of any prison struggle? – and whose worst fears about
inmates taking over the asylum were materialising before their eyes. The
event lasted some two hours in which we were able to mix freely, rather like
at a garden party, except indoors. Sinn Fein was to endorse the GFA in 1998,
at a special Ard Fheis following the delegation's visit.

In an extraordinary and rapid turn of events, as part of the GFA all political prisoners were to be released in a process according to their time served, and the last were to be freed in July 2000. Our mood throughout the republican Blocks was jubilant, although tempered with a certain wariness that the political negotiations might collapse. I was quite confident in terms of progress, and very content, as I expected to be one of the very last to be released, given my fifty-year tariff. Those who had served longest would be released first. Lifers who had completed eleven years were to be included. However, the provision was not extended to those of us transferred from England. The scheme was run by the NIO Prison Service, while we remained under the auspices of the Home Office. Yet another JR was initiated by Paul and Tommy, challenging this discriminatory practice of the Home Office. The matter was dealt with by the Sentence Review Commission, chaired by the South African human rights lawyer Brian Currin, which found against the Home Office. The outcome of the decision was immediate. Tom, Paul and my co-accused Gerry McDonnell were released that day. I was now due for release after completion of fourteen years – four months hence.

Further developments in the pre-release parole provision meant I was 'back-paid' more than a hundred parole days which had to be taken before my eventual release. The development actually added to the time pressure I was under to complete the first draft of my doctoral thesis (but wisely I kept that concern quiet). The pace of these developments was unsettling and led, I sensed, to a heightening of 'gate fever' – the obsessive anticipation of freedom. News reports on the continuing negotiations would be rigorously parsed for indications of further movement on early releases. I was reminded of the mood among us during the winding down of internment, and the fears that something unforeseen might occur to set matters back. We were in the countdown to release but the plug might still be pulled. Another concern, and one that I shared, was that too much weight would be attached to demands for amnesty. We understood well that the British saw the political prisoners as a bargaining card. However, none of us would willingly allow progress to depend on playing their hostage games.

Although much had been achieved during negotiations between Sinn Fein and the British, an amnesty had not in fact been secured, and all lifers were released under licence, meaning that we were liable to have

our licences revoked and be returned to complete our tariffs should we
'reoffend' – or if a British secretary of state deemed it politically expedient
(the fate, for example, of Ardoyne republican Sean Kelly, who was returned
to prison because of political pressure from unionist quarters). But these
matters were out of our hands. I focused on juggling parole time and study
time – an altogether positively different category of problem, unforeseeable in the darker days in the SSUs in England.

In another totally unforeseen development, in December 1998 I received
a letter that was to mark a major shift in my life. Harvey Thomas, who
had been injured in the Grand Hotel explosion, wrote to me:

Dear Mr McGee [sic],

*This is not an easy letter for me to write – and it has taken me a long time
and much Prayer before doing it! It is a personal letter – I cannot speak for
others who were injured – or who lost family members in the Grand Hotel
in 1984.*

*I was the Producer of the Conservative Party Conference in Brighton –
and the Occupant of room 729 – immediately above the Room in which the
bomb was placed.*

*As you prepare to leave the Maze Prison, I felt that – as a Christian – I
must write personally to say that God forgives each of us, if we repent and
put our faith in Jesus Christ. In the Spirit of Christ's teaching, I offer you
my own forgiveness!*

*The Bible urges us to be Reconciled to each Other – as we can be reconciled
to God through Christ – and that is my motive in writing to you! I hope
that you will receive this letter in the spirit in which it is written. I enclose
a copy of 'In the Face of Fear' that I published in 1985. I hope you find it
interesting.*

*I pray that as you return to your Family, you will also feel the Spirit of
Reconciliation and come to know God's forgiveness.*
Sincerely,
Harvey Thomas CBE

The clear sincerity therein expressed caused me much soul-searching. I
read it, and read it again. I read it inside out. Whatever injury this man

had suffered was down to me. On 15 December I replied from B Wing, H-Block Three:

Dear Mr Thomas,

Thank you for your letter and the copy of In the Face of Fear. I have given much thought to both. Your account of being buried in bomb-rubble and of drawing strength from your religious faith, along with thoughts of your wife and the imminent birth of your daughter, is a deeply-moving testimony (all the more poignant because my wife gave birth to our son in recent days).

While I do not share your evangelical views – indeed, I am not a Christian and, beyond a vague notion of a divine purpose to life, I have no religious faith to speak of – I respect the depth of your conviction. I also respect the moral courage of your decision to write offering me your personal forgiveness. As you indicated in your letter, it could not have been an easy journey to arrive at that frame of mind and then decide to contact me.

Your generosity of spirit demands a fuller more open reply than I am able to offer at the present time. For now, all I feel I can state is that I do believe firmly in the need for reconciliation. I use the word in a political rather than a religious sense. I see reconciliation as an endeavour to be pursued as much as an end, and entails the fullest allowance and respect for difference; and politics when guided by the spirit of reconciliation becomes the art of harmonising diversity. Dialogue is always a crucial first step. As you say in your book, 'at the heart of every failure in the church and in politics is a failure in communications'.

I wish you and your family well.

Harvey Thomas replied quickly, requesting a visit. At this point, I thought it prudent to consult with the camp staff, who would have a better grasp of the bigger picture. I was advised that should the media get wind of such a visit, any adverse publicity ensuing might jeopardise the implementation of the early release programme. The early release of political prisoners was a deeply divisive and emotive issue for many. But the policy was a cornerstone of the Good Friday Agreement, and indeed, the early release of captured combatants is a crucial condition in any genuine post-conflict or conflict-transformation process. Media controversy might potentially derail its further development. With that in mind I decided not to risk meeting Harvey. I regretfully declined a prison visit with him at this time, but had definitely decided to meet him when the moment allowed. I will say more about Harvey in later chapters.

Less than seven months later, on 22 June 1999, I was released under the terms of the Good Friday Agreement, fourteen years from the day of my capture, despite the home secretary Jack Straw's attempt to block my release in the High Court, possibly as a face-saving exercise to offset much media criticism of images of me exiting the prison turnstile for, I hoped, the last time.

13
My God! Him Too?

Were it not for the peace process, my projected date for consideration for release would, under the fifty-year tariff, have occurred in 2035 – when, if spared, I will be eighty-three. I was forty-eight. The officer commanding the IRA political prisoners in the Blocks had marked my cards that the press were lined up three deep at the gate. I had anticipated as much. So it was no surprise that I emerged from the turnstile to face not only the light of freedom but a phalanx of reporters and snapping cameramen. Waiting friends, among them Martin Meehan and Mickey Pierce, guided me through this unwanted attention. I didn't respond to questions from the press. I was in the waiting car and out onto the main road before I even properly greeted my welcoming comrades. They drove me home to Belfast via seemingly affluent, tree-lined unionist areas, reminiscent of that journey in November 1975 (again, I did not look back – see chapter six), before reaching a friendly house in the New Lodge area, where a feast of a meal awaited me.

Pictures of me emerging through the prison turnstile appeared in all the papers. I was conscious after the OC's warning of how pictures of my release would be widely circulated. I prepared my best poker face, not wanting to appear jubilant. In truth, I wasn't. All my senses were flooded by the reality overload of freedom. The one thing you dare not do in prison is display what is going on in your head. It became habitual to disguise emotions. I was well practised. Some were looking for signs of repentance. Indeed I had experienced feelings of remorse, for *all* that had been lost, but my head that day was fully geared to register the moment; and it was a moment of joy, of survival. Time for reflection on the past, and on the future, would wait.

After the whirlwind first hour, it is surprising how quickly I acclimatised. Pre-release paroles helped enormously in the adjustment to what felt like my return to planet Earth in a space capsule. The days and months that followed were replete with simple, modest but powerful experiences, to the point of concussion. Every sense was heightened, nothing commonplace, for in prison one is denied so much that is taken for granted in the external world. The pleasure of walking streets, during daylight, at night. Climbing stairs. My first time using a mobile – a Nokia brick, outdated even then. Passing conversations with total strangers who recognised me from the news. Revisiting intimately known districts in Belfast, now so different from when last there, after an absence of twenty-two years, either on the run or in prison. During those decades away, I had often consulted an outdated mind-map of once-familiar streets. I had comfort dreams of returning to old haunts. Now there seemed few points of reference in the actual urban landscape as it had developed. Some of the witnessed changes were welcome. Others, quite shocking. The Market, as I recalled the old district from the early and mid-1970s, had disappeared. On the other hand, Unity Flats, which had reverted to its original name of Carrick Hill, now boasted some of the best public housing in the city, due to the campaigning efforts of local residents, republicans to the fore.

Reactions to my release, and to that of other political prisoners, were predictable. Clearly a bitter pill for many to swallow. One memorable example does stick out. Margaret Thatcher's friend, General Pinochet, while awaiting his deportation from Britain back to Chile to face allegations of human rights violations, gave an interview in which he criticised the prisoner release programme. And when told of my release, he commented, 'My God! Him too?' To have caused him one minute's consternation definitely drew some of the sting from those fourteen years.

While on one of my home leaves, I had sought out another old comrade to ask for advice. I wasn't sure how I might contribute to political developments. I couldn't see how reporting back to the IRA was an option. In a sense I felt redundant. There didn't seem to be an obvious role for me. He advised that I should take a year out, to pick up the pieces after so long an absence. The ceasefire seemed solid. I believed the war was over. The war had lasted nearly thirty years. But building the peace and making further political progress might take decades. There was plenty of effort still required down the line, I was assured. It was good advice. It is highly doubtful that any political movement could absorb overnight the influx of hundreds of newly released activists. I decided to focus on finishing my doctorate, but with a firm view that I had some future role to play in furthering any outstanding work on the ground. Having a doctorate might open doors, gain me a platform or lectern to explain the past.

I had married in prison in 1997 and had a six-month-old son. For the first six weeks after my release we lived in Lenadoon on the outskirts of west Belfast in a flat owned by Martin Meehan, generous always to a fault, who had let my wife and son stay rent-free. From the window of the flat I had a view of three wall murals commemorating the struggle and celebrating Irish culture. I was glad to have left behind similar images in the Blocks. That linkage between the H-Blocks and our districts, of seeing the murals in the context of freedom, caused me an overwhelming sense of being hemmed in, of claustrophobia, as if I hadn't fully been released. The cultural trappings of conflict had still to be dismantled for the peace we all sought to be fully achieved; there was another time lock to be unpicked before we might relish true liberation. Mindsets too had to change. Dealing with the legacy had become a pressing imperative.

My core political beliefs had not changed. I still believed that partition was a crime perpetrated on the people of Ireland, all of them. And that as long as the border existed it would act to put a break on any meaningful extension of democracy.

However, there were practicalities which had to be faced. I had changed in other ways. Just being older made a difference, of course. I could think of many more reasons not to fight. Thought itself was inhibiting. All those years, in prison and on the streets, I had held my nerve. Now I wanted to be less guarded, less suspicious, less inclined to look over my shoulder. Ever alert in prison, I realised full well the continuing need for vigilance now I was released. But now out on the streets, it became apparent that I was no longer as sharp. I was followed on foot that first week. I only found out days later. A woman had called into a local Sinn Fein office to report that she had witnessed two guys whom she believed to be loyalists tracking me. They backed off, apparently, when I stopped to talk to someone near Union Street, close to the old Unity Flats. I had been totally oblivious to this sinister scrutiny. Around the same time, a car I was in was followed from north to west Belfast. The driver cottoned on and deliberately drew the tail into diversionary backstreet turns to expose them for sure. After that I avoided the city centre.

In the weeks before my release, despite all the pre-release tensions – the gate fever – I somehow managed to find the composure to complete a first draft of my doctoral thesis. If I hadn't, it is doubtful that I could have finished the task outside. Far too many distractions. There was a deadline for submission of the completed thesis. Luckily, good friends from the New Lodge district gave me the use of their home for four days while they took a break from Belfast over the Twelfth, the height of the Orange marching season, which traditionally marked an exodus of nationalists from the city out of harm's way during this seasonal 'cold spell'. I could use their daughter's computer. Perfect! I worked solidly throughout the four days, snatching catnaps and only once setting foot outside the door, until I managed to whip the first draft into submittable form. Even so, I fully expected to have to do a rewrite following the viva, which was set for September. That would entail at least six months of intensive work. I wasn't convinced I could summon further energy for the task, let alone the time.

There was one intrusive, unsettling moment in the midst of all that labour. I received a midnight visit from two comrades from Sinn Fein warning that the *Sunday Mirror* was running a story the next morning (11 July 1999) accusing me of being anti-peace process. That edition, they explained, had a photo of me and one of the Sinn Fein president, Gerry Adams, under a banner headline reading: 'I'll kill Adams'. The report began, 'IRA master bomber Patrick "Mad Dog" Magee has threatened to kill Gerry Adams for "surrendering" to the peace process.' It alleged I boasted that I would 'see to' Adams if, as reported, 'the terrorists were forced to give up their weapons'. A laptop belonging to a Whitemoor Prison official had found its way into the hands of the tabloid. It contained copies of reported remarks of Irish republican prisoners in the SSU – transcripts of mail and phone intercepts expressing criticism of the republican leadership, as well as hostility to the peace process. Phrases such as 'sell out' and 'traitors' set the tone. All of which were attributed to me. Except I was never in Whitemoor, and was known to be a supporter of the current peace strategy. The journalists concerned had made no effort, to my knowledge, to contact me for a comment or to verify the authenticity of my alleged dissension.

During ensuing days, I found quite a few old comrades looking at me suspiciously and, given the power of the written word, wondering whether there was any substance to the story, despite the fact that Sinn Fein had very promptly issued a statement outlining the facts, thus clearing my name. I was, however, saddened that any credence could have been attached to the article.

You need to understand how tightly knit to the point of claustrophobia Belfast is. One minute you're in favour, welcomed, pints bought for you; the next, the subject of innuendo, backstabbing, suspicion, hostility, snide remarks. This wasn't universal. Anyone who really knew me at least knew to suspend judgement. But at that time I found it difficult to deal with. I've since grown a tougher hide. And had to.

This unwelcome attention coincided with my wife expressing a desire for us to move south. She was unhappy in Belfast. I was ready to put distance between this unpleasantness and our need to just get on with building a home. I sought help about moving to County Kerry, a place I had always loved, and within a few months managed with the help of local Sinn Fein to rent a house in Tralee. But before leaving, I sought legal advice in Belfast with a view to suing the *Sunday Mirror*. I was advised that to win the libel case I had to prove that my character and good name had been damaged, and that the *Sunday Mirror* would respond with the line that as 'a mass murderer' I had no good character to impugn. With that logic the press can say whatever it chooses about ex-POWs. There the matter rested, until two years later, by now settled in Tralee, I sought further advice, from a local solicitor. He advised that in the new context of peace, and because of my (by then) known role as an advocate of reconciliation, a Southern jury might think differently. After a protracted legal process in the South, I eventually settled out of court when the *Sunday Mirror*'s representative admitted in the Dublin High Court that the newspaper's report was false.

I didn't allow any of the brouhaha over the offending article to distract me from completing the final draft of the thesis and submitting it for approval. The viva duly took place in September at the University of Ulster's campus at the old art college in York Street, Belfast, which meant a journey north from Kerry, the first trip back since moving to Tralee. The Derry-born author and one of the founders of the Field Day Theatre Company Seamus Deane was the external invigilator. He told me to relax, that I had earned the doctorate. A crucial criterion is that a doctoral thesis must be a contribution to knowledge. Deane expanded that there was much in my research that he had not known. As mentioned, I fully expected to be required to submit a rewrite, so this news came as a wonderful relief. Then I was informed that the panel had to go through the formality of the examination, before they proceeded to forensically deconstruct my argument. In Castlereagh I would have chosen to remain silent. But at least I was spared the rewrite. Ordeal over, I celebrated in McElhatton's Bar nearby, accompanied by panel members. Anyway, I now was entitled to add DPhil after my name and Dr before it, or could once bound copies of the thesis had been lodged with the university library.

I rarely use the title *Doctor*. I have seldom spoken or written in an academic capacity. Politicians are often wont to do so. Their choice. This can smack of elitism, although not necessarily. But I would feel uncomfortable, unless I was speaking or writing as an academic. I think any title can put a barrier between you and the audience.

This was a huge personal milestone. Now I could think of what next with my life. What were the options? The obvious choice was an academic career. I saw this as an opening through which the Irish republican perspective could be forwarded; an antidote to the hold of anti-republican revisionism; that is, the examination of the past from a unionist perspective. I did enquire about the possibility of lecturing in the USA. I contacted Notre Dame and Boston College, and through the critic John Sutherland, with whom I had corresponded about my thesis while in prison, I made contact with UCLA. The prospects of doing a coast-to-coast tour over two weeks looked promising. But then a mischievous article appeared in the *Sunday Times*, written by Liam Clarke, claiming I was scheduled to do the American circuit at $10,000 per lecture. I had then no experience of public speaking. I doubt if I would have made more than enough to cover the costs of the tour ($200 per lecture was the honorarium quoted), but I saw it as a means of testing the water and a signpost to my future options. However, after Clarke's piece, interest suddenly waned, or potential dates were deferred to the following year – and then forgotten. That first year after release was a struggle financially. The only work I could get was as a casual labourer. Twice I had to leave Tralee to work in Dublin, on each occasion labouring on building sites.

Bill Rolston of the publishing company Beyond the Pale, who had written extensively about Troubles fiction, encouraged me to publish my thesis. This would require me to emend the thesis to make it less academic, more reader-friendly. In itself the task entailed quite a bit of effort. I submitted the final version to Bill, and the book was later published in December 2001 and titled *Gangsters or Guerrillas?* In fact, the title was Bill's idea. There things settled until in August 2000 I heard from Coiste na n-Iarchimí, the republican ex-POW group, that Tom McGurk, a journalist on the *Sunday Business Post,* wanted to interview me. The interview took place in his home in Dalkey, south Dublin, and appeared soon after. This was my first interview, and it was lengthy, covering much more ground than many subsequently given to date.

There was, of course, a focus on Brighton. I expressed regret that lives were lost while at the same time holding to the necessity for the operation: 'Did the Tory ruling class expect to remain immune from what their frontline troops were doing to us?' When asked whether I thought about the victims, I acknowledged that, yes, I frequently thought about those I had hurt. I also for the first time revealed having had contact before my release with someone injured by the bombing. I was, of course, referring to Harvey Thomas, but I would not have compromised his confidentiality. And some three months before actually meeting Harvey for the first time, I said that 'perhaps the time is now right to make contact again'. Neither did I reveal that someone else connected to the bombing had expressed an interest in meeting me, although at this point I lacked knowledge of who this person was, and no arrangements for a meeting had been proposed.

Perhaps the most controversial point I made, and one seized on in the subsequent media response to the interview, was the contention that if Margaret Thatcher had been killed then her death might have been counterproductive. With the benefit of hindsight, this is a plausible argument, for in the absence of her death, and without a larger number of dead and injured, the IRA had sufficiently proven its capacity to strike at the heart of the British political establishment. I claimed that 'the awareness that it could have been worse … actually gave the IRA more leverage than if they had killed her'. But this, I think, reasonable view – a thought experiment, really – was twisted by the media to falsely claim that I was asserting that if Thatcher had died the operation would have been a major setback to the republican cause.

Soon after its publication I was contacted by the *Marian Finucane Show*, RTÉ One's flagship morning talk show. They wanted a live ten-minute interview. I had never spoken publicly before but felt I should agree to the request.

Marian Finucane was impressively professional and good at putting me at my ease. I was to talk with her up to the first commercial break. But during the break she said that her other guests were delayed and asked if I would talk on. I ended up talking to her for the entire programme, that is, for about fifty-five minutes. I had mentally prepared for ten. I was pleased that I hadn't frozen or mucked up. (Sadly, Marian died in January 2020.)

The interview caused a storm in the following days, with irate letters to the *Irish Times*, etc. One letter, from Muiris Mac Conghaill, a former controller of television programmes for RTÉ, accused the station of capitulating to terrorists by giving me airtime. He added that my appearance was 'a considerable psychological victory for Sinn Fein'. A few days later, commenting on the interview, Dr Conor Sweeney, a lecturer in broadcast journalism, wrote an article in the *Sunday Independent*, which similarly asserted that 'the Provos ... try to use the media as a weapon in their struggle for power'. This was despite me stressing at some pains that I was speaking only for myself and for no one else.

This was a breakthrough moment. In addition to the media attention, an article I had written for the London-based *Irish Post* was issued around this time: a short survey of Troubles fiction, based on my doctoral thesis. I gained much in confidence from having now had three successful incursions, back to back, into the world of media. Enemy territory for me, and yet I had come through not only unscathed but with a feeling I had usefully contributed to the task of countering the misrepresentation of republicanism. Some general perception of a future purpose began to coalesce from these early forays into the public realm. What better way to challenge a misrepresentation than to present yourself for the Other's critical scrutiny? This was definitely something I now felt confident about doing well. And not despite but *because* of being a republican. I had stumbled upon a path that apparently fitted the direction of my entire involvement in the struggle to date.

Nevertheless, I continued to be wary of the media. For example, around this time I was contacted by an associate producer, Nava Mizrahi, from

Brook Lapping Productions, which had won acclaim for its documentary *The Death of Yugoslavia* (1996). The company proposed making a documentary on the peace negotiations leading up to the GFA. Despite several reassuring meetings with Nava, I decided against being interviewed for the subsequent documentary, *Endgame in Ireland* (2001). I was unsure of how far I might speak independently of the movement, despite the newly realised sense of competence as an interviewee. I had found a voice. But how to use it to best effect? The evidence was pointing clearly to a role in dealing with the legacy of conflict. In my final months in the Blocks, Harvey Thomas's letter had opened a door. While contemplating how to approach Harvey, that other possible connection with Brighton again came to my attention. I was to meet a woman whose father I had killed.

14
Bridges *Can* Be Built

On 24 November 2000, sixteen years after the bombing of the Grand Hotel in Brighton and seventeen months after my release, I sat down and talked with Joanna Berry, whose father, the Conservative MP Sir Anthony Berry, was one of the five people killed.

During the week of that encounter I had been labouring on a building site in Dublin. Previously sought openings in the academic and legacy fields had failed to materialise. Life since my release had been a struggle financially. As a recently released republican POW, with Christmas looming, casual work was all that I could get. As was said then, crumbs from the Celtic Tiger. Several former republican POWs were working along with me on the site (a huge business park), one of whom I'd known from the internment cages. I remember the resentment of some of the unionised workers because of the presence of non-union labourers from Belfast. To some we were refugees, in the way that term had evolved because of a creeping partitionist mentality.

Dublin had changed. The numerous yellow cranes disrupting the capital's low skyline signposted its then-insatiable demand for modern office blocks and shopping centres, testimony to Ireland's recently acquired affluence. I had known a different Dublin, having been on the run there from the North in the early 1980s, a far from happy period and, in certain regards, one evoking a colder recall than my years in prison. Now, twenty years later, I was back, full circle, although not having to dodge the interest of the Garda Special Branch and at least now free to work, albeit labouring of the most menial kind. My two degrees seemed of little relevance.

The practice in the construction industry then was to knock off early on Fridays. After lugging bags of cement and plasterboards up flights of concrete stairs since eight that cold November morning, it was a relief to leave before four. At forty-nine, I was wrecked, fit only for bed, but usually with the weekend in which to recoup before Monday. This Friday was different.

All day I had been waiting on a call to find out whether tonight I would meet Joanna Berry. Indeed, I had been anticipating this moment since the summer, when I heard that someone 'connected to Brighton' wanted to meet me. The day before, the Thursday, I'd finished work at the more usual time of six, thinking only of a long soak then bed. I got a call from Coiste na n-Iarchimí, the Irish republican ex-prisoners' support group. Sleep would have to wait. I was to meet someone called Anne Gallagher at O'Shea's Merchant, a bar on the south side of the Liffey, a 'culchie' bar famous for its traditional music and set dancing and in sight of the historic Four Courts across the river on the Liffey's northern bank – not a bar for an early night. Anne Gallagher was there to arrange my meeting with Joanna Berry.

During the late summer Ella O'Dwyer, my co-accused in the seaside bomb blitz campaign, had phoned me from the Dublin offices of Coiste in Lower Dominick Street. A woman whose father was killed in the Brighton attack wanted to meet me, as the only person charged. This was the first time I had heard of Joanna Berry. She had first broached the idea of meeting me with Coiste members attending a conference either at Corrymeela or Glencree. I was later to hear from a former POW that it was he who had passed on the request. Joanna had also talked with Martin Meehan. Martin, my comrade who had met me at the prison turnstile, later revealed that he hadn't relayed Joanna's request because of his concern (comradely rather than paternalistic) that it was then too soon after my release (Martin died in 2007). Anyway the message did the rounds until Ella's call.

I had misgivings. I think understandable. Ella was able to assure me that Joanna Berry had impressed those she met with her openness and sincerity. I asked, and was reassured to hear, that she wasn't seeking to confront me but rather to gain an understanding of the conflict that had robbed her of a father. Nothing definite was being proposed at this stage – no venue, no date – but I wanted to be notified the next time she or, indeed, anyone should express a similar wish for contact. I believed then, and now I am even more convinced, that it is incumbent on republicans to avail of all opportunities to articulate our perspective, grievances and objectives, particularly given the backdrop of the decades-long suppression of the republican message.

An inchoate thought had been gathering, bereft of the language then to give it shape and force: the Brighton bomb was an IRA operation, but I held a personal responsibility; I couldn't hide behind the IRA, however justifiable its actions. Now I was hours away from meeting this woman – a daughter of one of the Brighton dead, herself a victim because of *my* actions. But the more formed feeling then was of detachment, and I still viewed a possible encounter with her more for its political than its human significance. A civilian victim of an IRA operation had sought a direct contact with the volunteer widely identified with that action.

Only a few years back it would not have occurred to me that one day I might be meeting someone connected with the Brighton operation. Not Brighton. I knew that part of any conflict resolution process must involve dealing with the legacy of culpability and pain; with the past, and with what today are termed legacy issues. But I thought this would at some future date mean meeting with former loyalist combatants, ex-British Army squaddies or Special Branch torturers. Brighton didn't seem to belong in the same reconciliatory universe. I reasoned that the British political elite would never countenance a face-to-face with someone so publicly identified with a prestigious attack on them. I thought *they* would never forgive; that I would always have to look over my shoulder because of my key role in the bombing. There was, of course, Harvey Thomas's letter, two years previously, and the proposal of a future meeting – an extraordinary development, and one yet to be pursued because of the pressures following my release. Joanna Berry, I understood, would be there representing no one but herself. But in my head, she was categorised as *they*; and *forgiveness* was outside of the equation.

A trusted comrade drove me to O'Shea's. Anne Gallagher arrived shortly after us. Because the contact had come through Coiste, I wrongly assumed that Anne herself was either in Sinn Fein or Coiste. Anne clarified that although hailing from a staunchly republican background, she wasn't a republican herself. Her brother was Dominic McGlinchey, the leader of the Irish National Liberation Army (which had split from the Official IRA in 1974), who was shot dead in February 1994. Other members of the family had also been imprisoned for their involvement in the struggle. She was herself a remarkable person (very sadly, Anne died in 2013). She was to become a good friend, and I was moved by what I learned of her experiences as a nurse at the Royal Victoria Hospital, Belfast, tending victims from all sides at the height of the Troubles. Anne founded the peace group Seeds of Hope, which aimed to build reconciliation through utilising the creativity and artwork of former republican and loyalist prisoners.

I asked Anne how she knew Joanna Berry. I couldn't help being cautious, even at this stage. I wanted as much information as possible. Anne replied that they had been friends since 1986 after meeting at a peace conference. The year surprised me – only two years after the bomb! Joanna Berry later corresponded with one of Anne's brothers while he was in prison. For some reason, however, Anne omitted a quite interesting detail about Joanna Berry's background. Leaving that aside for the moment, the upshot of the meeting was that I was to wait on a phone call the next day, Friday, when Anne would give the time and location of the proposed meeting.

Then the call. Again accompanied by my comrade, I crossed town from Ballymun, this time to Blanchardstown – a once comparatively prosperous suburb sprawling out of the city to the west, but then an area much troubled by drug crime – to Anne's house, where Joanna Berry was staying before their attendance the next day at a victims' project at the Glencree Centre for Peace and Reconciliation in the Wicklow Mountains.

We got to Anne's about seven. At the front door, I guess I rang the bell. The full import of the moment intruded. I was suddenly lacking in what now seemed the stupid confidence that the meeting would be nonconfrontational. If roles were reversed and I was the victim waiting to meet the person responsible for my pain, my anguish, my loss, how might I react when face to face with the killer? It is conceivable, regardless of a genuinely expressed desire for rational dialogue, that control over understandable emotions might slip and that I might lash out. Seconds beyond this doorstep was a woman whose father I had killed. Mightn't she now be assailed with doubts, or with thoughts of revenge? Her response couldn't be predicted. Albie Sachs, former judge on the Constitutional Court of South Africa, chief architect of the post-apartheid constitution and former ANC activist, has described how he almost fainted after shaking the hand of the man responsible for the car bomb in which he lost his right arm

and left eye.* This could so easily end disastrously; set matters backwards
rather than contribute in however small a way to the nurturing of the
peace process.

Anne Gallagher opened the door and warmly ushered us down the
hallway to her kitchen, the table still uncleared from an earlier meal.
Anne's was an open house. She introduced me to Joanna Berry, who had
been helping to clear up after several departed guests. Joanna seemed very
calm and centred. If she was nervous, she kept it well hidden. She was
disconcertingly far removed from the stereotype of a Tory MP's daughter
I had lazily assimilated – prim, tweedy, blue-rinsed. I had been expecting
someone much older. Instead, she appeared to be in her late twenties –
rather tall, slim, in black leggings and a hippyish turquoise smock. I sensed
no hostility at all. She spoke first, thanking me for agreeing to meet her.
What could I say to that? All I managed was to return the 'thank you'.
She was so polite. Then Anne offered dessert, all that was left. We sat
down around the kitchen table, Joanna at an angle facing me. I couldn't
eat. I couldn't talk. The others picked up the slack with some polite
stopgap exchanges. About what, who knows? It could not have been more
awkward – for me.

What were the rules? Was there a precedent? A guidebook? Who could
either of us have approached for guidance? A threshold had been crossed.
None of this could have been foreseen. I think I felt inhibited in front of the
others at the table, all of whom were sympathetic and supportive; tongue-
tied at the thought of them being witness to any outward expression of my
inward emotional churning, and feeling unable to be as frank and open
as the significance and gravity of the moment demanded. This was a very
private, scary moment. And one nothing previously had prepared me for.

One unalterable factor, intrusive and unsettling, continually asserted
itself: I had killed this woman's father. Placed in the same situation I
would be grateful for one iota of the calm integrity she exuded. Nothing
in her demeanour or conduct betrayed any hint of hostility or bitterness.
Instead, she epitomised dignity and poise.

As for who asked first whether we might talk alone, I cannot recall.
Perhaps Anne, socially astute, recognising the signals, enquired whether

*Interview by Jonathan Derbyshire, *New Statesman*, 31 October 2011.

we preferred privacy. That insight would have been in keeping. The conservatory, she suggested, was perhaps more suitable.

Her conservatory was built onto the side of the house, looking out onto the back garden. The room was bedecked in cushions and soft drapes, candlelit, as if arranged for a Sunday magazine photo shoot, a perfect setting to put us at some semblance of ease in normal circumstances. We sat facing each other on wicker chairs, politely distanced. Looking round, I could see several works of art, either stacked or informally displayed, including one by Michael Stone, the loyalist assailant of Milltown Cemetery infamy – of a Gothic window assuming the shape of a bullet – the one jarring note. Except for the distraction of coffee, we were left undisturbed, Anne entering and exiting only to check whether we needed anything else. Otherwise, we talked alone. For some three hours.

Three hours! With hindsight, I attribute our need to talk alone to a mutual recognition that nothing less than complete, most profound honesty was demanded and that any third, uninitiated party might somehow corrupt the pure solemnity of the ritualised moment. As for what was said? It was one of the most intense encounters I have ever experienced. We seemed to inhabit a different temporal order. Yet I cannot recount verbatim what was exchanged or all of what was shared. Time seemed to tick by to a point of unhurried closure.

I had come, of course, with an idea of what was expected of me and of the issues and questions likely to arise. Despite the forethought, I was tentative. I remember wondering what the other Brighton victims would make of this. What would Harvey Thomas think? I was all too conscious of expressions of hostility towards me subsequent to my arrest and my public identification with the bombing.

And she would have expectations about me, about her father's killer. For years I had been demonised as 'the Brighton Bomber'. The only corrective to the misrepresentation open to me was to present myself honestly, for better or worse. I had to begin by stating something about my involvement in her father's death. What else was she here for? Justifying the operation – the targeting, the bombing, the political and personal consequences, the intent – to the daughter who had lost her father may seem to many as insensitive, perhaps obscenely crass. But that is how I began, and there is no way to finesse what I had to say. Joanna was there precisely to hear my perspective.

What would be the point of anything less than the fullest candour? I shared my perspective. I believed that the targeting of the Thatcher administration was a legitimate act of war. Which isn't to say that I could reveal operational detail. Parameters for what was to follow had to be clearly set. But I stated to her that I would be as open about Brighton as possible; that as a republican I felt obliged to explain our beliefs and intentions when asked. As I've said, this was against the backdrop of the gross distortion of the movement's aims as reported. I felt a political obligation to explain when a platform was offered or when answers were sought. That obligation underlay my reasons for readily agreeing to the meeting. But it had to be acknowledged that there were aspects to the Brighton operation, again specifically operational detail, that I couldn't and wouldn't discuss. She appeared to have long accepted this condition, and demonstrated that she knew and understood my position. She had had discussions before with republicans. Perhaps she preferred to be spared the detail of this dimension to her father's death? Or so I may have thought then. Within that constraint, we proceeded.

Joanna's questions and comments revealed her as knowledgeable about the causes of the struggle, for this was an exchange. Moreover, judging from her informed remarks about people and places and events, she clearly had developed affection for Ireland, in recent years having been a regular visitor. She had come a long way in her personal journey of understanding, after years invested in trying to grapple with issues of cause and effect, and of asking why, as she put it, she had so cruelly and suddenly been projected into the conflict as a casualty from the moment the bomb detonated.

Joanna also revealed an interesting insight as to why she kept returning to Ireland – she described her isolation as an English victim, without recourse to support. This she shared with other English victims of IRA operations who, geographically dispersed from Warrington to Bishopsgate, Birmingham to Brighton, were without community support and who had little or no opportunity to talk through their losses with others who had similarly been bereaved. Today, Colin Parry, whose son was killed by an IRA bomb in Warrington, has made truly remarkable progress in providing a safe space in which to address the need. At that time, there simply was no group, and few individuals, to whom Joanna and other victims could turn in Britain. Ireland offered the chance to share her and their pain with others, many others, who had been traumatised and damaged by the conflict. In Ireland she was not alone; the currency of trauma was readily accepted within communities that had suffered greatly.

At a midpoint – I cannot be more precise – Joanna offered to read a poem she had written in May (just six months beforehand) called 'Bridges Can Be Built (by a Woman from England)'. It was an amazing, almost hypnotic recital. Here it is in full:

Fires rage in my heart
The heat heals the pain
Bridges can be built

As a human being
I listen to your suffering
You offer me your story
The pain of war
I learn
Bridges can be built

You are my enemy I was told
Be a good girl
Speak only your words
And then I met you
Bridges can be built

Truth is more important
I will speak out for the healing of the world
Take courage
Take spirit
The game of the tribe is not for me
Bridges can be built

The clothes of prejudice now stripped bare
As I open to you
Leaving my bare soul
That can love you all
Bridges can be built

With the eyes of knowing
I move from us and them
Our differences disappear
The unity of humanity remains
Bridges can be built

Your sons could be mine
I could be your brother
Planting the bomb that killed the little boy
Bridges can be built

And now I stand alone with you who killed my Dad
There is a place inside me that knows you acted your truth
Challenging injustice and oppression
My Dad was in the way
Bridges can be built

I miss my Dad
And cry for the grandda my girls cannot know
Tears of grief for all who suffer
We are one in our loss, in our pain
Bridges can be built

Sometimes I feel that my heart heals as Ireland heals
I am sorry for the suffering imposed by my tribe
I acknowledge your struggle
Bridges can be built

My heart burns for peace, justice and equality for all
The passion of knowing that
Bridges can be built.

Reciting the poem in full to me was obviously a very important restorative
action for her. Lost for words, I asked if she had written before. The poem
was her first in twenty years, she replied. What struck me most the first
time was how accurately the poem seemed to prefigure the spirit of our

actual meeting. One line in particular: 'And now I stand alone with you who killed my Dad'. The sentiment was so personal that it is unthinkable that she would have considered the recital if she had any doubts about my sincerity. How was it possible that her imagination after such pain and loss could anticipate this encounter? How could she so correctly realise my viewpoint and foresee my response? I was simply awestruck, disarmed at her apparent lack of bitterness, her magnanimity and perception, her understanding and compassion for my perspective. I felt more than challenged. Humbled. It would have been easier to deal with anger.

A different, distinct change in the dialogue began. She told me something of her background. And it was a notable background. She was a first cousin of Diana, Princess of Wales. I am sure that neither Ella O'Dwyer from Coiste nor Anne the previous evening had mentioned this detail. However, this connection didn't quite register beyond the beginning of the thought that there was need for care in case our meeting might become public, more for her sake than mine.

And then Joanna talked about her father. Theirs had been a close, loving relationship – the very independently minded daughter of a Tory MP. I imagined that must have made for some interesting exchanges. Joanna described how they had reached an understanding, that they both believed in peace – Joanna spiritually and her dad through his political work. Her sharing of this appreciation was very touching. She trusted me in sharing. She would never have done so, otherwise. I started to see her father differently. No, that is not it – I began to see him for the first time. Before that conversation, Joanna's father was a cypher. Her loss of him was palpable in that room. For the first time I opened to the recognition that I was guilty of something I readily attributed to our enemies. That they had dehumanised Irish republicans is a truism, but I too had failed to appreciate the full humanity of our political foes, finding it easier to comprehend them as oppressors, fascists – we were not immune from the application of 'thought-terminating clichés'. In that moment, an 'enemy' began to assume a human face. I struggle, really, with the words to describe the experience. But I started to see Joanna's father in a fuller light and to begin the process of understanding his view. All that I came to admire and respect in Joanna was surely due in part to his gift of values so obvious in her? And that also was a measure of the loss. Joanna's loss of her father. She revealed that she also had three young daughters. Their loss of a grandfather had now to be appreciated. But loss also in terms of my own humanity. For war does rob combatants of something of what it is to be human, of an essential capacity to empathise and to see the world through the eyes of others. There is a brilliant passage in John Banville's novel *The Book of Evidence* that crystallises this failure to imagine another's humanity: 'the essential sin … the one for which there will be no forgiveness: that I never imagined her vividly enough, that I never made her be there sufficiently, that I did not make her live.'*

At some point, she asked to be called Jo. That would take a while to become habitual, unsure as I was of what degree of familiarity was appropriate. She also mentioned having given an interview as far back as 1986 for the *London Evening Standard*, before I was sentenced, in which she said, 'I forgive the man who killed my father.' Furthermore, she stated that one day she wanted 'to meet her father's killers' – to understand, to walk in the footsteps of the bomber. She had received hate mail from that period. She gave me a copy of the original edition, dated Wednesday, 22 January 1986. I've since wondered how I might have responded had I read the article when published. Then, I was being held on remand at Brixton Prison, too absorbed in the looming Old Bailey trial to take in much else. If I possess any degree of insight into my own mind, I am sure I would have been deeply moved and open to the prospect of future contact, possibly through correspondence.

At the conclusion of the meeting, as we moved to the door of the conservatory, Joanna and I hugged. It was spontaneous. I told her that I was sorry that I killed her father; that 'I want to help in any way I can'. Also spontaneous but profoundly meant and felt. Then Joanna – Jo – said, 'I'm glad it was you.' It was such an extraordinary thing to say. I didn't know how to, or whether I should, respond. I was left floundering. Perhaps nothing of significance was meant – no more than a clumsy exiting remark.

Jo returned to England, I had to work on in Dublin to put money by for Christmas. But there was hardly a moment during the days following that I wasn't absorbed with thoughts of what had happened. For something

---

*John Banville, *The Book of Evidence* (Picador, 1989).

had happened, and I was left with the presence of the loss. Our meeting felt like we were at the beginning of an experiment, without precedent – to somehow reconcile that loss with the human need to understand. I was left feeling almost bereaved, wanting this exploration to continue. It did not occur to me that Jo might feel the same.

15

Facing the Enemy

That first meeting with Jo Berry took place nearly two decades ago, at the time of writing (February 2020). I knew it then to be a moment of profound significance to me. While still in the Blocks, I foresaw that after release I might play some role in dealing with the past. The letter from Harvey Thomas certainly opened up that as a possible future commitment. As a former combatant, I saw this as a political *and* moral obligation. The movement, we, I, had caused pain and loss. That we might justify our actions; that there was a context; that there was often no intent in terms of much of the suffering caused – all this is true. Nevertheless, we were culpable for loss and suffering. Dealing with the legacy is a necessary concomitant of all conflict. But I had no prior insight as to the depth of feeling that talking with a victim, with Joanna Berry – now Jo – that evening would awaken in me. I was too hardened by my experiences. In the moment of confronting the pain I had caused to this woman, I began a different, more challenging reappraisal of the past. This line of thinking consumed me in the days that followed.

There were so many unanswered questions swirling around in my head. Where was her anger? What could she have meant – 'I'm glad it was you'? I desperately wanted another chance to continue the dialogue. I do not say that lightly. I also understood that it would be entirely inappropriate for me to contact Jo. It was quite conceivable that she was now regretting our meeting. Further contact might cause her more trauma. To widen the point, there are instances when prisoners have contacted their victims to express sorrow. This is perhaps laudable, even to be encouraged, when arranged through a third party and not necessarily part of a sentence review process. I can see how such an initiative might help a victim. Consideration of a lighter sentence did not apply to me – I had been released from prison more than a year before I heard of Jo – but I nevertheless believed that some might see contact as a self-serving or a cynical exercise.

Especially because I had not renounced the armed struggle. While sincerely regretting any hurt caused, I knew that our struggle was justified. I still do. The essential regret is that it was necessary. Why would I, unsolicited, inflict that defence onto any victim?

Meeting Jo Berry was envisaged from the beginning to be a one-off event. What I hadn't allowed for was that she had her own need for answers from me. Jo contacted Anne Gallagher and together they made the arrangements for a second meeting. This would take place on Sunday, 10 December, sixteen days after that first meeting. Our dialogue had provoked more questions than answers. It had ended too soon. There was an evidently mutual need to continue where we had left off.

Anne, too, had recognised that something profound had happened. A deeply spiritual person, she was tireless in her involvement in charitable causes. Her home was a sanctuary for many troubled people, who gravitated to her positive welcoming energy and strength. She also recognised, certainly more than me at this point, that the dialogue with Jo held enormous potential in terms of an example of reconciliation. I got another call from Anne. Would I meet Jo coming off the ferry tomorrow? I was to meet Anne first at her home, then she would drive me to meet Jo at Dublin Port. I had got my wish.

However, Anne had made a further arrangement that I was not privy to. On my arrival at her home, Anne introduced me to Michael Appleton. Michael, from Belfast, was a documentary film-maker. He had collaborated with Anne on filming interviews with several former activists, both loyalist and republican, for a Seeds of Hope archival project. Anne's idea was that the second meeting with Jo could be video recorded by Michael for inclusion in the archive. A sound engineer and cameraman just happened to be a call away.

Naturally, given historic media bias, plus the usual paranoid stirrings, I had concerns about filming. I was still on high alert for Brit 'dirty tricks'. Might I say something inadvertently or be induced to reveal details that could either cause embarrassment to the movement or even lead to prosecution? Not least my own. I had been released on licence, meaning that I could be returned to prison to serve out life times eight should I be judged to have reoffended. These were early days in the peace process. I felt bounced by Anne, having to make a decision on the spot. And yet (a matter of surprise

to me, even now, looking back) I still went along with it because I instinc-
tively grasped the merit in promoting the dialogue with Jo.

She had already agreed, of course. And I could pull out at any time. I
was reassured to hear that Michael's company, About Face Media, had
a number of very worthwhile productions under their belt, including a
moving documentary series covering the work of a children's hospital.
His brother, Dodie, also is an award-winning film-maker. An additional
feather in Michael's cap was that he had already conducted an interview
with the greatly respected republican veteran Billy McKee in the old cells
of Crumlin Road Gaol. Another matter, not immediately realised but
which did cause me some concern later when I heard, let me admit, was
that Michael's father was a former Diplock court judge who had tried
numerous scheduled (Troubles-related) cases in the North. I wondered at
Michael's core attitude to Irish republicanism, even though he came across
as progressive and liberal. Anne duly drove me to the ferry, Michael and
his crew accompanying us in their van. Jo's arrival and the subsequent
dialogue back at Anne's were videoed.

The first filmed session was set up to capture the essence of the first
meeting a mere two weeks before. The conservatory was again used; the
same seating arrangement, cushions, etc. The lighting may have been
brighter for the camera. The conversation, however, began in a stilted
fashion. We were required to reprise the same ground. We both felt this
was a bit contrived, but necessary in terms of attempting to convey the
dynamic of the original dialogue. Anyway, I think we would have started
our second encounter with a review of the first, which could have proved
equally stilted to begin with. I had questions but they would have to wait
until the right moment. At some point, though, we both seemed to forget
about the crew and the camera and to have a genuine exchange, although
referentially bound to that first encounter. This was only possible, I think,
because of our shared belief in the significance of what we were doing.
We both realised that this might be relevant beyond our own needs; that
by seeing what was possible, others might surmount their own fears and
concerns and be prepared to challenge their demons.

Jo explained that she hadn't been able to sleep well back in England
after our first meeting. I too had had some difficulty. There is a phrase
used by therapists that identifies well feelings following upon the heels

of dialogue of this level of intensity: 'the re-entry problem'. During and immediately after that first meeting we both felt high, due I believe to a sense of weightlessness brought on by the unburdening to each other of our stories. But later, gravity takes over and back on the ground, there is a feeling of being low, of guilt. Has either of us gone too far? Revealed too much? It is a crash landing from a previous high, and can leave the individual emotionally drained and vulnerable. This is where support is most needed. Without any support, with no third party to consult, it was hardly surprising that Jo should find it difficult to sleep.

Before leaving to catch the train to the ferry, Jo had a conversation with her three daughters to explain why she was travelling to Ireland to meet me. One daughter, only seven years old, was furious and very upset. She wanted to come too. Jo passed on her message: 'Tell Pat that was a very bad thing he did to kill my mummy's dad.'

As you may imagine, that left me speechless. Out of the mouths of children! Now I did sense the camera's intrusiveness. And, of course, no matter what we can achieve as two human beings meeting after a terrible event, the loss remains. Neither forgiveness nor understanding can fully embrace that loss.

In the silence of the moment, Jo again read her poem, 'Bridges Can Be Built'. This had been clearly important for her on first recitation. Despite the camera, I found myself again moved, again astonished at how her words had prefigured the spirit of that first meeting. Although conscious of the camera, I determined to ignore its presence and to honour her magnanimity of spirit.

This hiatus in the dialogue allowed me to ask the question that had perplexed me since that first meeting. Jo's words: 'I'm glad it was you.' What had she meant? Jo smiled at the reminder. She hadn't meant to say anything provocative. Her witnessing of how moved I was in that illuminating moment of recognising her father's humanity had caused her to say that. She further explained that the person who killed her father might have not wanted to meet her, nor been motivated to understand her perspective. The meeting seemed to dispel that fear for her. It was crucial to her and justified the risks she had taken. I also came to understand that her commitment to bring something positive from her loss was a deep motivation, and that my response to her had opened up the prospect of a collaborative contribution to reconciliation. And her wider political goal of transforming her tragic loss was also matched by a deep inner spiritual conviction. She talked of healing. This in essence underlay her desire to 'build a bridge', a constructive, transformative spiritual step in her healing process.

During a later recorded session in February, Jo elaborated further, saying something that has particularly stayed with me: 'With you ... I have the most broken relationship in the world.' She defined her own spiritual quest in these terms: that she believed in the human family; that we are all one. But when the fabric of this relationship is damaged or breached, it is imperative to heal the wound. At a very early stage – within days of the bombing, in fact – she had reached a powerful spiritual conclusion: 'I'm not going to let my father's death lock me into just seeing you as a perpetrator. How can I bring something positive? I always felt this but only now know what to do.' Our meetings were a first step in a new journey for her. For Jo, 'the most broken relationship' in her life, the most difficult bridge to traverse, was the gaping wound inflicted when in killing her dad our paths crossed. We both felt that our dialogue took the shape of a healing journey.

I have no religious belief. From an early age I rejected religion; rejected, that is, organised religion. I have met many very fine religious people: priests, nuns, missionaries. Some of them have had an impact on my thinking after leaving prison, contributing insights and encouragement. There is such integrity in Jo's spirituality as she expressed its core value – there are many formulations, but the one I relate to most, even if merely as a metaphor, is this sense of the unity of the human spirit. Part of me wants to share her vision. The best I can do is believe in the best that people are capable of. I was a witness to so much that confirms my belief in the value of community – of what people can achieve together, despite terrible odds, privations, suffering, danger, threats, loss. Having witnessed that spirit, I will never lose belief in the power of the collective.

The breaking down of stereotypes was a two-way street. Over the course of many meetings, but it was a realisation that began to form from the beginning of our conversations, I was learning that Jo's father had been a decent man. I grew to see a stunningly simple truth: the goodness and intelligence and value I perceived in this woman must in some measure have come from her father. And I had killed him. I had killed a fine human being. It had evidently been more comfortable for me to live with the perception that as a Tory he was simply the enemy, a warmonger, driven by greed, without a personal moral code or a rounded background. I too was guilty of demonising the enemy. Now I had learned from the experience of meeting the Other, and in my former ignorance, delusion, arrogance, I hadn't foreseen how valuable and how liberating that lesson would be in terms of my own humanity and perception of the world. This realisation cut through all the layers of defence and denial, the justifications, reasoning and rationalising.

We concluded the first filmed conversation in Anne's conservatory, perhaps more for practical, editorial needs rather than having finished talking. We were required to give solo interviews, to comment separately about the experience just filmed. I had overcome my reticence about talking so personally before the camera. We both had risen above formulaic responses, despite the awkwardness of the camera recording every fraught and candid moment, some painfully frank and deeply poignant. The process was harder on Jo, I felt. She was particularly vulnerable because she was having to relive traumatic experiences as she spoke her emotions at her father's death and the impact on her family. She was, of course, arriving at her own judgement of the evening. In her interview with Michael Appleton, in Anne's kitchen, Jo also touched on this consequence of the camera's intrusiveness: there was 'more of him present without the camera'.

We heard subsequently that the recording wasn't technically satisfactory. Neither were we happy with the attitude and demeanour of the two technicians, on camera and lights. They seemed surly, possibly disapproving. I may be doing them an injustice, but I am reflecting what I then believed. I discussed this with Anne. She revealed that they were the same crew who had filmed Billy McKee for her archival project and that he hadn't been happy with them either.

Another consequence of the first meeting with Jo was an approach on my behalf by her to Harvey Thomas. Our first face-to-face contact came as a direct result of my meeting Jo. I mentioned to her that I had received a letter from Harvey before my release. She knew Harvey. In 1986, they had been interviewed, although separately, on an edition of *The Human Factor* (TVS). I asked whether she could set up a meeting. Anne agreed to host the encounter in her home and it duly took place before Christmas.

Harvey is a big man. Standing at six feet and four inches, weighing twenty stone and wearing size sixteen shoes, he has quite a commanding presence. But I found Harvey to be likeable, voluble, hearty and extremely decent. He showed no animosity towards me. A consummate communicator, Harvey had been a member of the Conservative Party for thirteen years, during which time he served as public relations coordinator for Margaret Thatcher and then for her successor, John Major. Before then, he had a long association with the American evangelist Billy Graham and organised his conferences worldwide, in over a hundred countries, I believe. He was also a regular radio contributor on 'God slots' such as *The Moral Maze* and *Thought for the Day*. At the time of our first meeting, he was an internationally sought-after public relations consultant. A particular meeting in that field led to his decision to write to me.

In 1994, during the general election in South Africa, Harvey Thomas worked as an election advisor to F. W. De Klerk. While there he also met ANC leader and presidential candidate Nelson Mandela. At one time, Harvey would have shared Margaret Thatcher's opinion of Mandela – that he was a terrorist. Harvey has written that meeting Mandela helped to convince him to make that initial contact with me in late 1998.

Our first meeting followed the same line as that with Jo, and took place a fortnight later at Anne's. I tried to explain what had motivated my involvement with the IRA – the political hat firmly in place. Harvey's response, instead, was a deeply moving description of his ordeal, with not a hint of malice towards the one person identifiable as culpable – me. He described his ordeal when the bomb exploded that night in 1984, sixteen years previously and very much still a traumatic recall, particularly when relating the impact on his family. He calmly described what had happened to him in striking detail – how the force of the explosion lifted him two floors from his room on the sixth floor before he plummeted several floors, where he was pinned against a joist and then covered in falling masonry.

Covered in ten tons of debris for three hours before his rescue, unable to either move or see, Harvey prayed. His overriding concern throughout the ordeal was for his wife, Marlies, who mercifully was not there that night. But she was pregnant with their first child and in fact overdue. How would Marlies react when she heard the news of the bombing? Marlies gave birth six days later to their first daughter, Leah. In one of those suggestive, mystic coincidences, I have a son born on the same birthdate eighteen years later.

Towards the conclusion of our first meeting Harvey produced a very battered, dust-covered leather-bound book. Harvey revealed that this was his Bible which was with him in the hotel room at the time of the explosion, later recovered and returned to him. He opened it and small bits of grit fell out onto the floor. Dust from the Grand Hotel had come to rest on the floor of Anne's conservatory. Harvey's testimony was especially moving, coming so soon after Jo's equally astounding eloquence and largeness of spirit. I was to meet Harvey again later the following year, an extraordinary day which I'll try to describe in turn.

Over the Christmas holiday, back in Kerry, I attempted to put the experience of meeting Jo and Harvey in writing. I had to make sense of it. Nothing can prepare you for listening to someone graphically describe, and with no apparent malice, how you caused them such deep hurt. It was clear that meeting victims and thinking a lot about reconciliation represented a continuity with and not breach with my past involvement in the struggle. Emerging from struggle, I saw the necessity of furthering the dissemination of the republican perspective, and that was achievable on two fronts: first, to live up to our need to be inclusive and to embrace the Other; second, by telling our stories, to break down the stereotypes on which ignorance of our struggle depended. The conflict essentially was about the exclusion from political and social life of the nationalist minority in the six counties. Nationalists had to struggle to achieve their own effective political voice. My doctoral thesis concerned the misrepresentation of the struggle and charted how through political struggle Sinn Fein ensured that its discourse could no longer be marginalised or ignored.

One consequence of the dialogue with Jo and Harvey is that I have become a much better listener. The frequent difficulty of our conversations caused me to slow my responses, to ensure that I replied in a thoughtful manner and that my meaning would be heard properly. Slowing the dialogue down to ensure each of you hears the other properly, to explain yourselves carefully, may be the best means of engaging with someone you have hurt or who has hurt you.

I thought hard about the significance of these meetings in terms of the benefits experienced and of their potential contribution to peace-building.

I began to explore how to structure a process through which any lessons learned might both help and encourage others, even if only in the negative – that is, learning from our mistakes. Having benefited from meeting Jo and Harvey, I was conscious of how beneficial such meetings would be for other protagonists and victims. But I also realised the inherent dangers of such encounters if not properly facilitated and supported. I recalled the apparent lack of empathy from Michael's crew. A 'safe space' was a given. In a sense, our experience was exceptional, due I believe to Jo's very early expressed wish to one day meet those responsible for her father's death. How then do you prepare others for such encounters? The germ of an idea for a reconciliation initiative began to take shape, and by January I had drafted a four-page outline of a project.

The idea for a title came naturally to mind from Jo's poem 'Bridges Can Be Built'. Building on this image of a bridge, I called the project Causeway. A causeway is defined as 'a raised road or path through a marsh or across water', which seemed a particularly germane image of what was required to contribute to reconciling the divisions within and between Ireland and Britain. There is also an echo in the name of the potential of alternative *ways* to advance a *cause* – alternative, that is, to violence, confrontation, aggression. The word *causeway* has a particular familiarity and mythological poignancy to an Irish ear because of the Giant's Causeway on the north Antrim coast, mythically linking it to Scotland.

As envisaged, Causeway would be independent, non-party, non-sectarian, and committed to conflict resolution through an exploration of the causes and effects of offence arising from the conflict. A cornerstone to the project was the recognition that a primary cause of political violence is the absence of peaceful avenues for resolving conflict; therefore, the project would seek to create a safe space and platform from which to prove the potential for resolving conflict through dialogue, providing an alternative to violence. I saw the initiative as seamlessly connecting with peace-building and reconciliation.

In summary, the project would aim to facilitate encounters between those affected by the British/Irish conflict; to achieve mutual understanding between encounter participants; to contribute to reconciliation through education, research, training and archiving; to exemplify tolerance; and to promote the benefits of a sustained dialogue process. These were the early ideas generated from the initial series of contacts between Harvey Thomas, Jo and me. Anne Gallagher was also supportive from the first.

I had found a commitment that was both a continuation and a clear break with the past. While no longer a part of the movement in a formal sense, I was convinced that Causeway and the collaboration with Jo would contribute to the essential task of furthering reconciliation, of building peace. I was fully engaged in, and stretched by, the task of both establishing Causeway and of tackling misrepresentation of the armed struggle and of Irish republicanism.

I was also aware, although I hadn't begun to put it into words, that there was an added significance to the dialogue with Jo. Anne had, however, more fully realised the potential for furthering reconciliation in the obvious symbolism at play, in terms of our very different backgrounds – political and spiritual beliefs, male/female, Irish/English – to the point of *personifying* the Other; Otherness.

Anne wanted me to join Seeds of Hope, but although I was interested in and admired the work she was doing, and was amazed at the extent and variety of her contacts, I was reluctant to commit to any organisation after my twenty-seven years' involvement as an IRA volunteer. I was definitely not a joiner. All the while I was putting more thoughts down on paper about what I had learned from meeting Jo and Harvey.

Realising that professional advice was essential, Anne Gallagher drew on her seemingly inexhaustible network of contacts and arranged a meeting for us with Maeve Stokes and Brian Glanville of the Psychology Department of St Brendan's Hospital, Dublin. We met them in February. I showed them my proposal. After reading it and asking many extremely well-informed questions, as you might expect, Brian and Maeve agreed to help us, acting in a voluntary capacity. Over several weeks, following many discussions, they used their considerable experience and expertise to help draw up guidelines designed to ensure the safety of 'victim–offender encounters'. Their interest in the project was more than academic because they also agreed to oversee the initial encounters once the project had been established. The Causeway encounter protocol later elaborated resulted from their efforts, the experience of the encounters between myself, Jo and Harvey, and the contributions of the many volunteers who subsequently agreed to participate in a training programme to test the protocol under their supervision.

I personally gained much from their professional input. Maeve gave me various articles she thought might help me understand more about issues of victimhood. One paper on post-traumatic stress disorder (PTSD) particularly caused me to examine my own state of mind. I was connecting with my own experiences, instances of trauma incrementally accumulated over thirty years, some of which I have referred to in earlier chapters. One paper contained a questionnaire to identify PTSD. I ticked nearly every box. I would never have called nor indeed thought of myself as a victim. I had made decisions in full conscience and could never think of myself as such; but after researching for the project I understood more fully that I *had* been traumatised, and I began to appreciate the extent of Troubles-induced trauma as it affected all participants and victims; whole communities, in fact.

The tangible result of the meetings was the establishment of Causeway, which aimed to facilitate similar encounters between victims and former combatants, a project warmly endorsed by both Jo and Harvey. We aimed to be totally inclusive – non-sectarian, non-partisan and cross-community. The membership of the management board reflected all the different constituencies. The goal as we envisioned it wasn't so much restitution as understanding. I think that is both an attainable and necessary goal – one achievable by extensive preparation before people are brought together. So you would be asking questions like, 'What are you willing to discuss?', 'What is the agenda?' and perhaps more important, 'What don't you want to discuss?' For example, obviously republicans would be reluctant to talk about operational matters, and I dare say this would also apply to all the other protagonists. But there's much that can be explored – so it's finding that out and setting an agenda. It's also important to have the right environment. The danger is that you can actually retraumatise people, and so we recognised the importance of creating a space that is psychologically safe.

While the development of the Causeway project proceeded, I continued to meet Jo. However, the original plan to contribute to a film archive expanded rapidly into a much more ambitious venture. Michael Appleton, moved by what he had seen of that second meeting between Jo and me, quickly realised the potential for a television documentary. I did wonder whether he saw potential in Jo's Princess Diana connection. Undoubtedly, our marked differences in background would present an intriguing added dimension of interest. Never on any occasion have I known Jo to make a thing of the royal link. In time I saw that Michael handled the matter with sensitivity. For the rest of our collaboration, he was assisted by a new technical team. Some of the original footage of our first filmed meeting, however, was retained by Michael and included in the documentary.

Over the course of the next ten months, whenever Jo and I met, Michael would be there to film the encounter. Our trust in Michael and his team grew and we both felt that they respected what we were trying to accomplish. At a later stage, Paul McGuigan, a Belfast man who had gained a considerable reputation locally as a director, came on board. That completed the team. In a very inspiring collaboration, we now had a goal in mind: our meetings were filmed for a projected BBC Two documentary, with the provisional title *The Journey*, which would feature as part of its prestigious *Everyman* documentary series dealing with important moral issues.

However, not all of our meetings were recorded. In April, I received an invitation from Jacinta De Paor, the director of the LIVE (Let's Include the Victims' Experience) programme at the Glencree Centre for Peace and Reconciliation, Wicklow. The programme had been running for about a year, although Jo Berry had been coming to Glencree since 1986. This was her sixth visit within this last year. Each of the participants was a victim due to the conflict. All were victims of IRA actions. Most came from England, victims of IRA bombs there in the 1970s, including a regular attendant who had been injured in the Birmingham pub bombings of November 1974. The programme gave them the space and safety to talk about their individual trauma. I felt very honoured to have received the invitation to attend. Chatham House rules would apply: anonymity had to be respected and what was said in the room must stay in the room.

The first plenary, all-group session took place in one of the larger meeting rooms. About thirty people of all ages found seats or sat on one of the many cushions scattered around. The facilitator asked each of us in turn to briefly identify ourselves and say why we were there. It was an intimate atmosphere. Clearly a lot of trust had been secured over the course of the programme. I was eighth in line to speak. I gave my name, said I was a former Irish republican activist and that I was grateful for the invitation. The baton passed to the next participant. I quickly sensed a chill descend. People were less open. I met with little eye contact. The session ended and we dispersed to adjacent rooms, nooks and corridors for tea or wine or a smoke and more 'one-to-one' discussions. I felt very excluded, although no one was uncivil. Then a man approached whose son had been one of the last British soldiers to be killed by the IRA. He invited me to join him and his wife for a glass of wine. He said quietly, 'Do you realise we weren't told you were coming?' I was shocked. 'No,' I said. 'If I had known that, I would not have come.'

On the second day I was approached by the organisers and asked if I would be prepared to join an 'inner circle' comprised of me and three others plus a facilitator. We would speak in turn, then ask each other questions before the rest of the group, who would then have the opportunity to also ask questions. This was risky, I sensed. Why should I trust them? There had been a behind-the-scenes discussion. I later learned that it was suggested I should be questioned by the whole group but that some had said this would be wrong. Nevertheless, I was to be put under a spotlight.

A LIVE project facilitator, a former priest, chaired the proceedings. The panel included a prominent former loyalist. I pre-empted the discussion by asking to speak. I repeated the point, already made privately, that if I had known beforehand that none of the participants would be informed about my attendance I would not have come; that I recognised that this was a safe space and that it was wrong to jeopardise that. I was fearful of retraumatising anyone. While it was important for me to convey this to the group, my remarks were also intended to be taken on board by the organisers. The discussion that followed was forthright but respectful.

Over the next two days many of the participants who had previously either blanked me or seemed cool towards me came up to me privately, in corridors, empty rooms and outside, and said that although they didn't like the way the organisers had not informed them about me, they admired what they described as my courage in facing them. It seemed to counter all common sense for me to be present when the group had not been prepared or given the right to absent themselves if they wished. However, over the next twenty-four hours most of them, singly or in pairs, approached me and repeated that they hadn't been told I would be there and how shocked they were when discovering who I was. I was individually thanked by many who said that they were glad to have had this opportunity to hear my perspective. There was some suggestion that the organisers had invited me in order that my notoriety but willingness to share about the past might jolt the proceedings out of a supposed comfort zone. I remained appalled.

The only participants who didn't talk to me or acknowledge my presence in any way were a group of young Protestant women from the Coleraine area. Some years later, in a conversation with one of the Glencree management team, I was quite shocked to hear that the same women were so traumatised at my presence that they barricaded their shared bedroom every night. For them, I was the embodiment of all they feared. While I was able to talk with the others and learn of their individual losses and grievances, I have no knowledge at all of what had happened in the cases of those women.

After a subsequent residential meeting in Derry with various victims and former protagonists, some of whom had attended the LIVE weekend at Glencree, I was offered a lift back to Belfast by the same former loyalist who had been part of the group asking me questions. Sharing the lift were the English couple whose son had been killed by an IRA sniper. After dropping them off at their hotel in Belfast, the driver headed for the city centre but stopped for a moment in Sandy Row. It was dark, the street deserted. From the car, he pointed to the site of a bar which, he claimed, had been blown up by the IRA. He lost a friend and was himself injured in the attack. He added nothing more and drove me on to where I had asked him to. I felt I had been challenged, tested, but also that he needed to share the memory at the spot associative of his own trauma. I also believed I could trust him.

Throughout 2001, while continuing to meet with Jo, I sought advice and support for Causeway. I was confident that, for me as a republican, this was the right course in furtherance of reconciliation, but it would have been arrogant to forge ahead without getting soundings from other republicans. I had to allow for the possibility I had made a mistake and had failed to see the bigger picture.

I arranged to meet a former comrade, the same comrade whose advice I had sought on pre-release parole two years before. I gave him a copy of my ideas on Causeway. He was polite, even supportive, but regarded the project to be, as he termed it, 'satellite activity'. I took this to mean peripheral to the main tasks facing the movement, in which I assume he considered I had a potential role still to play. Perhaps he was right but I didn't agree then. Now the movement has fully embraced the concept of building relationships with those we have harmed, regardless of the legitimacy of our past actions. But I acknowledge that at the time many republicans would have thought that what I was attempting to do was premature, a sideshow beside the stellar task of further developing Sinn Fein.

Later in the spring, I contacted my co-accused in the seaside bomb blitz, Ella O'Dwyer, who was still working for Coiste na n-Iarchimí in Dublin on behalf of republican ex-prisoners. I brought Ella up to date on what I had been doing. She said, tongue half in cheek, that there was a rumour circulating that I had been 'captured by the Moonies', implying that I had 'found religion' in a David Icke-like moment of epiphany. As they say, there had been talk, and by the tone, it was disparaging. Memories of the Peace People still rankled. Anne Gallagher would have been misunderstood by many in the movement as belonging in the ranks of the 'peace for peace's sake' brigade. Ella quoted a former Blanketman and fellow Coiste member as saying in regard to Seeds of Hope that he 'wouldn't touch them with a barge pole'. While I understood their reservations, I believed there was great merit in the documentary project. I also now believed that I could possibly do more outside the movement than from within to in some measure make a contribution to the peace process. I had wrestled with the concern that my notoriety might prove insurmountable and that many people might confuse the message, thinking my motives to be self-serving. In a sense they would be right, for I must acknowledge that the meetings helped me. I had learned to live with the epithet 'Brighton Bomber'. Having little choice. Perhaps I could make virtue out of necessity by exploiting that notoriety by utilising the interest, opportunities and platforms ahead to raise the issue of misrepresentation? I saw meeting victims as being part of the imperative to break down misrepresentations.

I spoke with Ella's Coiste colleague on the phone and we arranged to meet at their Belfast office. The meeting took place soon after. At the office, it was explained to me that Seeds of Hope was perceived to be anti-republican and would work with the RUC. I answered that I didn't regard them as anti-republican, although Anne had always opposed the use of violence. I explained that Seeds of Hope was a non-sectarian, inclusive organisation that would indeed embrace ex-RUC members committed to its broad vision. This inclusivity was its strength. While I understood Coiste's concerns, I was also disappointed. A further meeting was arranged for the following week in order for me to put my view more fully. At that meeting, the long-established involvement of Sinn Fein in outreach and reconciliation work was stressed. Ella and Martina Anderson (another of my co-accused in the seaside bomb blitz) were both active in outreach work and supportive of my work with Jo Berry. Martina would later lead Sinn Fein's unionist outreach initiative. She was elected as the Sinn Fein MLA for Derry in 2007, and from 2012 was its Member of the European Parliament. Jo Berry had met Irish republicans as far back as 1986. Under the radar, quietly, discreetly, reconciliation work was ongoing. It was also explained to me that a group from Coiste had attended an event held at Glencree the previous year, on the basis that former British soldiers or state forces would be there as former combatants. Instead, it was revealed that from the start of the encounter, ex-squaddies were there as victims and casualties – that is, of IRA operations. Republicans attending were considered the perpetrators. Coiste had elaborated an entirely legitimate concern. I would never have agreed to meet any former protagonists except on the basis of a mutual wish to understand each other's perspectives. However, I did not believe that Anne Gallagher would ever be a knowing party to any attempt to criminalise republicans. I explained to Coiste that I believed there was an opportunity for valuable work to be done outside of the republican structures as a bridge or mediator between republicans and those who we would like to reach with a view to dispelling myths. There the matter rested.

Within a week of that meeting, I met Ian White, the director of the Glencree Centre. The meeting took place at the Shelbourne hotel, Dublin. Ian introduced himself as a 'Belfast Prod'. He offered me a job – to work on establishing a combatants' programme. The general idea, he explained, was to bring former republicans to Glencree to meet former British soldiers. Given my recent meeting with Coiste, I raised their concerns. Ian admitted that the British Ministry of Defence was financing the project and that they wouldn't recognise republicans as equal protagonists. I had to refuse and argued that the project wouldn't work because republicans would have nothing to do with it, as it promoted the idea of a hierarchy of victimhood and of culpability. He agreed, sincerely, I think. I did say that I was still prepared to work with Glencree as a consultant. Nothing further happened – disappointingly, because I believed there was huge merit in the centre's work.

Another consequence of meeting Anne's extensive range of contacts was an invitation to attend, with Anne, a conference in the USA. Representatives of a group called LA Gang Intervention had been in Belfast the previous December. Following conversations with the group about my hopes for Causeway, they invited me out to California. I had serious doubts, given my profile, whether I would be allowed entry to the States. Section 212 of the US Immigration and Nationality Act 'prohibits the issue of a visa to any alien who has engaged in terrorist activity'. There would, undoubtedly, be opposition to me getting a visa. I had in mind the backsliding that occurred following the *Sunday Times* article over my wish to lecture there in 2000. However, Ron Noblet, the group's main financial backer, insisted that he would use his political contacts to get me in. In April, I applied for a visa at the American Embassy in Ballsbridge, Dublin. In early May I was interviewed there by the first secretary, Leigh Carter, and her replacement, Kim Kelly. They were interested in my work with Jo and Causeway, and also very well informed about what had transpired at Glencree during the LIVE programme earlier described. Chatham House rules had somehow been breached. They said they would support my application but that the decision wasn't theirs. Three weeks later I received a call on my mobile while in Dublin from Kim Kelly, by now in post as the first secretary, to inform me I hadn't been given the visa. However, with Leigh, she had approved my application and this would be on the record were I to reapply a year hence. Political sensitivity over the recent execution of Timothy McVeigh, found guilty of the Oklahoma City bombing, 1995, was cited as the primary reason for the refusal. What if I reapplied in six months? 'Let the dust settle,' she said. She wished me well with Causeway.

Throughout the year I continued to meet Jo. She would take the ferry across the Irish Sea quite regularly. In Ireland, we would meet at locations such as Glencree, as mentioned, and also at Clonard Monastery in Belfast. We talked of many fundamental issues: of misrepresentation, of injustice, of those asymmetries of power which by their nature formed a hold on progress.

Some of the most poignant exchanges concerned Jo's seven-year-old daughter's continuing questions for me, picking up from that earlier message for me from the first filmed interview in Dublin:

'Is Pat sorry for killing my grandad?'

Jo had answered her, 'Yes, Pat is sorry.'

'Does that mean my grandad can come back now?'

And Jo related a further conversation with her daughter, who requested, 'Please ask Pat, did he not see my Grandad Tony in the hotel? Did he not know he was there?'

Other very difficult conversations took place at Orlagh, an Augustinian religious retreat in the Dublin Mountains, where we spent two days filming with Michael and the crew. Jo confronted the issue of violence. Throughout our earlier dialogue I had continued to explain my support for and involvement in the armed struggle. Jo was able to deal with this with huge objectivity and understanding. She was very well versed on British involvement in Ireland. But the intensity of our conversations, in which I was justifying the IRA's campaign in terms of our lack of power and options, and therefore her father's death, suddenly became too much for Jo. She let the tears fall. I remember the depth of feeling in her words: 'What about those who even now believe they can't be heard, are they likely to kill more people? When is it right, when is the suffering worth it?' Despite the tears, there was restraint in her words. These were powerfully heart-wrenching, cathartic moments. I later saw footage of an interview she gave immediately after, in which she reflects on my defence of the use of violence. More anger was vented: 'How dare you think that your cause could justify killing my dad?' None of it was easy. We drew on a well of trust attained over the course of many exchanges. We continued to meet in our belief, which deepened in the process, that our dialogue might stand as an exemplar of the type of engagement with the past necessary for reconciliation.

To repeat an earlier point, sometimes we both felt that the presence of the camera detracted from the simple need to be as frank as possible, despite much sensitivity on the part of the crew. We really needed a return to the privacy and security of Anne's conservatory. But equally, we both appreciated how important it was to start a public debate. The documentary was the best means on offer to achieve that end. But –

and it's a huge 'but' – despite the camera's presence, we managed to enter astounding moments of candour and closeness to the loss, as surely exemplified at Orlagh.

We could never have foreseen that an event on the international stage would nearly put an end to Jo's further participation in the documentary. In early September Jo and I attended a Seeds of Hope conference organised by Anne in Rossnowlagh, a beautiful seaside location in County Donegal. Harvey Thomas also attended. We all spoke and shared our optimism for the future. It was the highlight of our public work to date. Back in Kerry after the conference, I woke to the news that a plane had crashed into the World Trade Center in New York. I then watched the live news coverage and, along with the huge audience worldwide, witnessed the moment onscreen when the second aircraft struck the building.

There is private footage of Jo in tears as she describes her feelings on hearing of the atrocity. She voiced serious misgivings about whether she could or should continue with our dialogue or with the documentary. The bombing also put into question whether the BBC would continue with the filming. Michael, too, had his concerns. On 12 September, Jo and Michael called me separately to share concerns that the documentary might be cancelled or rescheduled. Michael called back later that day to reschedule the next filming for 17 September at the BBC in Belfast instead of on location.

After a few days of quiet, private reflection, we all independently regained our strength of purpose in continuing the process. The way the world was shaping up, there was arguably a greater need to demonstrate the power of dialogue. We completed the final interviews on 17 September. Now there was a transmission date: 13 December. The remaining time was much filled by wrangling over contracts and the editing process.

As the date of transmission loomed, and given the obvious sensitivities involved, Jo was determined to contact all those affected by the Brighton bomb. She was consumed with worry over the documentary's possible reception. She was conscious too of the hate mail she had received after her public statements in 1986! She wrote to all those injured in the bombing or who had lost loved ones. As the broadcast date drew closer, Jo faced the task of informing not only other Brighton victims about her collaboration on the documentary but also members of her own family who were unaware of her contact with me. I decided that out of courtesy I should also meet Harvey Thomas again to give him a personal update on the filming and also on what we were trying to achieve with Causeway.

It was arranged that Harvey would meet me at Stansted Airport on 17 November. To my great surprise he turned up accompanied by his daughter Leah. I was totally unprepared for this development. As mentioned earlier, Leah was born within days of the bombing. I had no knowledge of how she might receive me. I gather that this was a spontaneous idea. Meeting Jo, then Harvey and now Leah, flew in the face of the conclusion reached by Causeway that such encounters – between victims and offenders – required careful preparation and facilitation. Harvey then surprised me further by inviting me to his home for breakfast.

He drove me to his home in Potters Bar, North London, where he lived with his wife Marlies and two daughters. Leah was sixteen then, and her sister Lani fourteen. I had breakfast with the family – beans on toast and very welcome.

During the meal, Lani addressed me, politely but firmly. She said, 'Do you realise that if Dad had died, I would not have been born?' That took tremendous moral courage – and perhaps physical courage also, for she may have seen me as a violent person, the man who tried to kill her father. A very humbling moment. I could only say with the deepest sincerity that I was sorry. The four of them – Harvey, Marlies, Leah and Lani, sitting round the breakfast table – accepted my words with great composure, warmth and generosity. In the years since, we have kept in touch. I always receive a Christmas card from them. Lani would later introduce me to her husband while visiting Ireland on their honeymoon. Following in her father's footsteps, she trained as an events manager. One of her first achievements as a student was to organise a public conversation between me and her father, which took place at St John's Church at Egham, Surrey, in 2008 (but I am jumping ahead).

Shortly after the meeting with Harvey and his wonderful family, I received a call from Michael Appleton: someone at the BBC had 'inadvertently leaked details' of the documentary to the media. This was not entirely unforeseen. The period in the run-up to the documentary's transmission in December was a nervous time for everyone involved. The biggest stumbling block appeared to be the concern of the BBC in

Bedford Street, Belfast, over my refusal to denounce violence. I regarded this as evidence of its institutionalised prejudice against Irish republicanism. I had my own issues with the documentary. I had objected to an early version which excluded all mention of a visit I paid to a memorial in Carrick Hill dedicated to Volunteer Louis Scullion. A still-frame view of the memorial was retained but my comments about having known Louis and about how he had died were edited out. I was furious. A compromise was eventually reached on this and a brief view of the monument was retained. I remained far from happy, but I still believed that there was much of merit in the documentary. The title was also altered, from *The Journey* to *Facing the Enemy*, which was itself a compromise on *Meeting the Man Who Killed My Father*, the latter only changed after Jo's insistence.

With a couple of days to go before transmission of the documentary, I realised a personal ambition with the publication of the amended version of my doctoral thesis. The launch of *Gangsters or Guerrillas?* took place at the Art Shop, Falls Road, on 11 December. Two days later, *Facing the Enemy* was first broadcast on BBC Two.

16

The F Word

That year, 2001, marked an early high point in the two decades since my release from the H-Blocks in 1999. I had met Jo Berry and collaborated with her in the making of a documentary, met Harvey Thomas and his wonderful family, and ploughed those experiences into a reconciliation project, Causeway. And before the year was out, I had seen the publication of *Gangsters or Guerrillas?* I recall first seeing my book on a shelf in Easons, Dublin – the thrill, alas, not matched by the sales!

I also ended the year on a high due to receiving very favourable feedback on the reception in Belfast of *Facing the Enemy*. It had been an anxious wait. I was still uncertain of how friends and former comrades might regard my *collaboration* – a loaded word. However, I was reassured when people would stop me in the street and say, 'Well done.' Many told me they admired Jo Berry. Nationalists had been demonised as a 'terrorist community' but this Englishwoman's willingness to try to understand had really touched them. The timing of the broadcast seemed to accord with a current mood that considerably more effort was needed to further the peace process. The period was marked by increasing sectarian tensions, culminating in the Holy Cross dispute, when loyalists violently protested against Catholic schoolgirls passing their area on the way to and from school. The documentary had shown what was achievable through contact and dialogue despite profound differences, in order to build trust and contribute to reconciliation. Could there be more profound difference than the fact that I had killed Jo's father, hurt Harvey and harmed their families? Former comrades, with some exceptions, however, seemed cagey about expressing opinions. I had acted independently, which always incites suspicion among republicans. This was not a deliberate choice; to this day I feel part of the broader republican movement. I never fail to vote Sinn Fein (although more likely these days to give second or third preferences, when proportional representation allows, to other worthy candidates or parties). I was motivated *as* a republican. I felt that the documentary was a contribution to building the peace.

Among those republicans who did speak favourably from the start was Martin Meehan, who himself had been very active in engaging with unionists and political opponents. Earlier that year, Martin had invited me to attend a meeting organised by the Meath Peace Group in Drogheda, where we had a useful roundtable discussion about the past with a representative group of loyalists and unionists. The public reception was even greater when *Facing the Enemy* was rebroadcast six months later – encouraging as well because the transmission competed with celebrations of Ireland's three–nil defeat of Saudi Arabia in the FIFA World Cup! By this time many more former comrades were expressing their support. Perhaps they had been cautiously ascertaining the community's reception in the meantime.

After the favourable reception of *Facing the Enemy*, Jo and I received many invitations to speak at public events, particularly in England; but in Ireland, too, although to a lesser extent, particularly in the partitioned North, where emotions after decades of conflict were still raw. I will say more later about the opportunities for dialogue that arose thanks to the documentary. For now, I will focus more on Causeway.

Throughout 2001, while collaborating with Jo on the documentary, I also continued with my efforts to develop Causeway. Many people were involved in establishing the project. Particularly supportive were Liam Maskey and his colleagues at Intercomm, the north Belfast–based cross-community development organisation. Through Intercomm I was to meet a wide cross-section of community activists who were to contribute to its eventual formation. It would be invidious to single out individuals, but Liam, along with John Loughran, was tireless in his support. Crucial endorsement at an early stage was also given by the leading loyalist Billy Mitchell. He died in 2006, a great loss to the task of building a peaceful future. Martin Meehan, as always, was fully supportive. It is instructive that both Billy and Martin had played key operational roles during the conflict.

With Intercomm's help, in the summer of 2001 I travelled to South Africa. I wanted to gain first-hand insights into the work of the Truth and Reconciliation Commission (TRC). In January, I had attended the Action from Ireland peace and justice conference in Kildare, at which I met Father Michael Lapsley, a New Zealand–born Anglican priest. Michael, targeted because of his opposition to apartheid, had lost both hands and an eye in a parcel bomb attack in 1990. An inspiring man, he listened with interest to my plans for the project. He extended an open invitation to visit him at his offices in Cape Town. Thanks to Intercomm, I was able to visit South Africa within five months of that meeting.

I travelled overnight by bus from Johannesburg to Cape Town, where I again met Michael Lapsley, this time at his very modest offices at the Institute for Healing of Memories. After I'd briefed Michael about the progress of Causeway since our conversation in January, he invited me to lunch. I expected an equally modest meal somewhere locally. Instead, I was surprised when he drove me up to the Rhodes Memorial, overlooking Cape Town, where at an outdoor restaurant the white 'elite' would dine. His presence caused a discernible stir in surrounding tables. As a prominent Anglican priest in Cape Town and human rights activist internationally, Michael Lapsley was a very well-known public figure. We ordered steak. Michael, eschewing advanced prosthetics, had hooks designed to serve Mass and to drive his car, but their utility did not extend to dicing sirloin. He therefore asked that his be served in manageable bite sizes. The hospitality was minimal. His request was haughtily ignored. I suspected he had brought me there knowing this would happen. I felt privileged when he agreed to let me do this for him. I had witnessed that there was much still to be done in terms of attitudes in post-apartheid South Africa.

While in Cape Town, I also visited the TRC headquarters, where I had a meeting with Lavinia Brown, arranged by phone before my departure from Belfast. Lavinia, an influential figure in her own right, was the personal secretary to Archbishop Desmond Tutu, who was in hospital abroad undergoing surgery. We had an informative discussion about Causeway. After a second long-haul bus journey, I also gave a talk at the Workers' College in Durban to an audience of trade union activists and student campaigners. I returned to Ireland encouraged by many supportive responses.

By October that year, I was ready to speak publicly about my intentions for Causeway. I gave a briefing at Intercomm to a wide-ranging audience of cross-community leaders involved in reconciliation projects. I had compiled a selection of video clips chosen from the hours of interviews recorded for the documentary to illustrate my dialogue with Jo. Further support and encouragement followed. Meanwhile, other opportunities to advance reconciliation beckoned.

One, which proved difficult, occurred in September 2002, when I was contacted by a producer of the BBC Two current affairs show *HARDtalk*, which had a catchment audience of between 100 and 250 million worldwide. It was difficult to let the opportunity pass. I knew the programme's format – it's in the title – but was concerned that the sole focus would be to challenge my support for the armed struggle. I sought an assurance from her that the interview would also include a question about *Gangsters or Guerrillas?*, which would allow me to discuss media distortion and misrepresentation. I also expressed concern that the interview would be aired on the anniversary of the Brighton bomb. For me to be seen to defend the armed struggle on the anniversary of the bombing would be interpreted as an act of gross insensitivity.

The interview was arranged to take place at the Europa Hotel, Belfast. The choice of location had a certain irony, for apart from being reputedly the most bombed hotel in the world, it was where the press corps famously filed their news reports, often concocted from British Army briefings.

A single room on one of the upper floors had been turned into a makeshift studio. The heat from the arc lamps was oppressive. Tim Sebastian, the interviewer, was already seated. I was immediately guided to the interviewee's chair by the producer whom I had been in discussion with over the parameters of the interview. No small talk, although I did ask for a dab of make-up – Tim Sebastian was clearly plastered in the stuff. She said it wouldn't be necessary. I half-joked that they must want to see me sweat.

Tim Sebastian launched into the interview. It felt like an ambush. He was relentlessly hostile. Questions about terrorism, civilian casualties, Colombia, decommissioning. None about the book. I think I won some points but felt that I was in the dock under Aussie rules. Sebastian did not proffer the customary handshake at the conclusion. I left the room concerned about how the interview would be received when broadcast, as claimed, two weeks hence. Instead, as I had suspected, it was broadcast on the anniversary of the bombing. The experience re-affirmed my view that the BBC should never be fully trusted in its reportage of the conflict (I declined a request to be interviewed for the show in 2019). I feared that the show would set back my efforts at reconciliation. Three days later Harvey Thomas called from Dubai to congratulate me about the interview, which he had watched via satellite.

The inaugural board meeting of Causeway was held in Belfast on 30 May 2003, and on 7 June 2003, Causeway was publicly launched at the Farset hotel in Belfast. The then lord mayor, Martin Morgan (SDLP), presided over the opening ceremony. Harvey Thomas had agreed to be a patron of the project and Jo Berry a board member.

Beforehand, I had received a call from the Multi-Agency Resource Centre (MARC), based in Belfast, to inform me that Liam Clarke, a local journalist, wanted an interview – the same Liam Clarke whose *Sunday Times* article in 2000 effectively scuppered my chances of lecturing in the USA. I refused. I later met Jo at MARC's offices in Bridge Street. She had also been contacted earlier by Clarke requesting an interview. I explained to Jo why I would not have anything to do with Clarke, who was widely suspected among republicans to be little better than a British agent. Jo, of course, would make her own mind up about whether to agree to be interviewed or not. In the end, she agreed to give the interview, conducted over the phone, wanting to spread the word about our work.

Later at the launch, I asked Jo how the interview had gone. She revealed that after giving the interview, Clarke had called her back and asked her whether she was 'romantically involved' with me – 'Absolutely not!' I think I was equally shocked, and concerned that this would be an angle pursued in the press to deliberately undermine the project. Jo seemed to make light of the incident but she did regret having agreed to the interview. Later that week, Clarke reported that Jo had 'denied being in a relationship' with me.

Although the launch went smoothly, in terms of attendance and media interest, on the eve of the launch tensions over the ongoing parade controversy resulted in a group calling itself the Combined Loyalist Military Command issuing a statement threatening any Protestant involvement in cross-community work. The success of the event was seriously undermined by the noticeable absence of many community activists from a loyalist background who – understandably, given the seriousness of the threat – had decided not to attend. There is no denying that this was a major disappointment for all concerned, who had given much to the project. We had decided to proceed in the anticipation that the impact of the threat would be short-lived. In fact, it was to prove a considerable setback.

Nevertheless, the launch of Causeway had all the face-saving appearance of success, if only in terms of being quite extensively and positively covered in local and (Irish) national media. RTÉ, for example, broadcast an interview with me that night. Also present at the launch was the journalist and broadcaster Peter Taylor, with whom I had been in negotiations for some while about an interview for an in-depth BBC documentary on Brighton. Our first meeting had taken place in Tralee, County Kerry, in December 2002, six months previously. The documentary was scheduled to commemorate the twentieth anniversary of the Brighton bomb, in the following year, 2004. Peter was there to record the launch of Causeway for inclusion in the documentary, later to be called *The Hunt for the Brighton Bomber*.

Another journalist in attendance was Marina Cantacuzino, who, inspired by *Facing the Enemy* and by reports of our public dialogue, had written to us beforehand to arrange an interview, which duly took place immediately after the launch of Causeway. Marina, spurred on by stories emanating from the war in Iraq, had established a peace initiative called The Forgiveness Project, a collation of interviews mounted on storyboards with accompanying photo portraits by Brian Moody of people who had established connections with those who had caused them harm, and who were willing to share their disparate, often conflicting viewpoints about 'forgiveness'. Marina wanted to include Jo's and my story in an upcoming exhibition. Brian took our photo for inclusion in the project. I was always uncomfortable with the thought that our dialogue was unique. Uncommon, certainly, but Marina's initiative, in which many personal accounts are catalogued of meetings between victims and offenders, proved that there were many other examples; that every situation of conflict generated individuals who wanted to understand why – why them? Why their loved one? Rather than stay locked in grief and perhaps self-destructive anger, or pain, even hatred, some sought to understand. This very human desire to understand can be mortally wounded by loss. Grief is a lonely path. We were not alone. This was so encouraging and vindicated all our efforts to publicly share our experiences.

Despite the insufficient cross-community support at the launch of Causeway – understandable, given the loyalist threats – we were delighted by the positive media coverage nevertheless generated. Now we could only wait upon initial client enquiries. We had hoped to bed down Causeway with a few positive facilitations. Indeed, there was at least the suggestion that one potential client was in the wings ready to begin the process. If we could demonstrate that the protocol worked in broad terms, this would enable us to lobby for funding and other resources.

However, there was no contact from anyone seeking to avail of the service. This was deeply disappointing to all who had contributed their time and energies to our shared belief in the evident relevance of the project. One criticism often raised was that the timing for such a project was premature. Clearly, the impact of the loyalist boycott of and threat to cross-community projects was also a major setback. The timing couldn't have been less conducive for encouraging potential client interest. I also have to accept (what from the vantage of today is glaringly obvious) that my notoriety may well have been off-putting, and perhaps served to handicap the project from building support more widely. I must conclude, therefore, that my public association with Causeway was a misjudgement; that it was an obstacle for many who might otherwise have contributed to the project or, more pertinently, availed of its service. I should have helped from the sidelines, and initially this was what I had envisaged.

I still reckon, however, that it is overly simplistic to think of the early demise of Causeway as an abject failure. While the project did fail in its primary objective of establishing a safe space for facilitating meetings between victims and offenders, many valuable lessons were learned about how such a process ought to be managed. It was also beneficial, I believe, to all who contributed to its early development because it highlighted in many ways unforeseen the problems and pitfalls any similar initiative would meet, and thus the experience and insights gained could well be utilised in future reconciliation work.

The disappointment over the failure of Causeway marked an appreciable change in the nature of my involvement with reconciliation work from that point onward. At this stage, I was out of prison four years, and to an extent carried along by events. I was certainly far less proactive, if no less busy. Whereas before I would be constantly thinking of ways to further the work, the sheer scale of what needed to be done to develop Causeway exposed my own unsuitability in terms of public notoriety for the task.

It was time to take stock. This was a major setback personally. However, if and when asked to speak at a conference, or to give an interview to a journalist or research student, I would readily agree. There was still considerable interest, particularly outside of Ireland, in my continuing dialogue with Jo Berry, although much of the focus was still, as suggested, centred in England.

At an early stage I began to tally the number of times I met Jo. I reckoned up to around the hundred mark, after which I no longer bothered to count. This is not to suggest for one moment that meeting Jo became easy or easier for either of us. After each conversation, we would each have to decide whether to continue to meet. And there were times when it would stop, without prospect of being continued (more on this towards the end of the next chapter). It could be legitimately argued that any time during a meeting that Jo left the room, her decision to return to the room could constitute another meeting. It is hard to conceive of a more difficult dialogue. However, after a week or two, an invitation to an event would usually arrive which offered us the opportunity to resume the journey.

We have spoken together at many universities and schools. One university (Galway) awarded us its annual peace trophy. Bradford University included our dialogue as an integral part of its peace studies degree course. We also spoke in prisons (to inmates and to staff); at peace conferences and seminars (at so many that I began to collect the name tags); at Rotary events; literary and musical festivals; public meetings. We have also given, together and individually, many media interviews, for the press, on television and radio. We have also worked with academics and collaborated with documentary-makers. We even sat for our portrait as part of a reconciliation project. One event would spur on an invitation to attend another. I was carried along in a quite comforting tide of interest in what we were doing, strengthened in the belief that accumulatively we were making a difference.

On each occasion that we shared a platform, the focus of our discussion was on our first meetings. For me that first meeting particularly with Jo marked a crucial personal development, which I was driven to share in the belief that it provided an entry point to a better understanding of the conflict. Our events always included a question-and-answer session, and it was during these that I gained the opportunity to test my personal motivations and beliefs. I was provided a rare privilege of having to look back critically over the past. There was no hiding from it; no rationalisation or certitude that could survive the intensity of the continuing dialogue with Jo and of audience responses. That was the essence of our journey. She trusted me in that process, however strained it became at times. She trusted me despite our differences, not least in regard to my continuing belief that the IRA's armed struggle was necessary. You can imagine how hard that was for her to bear.

Some of the projects we were jointly involved in or lent our support to were potentially significant in terms of furthering the debate on the need for dialogue, inclusion and understanding, the prerequisites of every peace strategy. All were opportunities to tackle misrepresentation – to challenge the labelling or othering that handicaps our search for peace and rights. Of these, perhaps Marina Cantacuzino's Forgiveness Project was most influential – for encouraging debate about the problematic issue of forgiveness and in gathering examples of its wide range of often-conflicting definitions.

I found the issue of forgiveness to be problematic. It seemed to mean different things to different people and in different contexts. Some understood it in a religious sense – that first one must atone. And did forgiveness mean that you somehow transcended anger? Marina had collated many examples of victim–perpetrator dialogues. Descriptions of various instances, drawn from many different contexts of conflict – war, crime, genocide – accompanied photographs of the participants. A selection of these were used in an easily transportable mobile photographic exhibition. The premise of the project was that there was no overarching definition of forgiveness. Indeed, at least one of the earlier stories exemplified the inability to forgive.

For example, Harvey and Jo are two very different people, each on a long journey towards understanding. For Harvey, a committed Christian, forgiveness – forgiving me – was a core test of his faith. For Jo, the need to understand 'why' transcended her anger and hurt. Some will perhaps never forgive. Others may be on their own point in the journey. I would never ask for forgiveness. We couldn't be prescriptive. The more I hear the term, the more aware I become of its complexity and contradictions, the more I see *understanding* as the key to reconciliation. The concept of

forgiveness, therefore, is deeply problematical. The brilliance of The Forgiveness Project is that it points out these difficulties while showing what
can be and has been achieved through contact and dialogue.

Marina's project was launched at the Oxo Gallery on the South Bank
in London in January 2004. Jo Berry and I attended the opening of the
exhibition, entitled *The F Word: Images of forgiveness*, in which our story
and photograph featured prominently. The title is brilliantly suggestive of
the difficulties alluded to. Archbishop Desmond Tutu gave the opening
address. The exhibition went on to tour many countries and continues
to tour to this day, updated with many additional exemplary stories.
According to the project's website, to date, the exhibition has been staged
in 550 locations across fourteen countries, to an audience exceeding
seventy thousand people. More than 160 such accounts have now been
collated by this wonderful initiative.

That summer, I was invited by Michael Lapsley to attend the Healing of
Memories conference on Robben Island. The *F Word* exhibition was also
installed as a backdrop and then was transferred to St George's Cathedral
in Cape Town. At the conference, I faced some criticism for insisting
that the IRA's armed struggle had been necessary. Nelson Mandela's
example was invoked by an American attendant. In response, I referred
to Mandela's autobiography, *Long Walk to Freedom*, in which he relates
how upon release he had stressed to reporters 'that there was no contradic-
tion between … [his] continuing support for the armed struggle' and his
advocacy for negotiations: 'It was the reality and the threat of the armed
struggle that had brought the government to the verge of negotiations.'
Mandela reiterated this line during a keynote address to thousands who
had gathered to celebrate his release in Soweto. In a conversation I had with
him at the conclusion of the conference, Michael Lapsley was supportive,
adding, 'Yours is a difficult message for people to hear but it is necessary.'

I visited Mandela's cell during my stay (I've read recently that this is
no longer possible to do). I also recall a conversation with a remarkable
Aboriginal Australian woman, a survivor of poverty, abuse and sexual
violence, who shared that she was proud to have Irish blood (she called me
her 'Irish brother'), and that Gerry Adams, during a recent tour of Australia,
had mentioned visiting the Irish Cemetery on Robben Island. She asked
me if I would help her locate it. We did manage to find it, overgrown

and neglected, on a small rise which afforded a magnificent view of Table Mountain across the strait. The story goes that a ship from Ireland bound for Australia had sought shelter on the island, then a leper colony. Some of the passengers were so moved by the plight of the wretched victims of this terrible affliction that they elected to remain behind. Over the years they died and were buried together in one of the most inaccessible cemeteries in the world. I remain deeply touched by knowing of their sacrifice.

Later that year, I attended an event in Brighton to commemorate the twentieth anniversary of the 1984 bombing. The event, partly organised by Marina, was chaired by the broadcaster Simon Fanshawe, who was inspired to do so by hearing Jo and me speak.

I had been asked a number of times whether I would ever return to Brighton. I always said no, without having to give it much thought, realising that to return might offend or be construed as an affront to the memory of those who had died, and to those who had been injured or traumatised. What conditions needed to be met for me to change my mind? Firstly, Simon Fanshawe's assurance that he would organise an event in a way sensitive to these concerns, at which I could speak openly, frankly, in the spirit of reconciliation. Secondly, that the event wouldn't be turned into a media circus. Thirdly, that Jo and Harvey would be agreeable (although I was fairly confident they would be).

I understood fully, nevertheless, that my presence would offend some, perhaps many. I had to weigh whether the goal of reconciliation would be furthered or undermined. How the event was to be organised could minimise the chances of bad publicity, negative media coverage or possible protests.

Inviting me was a brave step on the part of the organisers. There was the danger that my motivation would be misapprehended: 'Is this a republican stunt?' The actual location in Brighton, St Nicholas Church, was kept secret from those who agreed to attend until the night before, when they were emailed the address. This was to forestall the event turning into a media circus, or worse, perhaps, a magnet for protest. But the afternoon passed off without incident and part of a transcript of the dialogue appeared in the next day's *Guardian*.

Later that same day I travelled to London at Jo's invitation to attend a similar event at St James's Church in Piccadilly. She had chosen the venue because it was here that she had sought solace two days after hearing the news of her father's death, and where she resolved not to become bitter and angry. There is a piano in the church and she played – a haunting, very moving improvisation – as she had often previously played. The audience was bigger than that of the earlier event, and overwhelmingly supportive, except for two people who criticised me for not renouncing violence. I fully grasped this as a punch I had to roll with, rather than counter on every occasion. However, this was often a matter of tension for Jo.

At some point during the course of 2003 I had begun to have concerns about my health. I eventually raised this with my doctor, who arranged a visit with a consultant. After a series of blood tests, I was diagnosed with prostate cancer. A biopsy indicated that if not surgically treated there was a high risk of metastasis. A prostatectomy was performed in January 2005. Mercifully, thanks to the surgeons and nurses of the cancer unit at the Belfast City Hospital, the operation and recovery were successful. However, the wind was knocked from my sails and it took me quite a while to fully realise how lucky I was to be one of the survivors. Many former comrades had died of cancer in recent years, the seemingly high incidence of cancer-related deaths among ex-POWs perhaps attributable to the effects of CR gas during the burning of the Kesh (see chapter five). In my twenties I had followed the coffins of many comrades killed in action, and of the many victims of state killers. Now I was increasingly attending the funerals of friends who had succumbed to cancer. It is inevitable in life that at a certain age you find yourself attending more funerals, the relentless signal that time is running short. Hardly a fortnight passes now without a funeral to attend.

After my post-operative recovery, the first occasion to speak in public came in May 2005, when I shared a platform with Bernadette McAliskey and Martin Ferris in support of a friend, Deborah Devenny, Danny Devenny's wife, who was standing in the council elections for Sinn Fein in the Short Strand. Regrettably, Deborah wasn't elected. I was soon as busy as ever.

17

The Field of Peace

One of the more personally engaging dimensions to my work with Jo, providing much insight, was our collaboration with others on their interpretations of our dialogues – academics, linguists, peace activists, artists, dramatists and actors. My doctoral thesis on the misrepresentation in fiction of the conflict argued that similar issues of distortion and of bias also shaped film and drama. Therefore, I was particularly fascinated to be a part of rehearsals, workshops and performances of plays based on our meetings, which provided opportunities to explain the dynamic of meeting Jo and other victims – and additionally the context of the conflict from a republican perspective.

My first experience of meeting artists was at the Barbican in 2002. Jo and I were invited to speak at a two-day conference there (31 January–1 February) by Scilla Elworthy, founder of the Oxford Research Group (ORG), which campaigned for non-military alternatives for the settling of international disputes, and for which she was thrice nominated for the Nobel Peace Prize. The focus of the conference was conflict prevention and peace-building. This was the first occasion I shared a platform in England with Jo; indeed, my first public appearance in Britain. The centrepiece of the event was a performance by actors from the Royal Shakespeare Company of David Edgar's new play *The Prisoner's Dilemma*.

Scilla had invited delegations from the military, media, arts and politics to attend the conference. Much of the tone was academic and cerebral. Jo and I were there to offer a more personal account. We gave a short, very well-received presentation expressing the essence of our first meetings: the impact on me of hearing Jo describing both her relationship with her father and her loss. I said that I now realised that I could have sat down and had a cup of tea with him. It wasn't planned, but meant; said in the moment. Jo was deeply moved. From the questions and commentary that followed our contribution, our being together made as deep an impression as what we had said. We had connected with the audience. The feedback was very positive and encouraging. From that experience, I learned not to fear expressing emotion, to trust my instincts and to have confidence in knowing my own mind. I have experienced many such moments when sharing public meetings with Jo. For me, this opened up a new approach for tackling the lack of understanding about the context of the Irish/ British conflict.

Also there was the film director Paul Greengrass, fresh from the success of his film *Bloody Sunday*, who showed an interest in our dialogue. We met and talked with him at the end of the event. There is a poignant scene in a film he went on to direct, *The Bourne Supremacy* (2004), in which the eponymous hero admits his guilt to a Russian woman, Irena Neski, for killing her parents. I did not get to see the film until much later after its release but then did wonder whether our conversation that day might have had a faint influence on his direction of that scene, so closely did it evoke the depth of the moment of encounter between victim and offender. Whether so or not, the scene brilliantly gives dramatic insight into the themes of forgiveness and reconciliation; into the power of drama to evoke those moments of clarity that arise through contact and dialogue. Clearly, though, by his attendance, these themes were of interest to him, and exemplified by our contribution on stage.

To coincide with the first anniversary of the Twin Towers attacks, ORG organised a three-day event called Transforming 9/11, at the Royal Opera House (ROH), Covent Garden, London. I gave a talk at a seminar organised by Mari Fitzduff, chair of conflict studies at the University of Ulster. Scilla Elworthy launched a new peace initiative, Peace Direct, dedicated to giving practical support at the local level to stop violence and to build peace. Jo and I were interviewed separately for a book in support of Peace Direct (*Unsung Heroes*, published in March 2004). We later spoke on stage at the Linbury Theatre within the ROH on the three nights. Other speakers included Ben Okri, Annabel Brooks, David Oyelowo, Julie Christie, Stephen Fry, Phyllida Law, Mark Rylance and Juliet Stevenson. The composer and singer Chloë Goodchild performed her 'world anthem', 'The Singing Field', inspired by the poetry of Rumi. On stage, Jo talked about how 9/11 had caused her to doubt whether she should continue our dialogue but that she had concluded that there now was even greater need for dialogue in the world. In my contribution, I addressed the imminence of a US invasion of Iraq, in what I described as the 'carefully choreographed drift to war', and said that Tony Blair and the other political leaders should follow Jo's example in not forestalling contact and dialogue. The event was contact rich, and we also met with representatives of the Israel/Palestine Centre for Research and Information, which led to a later invitation to attend their conference in Antalya, Turkey.

Scilla was also instrumental in arranging for me to talk at a workshop organised by the director Max Stafford-Clark in London for a future production called *Talking to Terrorists*. Also there to give advice was the Russian defector and former Russian Federal Security Service (FSB) officer Alexander Litvinenko (later to be assassinated by radiation poisoning). As ever, I saw these events and initiatives as almost transcendent opportunities for countering misrepresentations not only of myself as portrayed in the media but more importantly of how our struggle was so misunderstood.

Talking to Terrorists is an example of verbatim theatre, in which the words of real people, as opposed to imagined characters, are scripted or montaged into a narrative drama. The playwright Robin Soans interviewed me at the Europa Hotel in Belfast. He was accompanied by the actor chosen to play me, Lloyd Hutchinson. Lloyd revealed that he had first made a regular living as an actor dubbing the voice of Gerry Adams during the broadcasting ban introduced by Douglas Hurd, which banned Sinn Fein from speaking over the airwaves. Broadcasters circumvented the ban by having actors dub over the voices of Sinn Fein spokespeople. A steady source of income thus dried up when the legislation was overturned during the early days of the IRA's ceasefire. I attended one of the first performances of the play at the Royal Court Theatre, London. Also there on the night was David Ervine, the leader of the Progressive Unionist Party, who is credited with helping to deliver the loyalist ceasefire in 1994. We spoke briefly and shook hands. His son Mark, who worked as a muralist in Belfast with Danny Devenny, later became a friend. I began to optimistically visualise all these disparate but connected efforts as part of a galaxy of activity within the influence of reconciliation.

In January 2006, Jo and I were contacted by a youth theatre group based near Liverpool, Action Transport Theatre. They wanted us to attend one of their rehearsals for a performance of a play based on our meetings, *The*

Bomb, written by Kevin Dyer. We duly attended a rehearsal with the full cast, production people, director and playwright at their base at Whitby Hall, Runcorn. It was fascinating to observe how these young actors interpreted our first encounter, as scripted by Kevin. It was apparent to me and to Jo that Kevin had misunderstood the dynamic between us in our meetings and reconciliation work, but particularly that first encounter, the broad basis for his narrative treatment. Our conversation was depicted as fraught, confrontational, violent. It was thrilling to watch in terms of the emotional impact conveyed by the cast, but also disturbing. For as rehearsed it echoed some of my fears that had proceeded the actual first meeting with Jo. Conflict is integral to drama, of course, but in the context of that first meeting, it might well have ensured that no further meetings were possible. The cast were very attentive. We explained our concerns – that it was the *absence* of anger and the willingness to listen which were at the heart of our continuing decision to meet and to further the dialogue. The cast showed great talent in then incorporating our concerns into the performance. As a drama, it worked well but still fell short, in my view, of faithfully realising the nature of our actual meetings. The experience of meeting this group of English actors, and others I have met, demonstrated the immeasurable value of engaging creatively with people possessing open, inquisitive minds; those prepared to rise above prejudice and not be hidebound by any received view of the IRA, or indeed any Other. That is why it was so fascinating for me to see at close hand how they reacted to me and to what I could reveal to them about the Irish conflict. The experience underscored the value in promoting, facilitating, encouraging local community arts. I imagined the impact of cross-community drama projects at interface areas in Belfast.

The Bomb successfully toured throughout England and received critical praise. It was also broadcast on BBC Radio 4. Kevin Dyer was awarded the Writers' Guild Award for the play. We attended some of the performances and met the audiences afterwards. In November, the play was staged in Belfast, at the Baby Grand, followed by a discussion chaired by the local broadcaster Ivan Little. A home audience always presents a greater challenge for me. For some, I epitomise the enemy. Ivan Little asked (mischievously, I thought) whether I regretted that Margaret Thatcher had survived the bomb attack. The intent was, certainly, to target her in particular, but I fielded that all deaths are regrettable in the conflict without the extra burden that her death would have laid on me.

In November 2009, to mark the twenty-fifth anniversary of the bombing, Jo and I were invited to speak at an event jointly organised by The Forgiveness Project and the All-Party Parliamentary Group on Conflict Issues (APPGCI). This took place in the Grand Committee Room of the British House of Commons, Westminster. Hardly the secret location that was required at the occasion of the twentieth commemoration in Brighton. Marina Cantacuzino hoped that our attendance would draw attention to the work of The Forgiveness Project and of the APPGCI.

For the day, we were assigned a PR woman to deal with the media and generally to guide us through the busy schedule. An interview had been arranged at the BBC's Westminster studios. We entered a security area at the same time as the Tory MP Ann Widdecombe was leaving after giving an interview. The PR woman tried rather ham-fistedly to bounce the MP into meeting me. I could not believe it was happening. Ann Widdecombe seemed equally appalled at the suggestion. She wouldn't look at me but, before deftly exiting through the security turnstile, remarked, 'I lost friends at Brighton.' I would never have contrived to meet her that way, nor indeed any victim or someone with a connection to a victim.

I should mention that I had a previous unscheduled encounter with a leading Tory. In July 2007, I visited the H-Blocks, where a conversation between me and my former academic supervisor, Bob Welch, was recorded as part of a video archive project. Afterwards, by coincidence, we briefly met Lord Gowrie, a former Direct Rule Tory minister of state, visiting the site on some other matter. Bob made the briefest of introductions, an uncomfortable moment, over in seconds, but we shook hands. Bob later confided that Lord Gowrie, whom he regarded highly for his interest in the local arts during his tenure as a minister in the Northern Ireland Office, wryly commented that he supposed it was his contribution to reconciliation. While I am on this track, in April of that year I also met Douglas Hurd (who as home secretary in 1998 had proposed setting my tariff at fifty years). Along with Jo and Harvey, we took part in a recorded panel discussion about the Brighton bomb for *The Reunion*, chaired by Sue MacGregor and broadcast on BBC Radio 4 in May 2007. Douglas Hurd was courteous, matching his patrician public persona. The recorded discussion was equally civil. Hurd had stayed at another hotel on the night of the bomb, but, of course, he had lost friends and colleagues. I was annoyed to discover that when the programme aired one exchange was cut: when I argued that the IRA were never defeated, the former home secretary and secretary of state had agreed. I cannot say why the admission was edited out, or whether Douglas Hurd had requested its deletion to save political embarrassment.

To get back to the event at Westminster – the same PR woman had promised an interview with Jo and me to a reporter with crew waiting outside on College Green. The reporter was rude to Jo when I didn't turn up. No one up till then had asked for my consent for an interview. In fact, I expressly stated that I did not want to give interviews, knowing full well there was a considerable likelihood that my words would be twisted to undermine the whole event.

Later in the day I met a Labour member of the All-Party Group. He wanted me to know that the Group had taken a huge political risk in extending the invitation to me, but that a reconciliatory gesture or apology from me would be helpful. I thought my presence there on the day 'a reconciliatory gesture'. I don't doubt that he was well-intentioned, but the request suggested the huge gulf in our differing mindsets about culpability for the conflict.

The room was full for the event, chaired by Liberal Democrat MP Simon Hughes, and consisted of a wide range of experience – in the fields of prison rehabilitation, restorative justice, etc. – and, of course, interested MPs from all political persuasions. David Cameron, the new Tory leader and future prime minister, although not present, had expressed his goodwill for the occasion. Jo and I spoke in turn and were courteously received. The occasion demanded absolute candour. I was conscious of the expectation of a 'gesture' from me. This was pressure. I repeated there the core message from my difficult conversations with Jo – that all deaths in the conflict were regrettable, but that I believed the IRA was justified in its campaign; that we had exhausted all options, while the British state, with all its resources and power, had chosen violence. One Conservative MP, Patrick Mercer, who had served with the British Army in Ireland during the conflict, complained that I hadn't expressed remorse, voiced his opposition to my presence there and left in protest. In an extraordinarily direct but nevertheless eloquent intervention, a Labour peer said he recognised that I was a 'man of integrity' and pleaded for some expression of remorse for all the victims. I explained that I was there as an individual and could not speak for the IRA. The IRA were already on record as expressing regret for the loss of life. I know that Jo was disappointed and perhaps had hoped for more. The next day's headlines judged that 'a defiant Magee' had refused to show remorse. I found it sad that, after my then nine years of working with Jo and others, the media were so wilfully deaf to what I was saying. All deaths in the conflict were regrettable; and I do not make the distinction between innocent victims and those who died as protagonists. My bottom line is that I regret that the conflict was necessary. War had come to us.

The film director Roger Spottiswoode, perhaps best known for directing the James Bond movie *Tomorrow Never Dies* (1997), was permitted to film the event, although I had no notification of his presence. He had interviewed me earlier in the year in Belfast for a feature documentary, eventually released in 2012 as *Beyond Right and Wrong* and co-directed by Lekha Singh. As well as dealing with the themes of restorative justice and forgiveness as related to the British/Irish conflict, the documentary also examined their relevance to the Rwandan genocide and to the Israeli/Palestinian conflict. The UN secretary general at the time, Ban Ki-moon, had agreed to the screening of the film for the General Assembly in New York.

I saw *Beyond Right and Wrong* at a pre-premier screening at the Soho Hotel, London, in January 2013. Jo also attended, and afterwards we shared a discussion about our participation in the documentary. It is a powerful, even disturbing documentary, perhaps particularly in the Rwandan section, and remains to this day deserving of a wider audience. However, I did have issue with the manner in which my own contribution was edited. I spent hours being interviewed, often being asked the same questions. I sensed pressure to go further in regards to expressing remorse. I was also interviewed in a reflective mood on location in the hills overlooking Belfast. All that was shown of the interview was a short depiction of me apparently tearful, when in fact I had been suffering from hay fever. The edit contrived to show me in tears.

Lord Alderdice, former speaker of the NI Assembly, who appeared in the documentary and who was also at the pre-premier screening, chaired a talk a fortnight later at an event that Jo and I spoke at called Choice: Empathy or Enmity, organised by Religions for Peace and held in one of the committee rooms of the House of Lords.

However, I am skipping ahead. A few days after the event at the House of Commons, I was again invited back to Brighton by Jo to mark the twenty-fifth anniversary of the bombing. Jo organised a screening at the Duke of York's Picturehouse in Brighton of a documentary about peace-building, *Soldiers of Peace* (2008), part of which featured our work together. In a Q&A session after the screening, which as previously was chaired by Simon Fanshawe, one of the issues raised was knife crime, then a concern in Manchester, where Jo was living at the time. Jo used the occasion to launch her charity Building Bridges for Peace. Much of the charity's subsequent focus would be on social issues affecting inner-city schools, and crucially the issues of racism and of gang violence. Simon reminded the audience of the tight security thought necessary for the twentieth anniversary event in 2004, when those attending were only informed of the location the night before. This time, details of the event were widely circulated, betokening, he suggested, much progress in local attitudes.

In another memorable event organised by Marina Cantacuzino, I was invited to share a panel discussion at the first annual lecture of The Forgiveness Project at St John's Smith Square, London, in May 2010. Desmond Tutu gave the inaugural lecture: 'Is violence ever justified?' The panel afterwards was chaired by the writer and broadcaster Edward Stourton. Talking of this matter is always difficult, and potentially harrowing, for victims and survivors. A fellow panellist, Mary Kayitesi Blewitt, who had lost over fifty members of her family during the Rwandan genocide, had to leave the stage in tears.

To further illustrate the difficulties involved in these always potentially fraught events, in July 2010 Jo and I were invited to the Tim Parry Johnathan Ball Peace Foundation in Warrington. The centre was established by Colin and Wendy Parry, whose twelve-year-old son Tim was killed along with three-year-old Johnathan Ball in an IRA bombing in Warrington in 1993. I had met Colin Parry before, when attending the centre. Colin wrote about it shortly after in the *Irish News* (15 December 2001), on the eve of meeting Martin McGuinness, then minister for education at Stormont:

I met Patrick Magee myself last week and we were able to talk for a short time.

I don't know if I could meet the man who killed my son but I told Jo [Berry] that I admired the fact that she had done so.

The occasion this time for my attendance in Warrington was for an event organised by Combatants for Peace, an Israeli–Palestinian initiative dedicated to the promotion of nonviolent protest over the Israeli occupation. Jo became upset after my very defensive response to a question from another panellist critical about the IRA's armed struggle. I felt put on the spot and totally failed to respond with the requisite sensitivity towards Jo's feelings and indeed those of others in the audience. Jo expressed her anger. We stopped talking for several weeks, months. There is always the possibility that any suppressed hurt and anger might break to the surface. As I have said, these were extremely difficult conversations and required great tact and support, one of the essential findings of our earlier work on Causeway. On this occasion I failed. To this day I find it truly remarkable that Jo, despite setbacks such as the one just described, continued to demonstrate that willingness to engage in dialogue. It is a humbling realisation that she has shown such trust in me. One of the Israeli participants remarked to Jo that he and others, including others among the Palestinians present, appreciated having witnessed our public disagreement which, paradoxically, made them feel better in identifying with the shared difficulties in these often fraught encounters.

Back in the Blocks, I had foreseen that one day I could meet and have conversations with former squaddies, RUC men, etc. – all those we saw as enemies. Over the course of the last twenty years I have got my wish, for on several occasions I have been able to share platforms with erstwhile protagonists. The experience has always been positive. None more so than when in October 2014 I met a group of former British Army veterans in Belfast. They were there as part of a Veterans for Peace (VFP) delegation on a tour of former locations they had served in during the Troubles. I met them with Jo Berry at Queen's University, Belfast, at an event chaired by Claire Hackett of Féile an Phobail (Ireland's biggest community festival and summer school). There were eight in the group, who had served in various regiments, in different locations and at different times, in Derry,

Belfast, South Armagh, etc. Four of the group were former Paras. Their leader, Ben Griffin, was a former member of the Special Air Service. We each in turn told something of our life stories. I got a real sense of connection with those guys. Each individually I could relate to, and even compare with comrades I have known in the IRA. There was no Other in that room. The event was videoed and is available on YouTube (as indeed are many events at which I have shared platforms with Jo).

The distinction is sometimes drawn between professional soldiers, like British Army squaddies, and those who form the spearhead of their communities' resistance, like IRA volunteers. Both are trained for combat but a major difference between them, demonstrably, is the level of resources available to the task. Any professional soldier will have that advantage. The training of the professional soldier, however, is designed to purge individual identity and to substitute group obedience to command, to a level which supersedes any nominal loyalty to country or mission, whether justified or not. I have no doubt that a squaddie may believe in his or her country's stated mission, but it is not a prerequisite. To obey is everything. For the IRA volunteer, however, the cause is everything and must be justifiable. The vets struck me as thoughtful and honourable, haunted by their individual experiences of service, and now individually attempting to undo the personal harm, as they argued, of their training and experiences. Ben Griffin memorably explained that his own experience of post-traumatic stress was part of a healing process; the mind's rejection of the indoctrinated unquestioning obedience required of the professional soldier by the reassertion of natural emotional responses. Ben used the term *de-indoctrination*. This process was a recovery of humanity in the individual.

In a further development, VFP invited me to speak at their annual general meeting in London in 2015. I shared the platform with two of the veterans who, as part of the vets' tour, had attended the meeting at Queen's University the year before. Also on the platform was the former POW and leading republican Seanna Walsh, who in 2005 had the honour of reading out the IRA's declaration of the permanent ending of hostilities.

The most formidable obstacle to future peace and harmony is the gulf between the 'two traditions' – that Other with whom we share the island. Jo often expressed her sadness that more opportunities to share had not occurred in the North. To the outside world the situation there may have seemed, and was often reported as, hopeless. I have been asked numerous times at events whether there were any signs to encourage hope for the future. I was fond of alluding to several cultural harbours of inclusion: boxers, bikers, punk and goths. Each as a distinct cultural phenomenon largely exemplified commonality and a rejection of the surrounding seas of division and fear, free of the tides of sectarianism and bigotry.

Perhaps the occasion of most hope for me personally was our meeting with VFP at Queen's. Former squaddies have appeared on various platforms during Féile an Phobail events. We also have talked at the Féile. But conversations with the Protestant communities, with unionism and loyalism, seemed elusive. And yet extremely meaningful and rewarding when they do happen. Another source of encouragement came from attending an event organised by the Belfast Interface Project where I presented to a group of loyalists from the Shankill and from east Belfast. The best part for me personally was the very good-natured discussion with a group of them following the stage address and Q&A session. It is deeply regrettable that more resources have not been earmarked for this area of reconciliation. Contact and dialogue are always positive but need to be nurtured and resourced, I believe, as an integral ingredient of the peace process.

However, there is no denying the enormous distance still to travel in reconciling our divisions. We all carry pain and loss. My dad's distant cousin Con Neeson was killed in an axe attack carried out by the Shankill Butchers (August 1976), and Mum's cousin Joseph Donegan died a terrible sadistic death at the hands of Shankill Butcher Lenny Murphy (October 1982). These killings and the many others should never be forgotten. But we should strive to find a means of ensuring that we do not remain locked in bitterness and pain. The most effective antidote I know comes from the healing power of contact and dialogue. Those two words, again.

In January 2014, Jo and I were invited to give a talk at the Skainos Centre on the Newtownards Road, in the loyalist heartland of east Belfast. This was part of a festival entitled Listening to Your Enemies. Our talk was chaired by the Reverend Dr Lesley Carroll.

There was concern that the event would not take place because of hostility from some loyalists outraged that I had been invited. My stance was to be guided by the advice of the organisers. In phone conversations earlier that day, I had been assured that the main loyalist organisations were supportive of the event going ahead. I was heartened by this. On that basis, I agreed. If they had advised otherwise, I would not have attended. It should always be the decision of the host community whether to precede or not. It is that community which has to live with the outcome, whether positive or otherwise.

On the night, myself and Jo had to enter Skainos by a back door while outside an angry crowd, estimated between fifty and a hundred, protested my presence. Stones were thrown at the police, four of whom were injured. The tension in the hall was palpable. What was said was perhaps of less significance than the fact of it going ahead.

One of the first to greet us was Andrew Rawding, a former British Army pastor who I had shared a platform with at Glencree in July 2005. All these former contacts have proved their value in promoting further contact and discussion. This was a big step for all who had a hand in organising the event. It was certainly a huge step for me and one I am proud to have made. There have been many instances of loyalists and unionists being invited to speak in nationalist venues. Far fewer republicans have been invited in the other direction. The invitation from Skainos set a marker in redressing the imbalance, one that will hopefully lead to further difficult but necessary conversations.

Towards the end, the audience were asked not to applaud but to allow the speakers to leave without signalling to the protestors outside that the event was about to conclude. We left in a police Land Rover, which dropped us off safely in the city centre. None of those remaining would have been in any doubt about the hostile reception waiting outside. The audience had to exit the centre to threats and insults. I have the utmost admiration for all who attended that night. Although there were threats after the event to raze Skainos to the ground, it continues to flourish, and is a shining testament to efforts of the local community to further regeneration and inclusion.

Some months later, I was attending a conference in Brussels. One of the speakers was a prominent loyalist. We got talking. Skainos was mentioned. He confided in a good-natured manner that his sister was very likely one of the loyalists involved in the protest that night. At a west Belfast Féile talk, Mervyn Gibson, leading Orangeman and former RUC Special Branch officer, ventured that the event was premature. I think it was David Ervine (the leader of the Progressive Unionist Party) who coined the phrase 'baby steps' in terms of reconciliation – slow but sure progress? Skainos was a huge step. It was a courageous step.

We travelled extensively with our message that contact and dialogue are the keys to understanding. We have spoken in Spain, in Portugal; in Germany, Norway, Austria, Bosnia, Kosovo, Turkey, the Netherlands, Belgium, Switzerland; in Lebanon, Israel/Palestine, Rwanda and South Africa. Many were recent war zones, their people slowly emerging from conflict, each seeking to deal with the legacy of the past and their demands for justice and the truth. At a profoundly human level, our willingness to openly share our stories seemed to embody the possibilities of hope for many who heard us speak. Each occasion would lead to further invitations. Jo has spoken abroad separately on numerous other occasions.

I described in the previous chapter my quite positive meeting in Dublin at the US Embassy. If it were not for the increased security procedures introduced following 9/11, there is reason to believe that I would have been able to travel to the States. Subsequently, I have received a number of invitations to attend conferences there, but have always failed to obtain a visa. This is an issue affecting all former republican prisoners. Our 'criminal records' prevent us from obtaining certain categories of employment and from travelling to certain countries. Our release fell short of amnesty, which would in theory have expunged our criminal records.

This was well demonstrated to me when, in November 2015, Jo and I were invited to speak at Ciudad de las Ideas in Puebla, Mexico, and at other events in Mexico City. The invitation followed our presentation at a peace festival in Sarajevo in 2014, where we met Dr Mauricio Meschoulam of the Universidad Iberoamericana, Mexico City. We were due to fly direct to Mexico City, but at the check-in desk at Heathrow I was told my booking was cancelled at the behest of the USA; while it was a direct flight, it would cross American airspace. We agreed that Jo should continue without me while the organisers were contacted. Once acquainted with the news of this setback, Mauricio insisted on organising an alternative route. That evening I took a flight to Madrid, but was again stopped there from boarding a direct flight to Mexico. Overnight, a flight to Colombia was organised, where I would get a connecting flight to Mexico. Eventually arriving at Mexico City International Airport via Bogotá, Colombia, however, I was detained for several hours and questioned by immigration officials, refused entry and deported. My passport was removed and not returned until my arrival back at Madrid, via Bogotá. At no stage was I formally advised that I was being deported or why. My journey began on the morning of Wednesday, 4 November and ended on my arrival back at Heathrow at lunchtime on Saturday, 7 November. I reckon I must have spent about thirty-five hours in the air over those three days. Despite that inconvenience, Jo was able to make a very effective and successful presentation in my absence. Against a backdrop of a huge photo of me, Jo stood beside two empty chairs and addressed the audience. One chair, she explained, represented her father; the other, my absence from the event. Jo read out a brief statement I was able to email to her as soon as my mobile was returned to me after landing back in Madrid:

> *Muchas gracias* to Dr Mauricio Meschoulam and to everyone involved in Ciudad de las Ideas. Jo Berry and I are honoured to have been invited to Mexico to demonstrate that despite profound differences, trust can be built and the mutual desire to explain, to understand and to be heard can be nurtured. What is more profound than Jo's willingness to try to understand my perspective given that I killed her father?
>
> A huge lesson learned from our exploration of difference, here simply expressed, is that to build peace we must strive to remove any obstacles to its attainment.
>
> This simple message proved too contentious for some in authority, who have prevented me from being with you in person today.
>
> I am equally honoured by the efforts made by Mauricio, and others I haven't met, to find alternative means to get me to Puebla today.
>
> But Jo *is* there and our message will be heard.

I remember a visit that Jo and I made to the Peace Museum in Gernika (Guernica) in the Basque Country, established to commemorate the terrible bombing of the town in 1937. The museum challenges our notions of what peace means by identifying its many constituent parts – that it means more than the absence of war; for example, the laughter of children, the respect for human rights, social justice; or what Albie

Sachs identifies in his memoir as 'soft vengeance' – the establishment of an inclusive, law-based society.* We had the privilege of meeting a man who had survived the bombing raid. The survivors faced decades of cover-up and lies to the effect that the sole culpability for Gernika lay with General Franco's German and Italian fascist allies – not with Franco. Very much on my mind was that back home in Ireland we awaited the findings of the Saville Report into the Bloody Sunday murders of fourteen unarmed civilians protesting against internment and for civil rights in Derry in January 1972. A further fourteen were wounded, none of whom were subsequently charged with, for example, possession of a weapon or attempted murder – the Brits had claimed that they had engaged arms only with gunmen. Within days of my return to Ireland, the Saville Report was made public. I witnessed people reduced to tears at reception of the report's finding of the innocence of those shot dead that day. We all knew the truth but those in power denied it for so long. I know of many young people of my generation who went to war because of those killings. The consequences of Bloody Sunday, of the abuse of state power, stretch for decades and are measured in destroyed lives, ruptured families, untold years behind prison bars, miles of 'peace walls' and of razor wire.

It has been said that peace is more difficult to build and to sustain than wars to start. The term *field of battle* is often used but the term *field of peace* is equally apt, I would suggest, to describe the pursuit of peace. For the pursuit of peace is a struggle. Even when the fighting has ceased the propaganda war will continue, with each side continuing to assert its version of a conflict's history, motivations, conduct. Peace may not be desirable to certain interests who might feel threatened by a political accommodation that weakens their power. Peace requires equilibrium; it requires safeguards to offset the imbalances in power which appear inevitably to lead to its abuse. Peace also requires the active engagement in reconciliatory activity. The reaching out of the hand of respect to the other. Most tellingly, when compared to the human and financial resources directed to 'security', efforts to promote peace are grossly under-resourced.

The past has to be understood to avoid the mistakes, the historical abuses of power, the miscarriages of justice, the pitfalls and cul-de-sacs of

---

*Albie Sachs, *The Soft Vengeance of a Freedom Fighter* (Grafton Books, 1990).

history. Gernika and Derry for me hammered home that reconciliation requires the truth, and not drawing a line on the past in order to protect those with the most power. If the Irish, and Basque, experience is anything to go by, there are always powerful vested interests threatened by the truth who are resistant to change, for real change requires an alteration in the balance of power towards more equitable, democratic outcomes.

18

Postscript

Post-conflict Belfast (there's an optimistic turn of phrase!) is best epitomised, for me, by a visit to the Sunflower Pub in Kent Street where, nearly half a century ago, I received my first direction as an IRA volunteer. Back then it was the Avenue Bar, a smoke-filled haven for local punters. In the midst of the Troubles, the bar was blown up and shot up by loyalists. People were killed; limbs were lost. As recounted earlier, this was a dangerous area. The security caged entrance is still there, one of the last, if not the last, in the city, a respectful memorial to those dark days. Now the young have made the bar their own. Students, artists and young professionals for the most part. It's rare to spot a local from the old district. These days it is an acoustic hub – folk, blues, jazz and Irish trad sessions. But no Guinness. Instead, a bewildering array of boutique ales and bespoke gins. Belfast itself, and indeed the North, is now a popular tourist destination. Hotels spring up but can't keep pace with the demand. Heartening also how skateboarding youth and buskers have staked their claim to the city centre. Theirs now: never ours then. We hated the exclusion that the centre stood for – where Orangemen could flaunt their triumph, but where no nationalist could parade until well into the 1980s.

Few now appear interested in or even aware of that history. Or at best they consider it academic and remote from the new reality. Snippets of conversation overheard, for it's a bar where people talk easily, suggest that the patrons come from every quarter of the city. It couldn't be further removed from the huddled, conspiratorial ambience of former times. It is now a microcosm of the shared future we all seek.

I have called in occasionally during the writing of this account, to sit on a barstool, dwell over a pint and tap into that past. The bar is a vestigial link, marking the day when, as mentioned, I received a whispered IRA command to attend my first gun lecture. Here's where I would also meet Dad for a pint. Joss too may have stepped across its threshold, although the old Carrick Hill had more than its share of rival hostelries. The ghosts are there to haunt.

We cannot draw a line under the past; we must strive to understand that past or potentially have to deal with conflict in the future. I am sufficiently realistic to expect that evidential detail of our historical trauma will continue to surface or be unearthed without satisfaction of the concomitant need felt by many for justice. Lost documents may surface; others will be released after the thirty-year rule embargo; memoirs and deathbed confessions may add to the mosaic. We will never get the completed picture. People in positions of power will take their secrets to the grave or beyond the reach of blame. It is difficult to imagine that any British minister or general will ever stand in the dock to answer for their culpability for the conflict; for sanctioning torture and murder; nor for the core injustice of partition, or for turning a blind eye to fifty years of unionist misrule, or for the conduct of Direct Rule. I am also aware that there are many victims of republican actions who are unlikely to achieve closure.

The extent of the human cost to all may blind us to how much we have in common. Republicans share with loyalists the lived experience of communal threat, regardless of how far the threat was and is imagined or concocted. From a republican perspective, the essential difference between our communities, despite the overlap of shared poverty and deprivation, is that Protestant communities historically were aligned with power and privilege. That is our understanding. The cohesive power of Orangeism, in James Connolly's analysis, was or is to subsume distinct class interests under the misperceived and deliberately fostered fear of Irish republicanism. This ought to be a focus for dialogue between communities who always shared much more than divided us. Reducing the sense of threat, and the suspicion and fear engendered, should be our mutual focus. Dialogue and contact, as ever, are the keys. And that neighbouring island across the water? Despite a troubled history, the connections are deep-rooted and merit fostering, but on the basis of respect and equality, and not exploitation and domination.

The immediate future is uncertain. We are in a period of transition. I believe we are capable of a mature appraisal of what is needed to maximise the economic and social potential within the island of Ireland; not separate from, isolated from, that other island – that other community with whom we share history – and without shedding one scintilla of cultural identity or political conviction.

The world is smaller on our handheld screens. We feel the pain of the child in Gaza or in Yemen or in Rochdale; we despair together over climate change and other global challenges and together must organise if we are to deal effectively with them. Intrepid journalists send images of events as they happen with astonishing immediacy. We are now, to a greater extent, alert to the pain and suffering of others in our global village. Empathy now can be harnessed to change the world. We should also recognise the clear and present danger that our electronic reach is exploitable by the powerful to limit our freedom.

I can look back on my involvement in the conflict at various stages – while active; in periods of incarceration; as a fugitive. There are many moments that signified change; development; awakening. Perhaps the most significant occurred nearly two decades ago at some midpoint in that marathon, three-hour dialogue I had with Jo Berry. The sudden awareness that what I imagined to be my openness to other perspectives – my preparedness to listen, to challenge, to question certainty – had shrunk; that there were conflict-inducing limitations to my perception of reality. That natural human ability to empathise had been diminished. All of us, all sides to the conflict, were locked into a mindset narrowed by the effects of that same conflict even as we emerged into the light of the peace process. Call it an epiphany. I recognise it as a moment of healing; a gradual reversal of the damage individually and collectively that the existential trauma of the conflict had accreted over decades, at each painful turn. I had failed to perceive the fullness of others' humanity. Now you can reason that the reduction of this perception in conflict is a survival mechanism. How could you function otherwise in a war setting? We reduce our enemy down to a scale more readily apprehensible in order to meet the challenge, to defend against and ultimately to defeat. It is as selfish as that. 'We' against 'them'. That is to label. And to label is to reduce to an essence. It may also be exploited to misbrand. To lie.

In all spheres of endeavour – in the sciences, philosophy, the arts – language evolves to match the complexity of insights gained. We live in an age of great complexity and contention. Yet in the political sphere, complexity is conveyed in a ridiculously simplistic resort to labels. It has always been so in that world. 'Fanaticism' has been replaced by 'terrorism' in this update of obfuscation. This is language in the service of power that acts to the detriment of us all.

The last and perhaps greatest obstacle to a shared future is the battle of narratives. There are those in this post-conflict situation who would deny any legitimacy to the republican perspective. The propaganda war continues to be waged; words continue to divide. In this light, we should look at all we have endured and survived and unleashed on each other, have difficult conversations and face uncomfortable truths.

I recall Jo Berry's anguished words from Orlagh: 'When is it right, when is the suffering worth it?' I have heard similarly painful questions echoed many times by former activists who, conscious of loss, are either supportive or critical of the present state of politics and of the peace process: 'Was the armed struggle justified? Was it worth the sacrifice?'

Some argue that the outcome was not worth the death toll. A pyrrhic victory. Did Britain ever consider the death toll when negotiating its withdrawal from empire? The question is rarely addressed. There are other questions. What about those in power, who have wealth, resources and the options these bestow; are they less likely to kill to preserve their privilege? Does their self-perception of entitlement and superiority legitimise their use of violence as a first response in many instances to calls for a more just society and distribution of wealth?

Britain partitioned Ireland through violence, political chicanery and the threat of a further escalation of repression. From one perspective, a unionist perspective, partition drew a line under the past and was intended to establish its own historical calendar, with 1921, the year partition was sanctioned, as year zero. Northern nationalists found themselves locked into 'a Protestant state for a Protestant people'. The grandparents and parents of my generation found themselves bereft of the means to address their grievances. All means had been tried. All had failed: marches, demonstrations, rallies, campaigning, lobbying, electoral politics within a gerrymandered constituency framework – the full range of open, democratic, constitutional means of tackling injustice. They had to endure repression and poverty in every decade. Eventually the pot boiled over.

In conflict, any conflict, we are all diminished. Outcomes are rarely definitive. We can survive; perhaps achieve some ends: more equality, liberty, justice. But often loss and pain at the personal level preclude any sense of victory. For some, nothing is worth the loss of a single drop of blood; others may take stock of future benefits, the ends justifying the means. To have prevailed against terrible odds seems a victory. If our enemies had indeed won, as we often hear promulgated in their media, we might have expected from them more magnanimity, a willingness to move on, instead of which there is the continual assertion of our defeat. I am satisfied that we prevailed. But at terrible cost.

When the Dalai Lama was asked why he didn't fight the Chinese, he took time to reply, 'Of course the mind can rationalise fighting back … but the heart, the heart would never understand. Then you would be divided in yourself, the heart and the mind, and the war would be inside you.' I wish I could believe in this duality of mind and heart. I dare say that the mental conflict I have experienced comes from the absorption of certain religious values from an early age. I certainly am not conscious of having been reared to hate or to hurt others.

And so I remain conflicted. This was not the life I might have hoped for. But I have had the privilege to share a gift not everyone can claim of their lives. I was involved in a collective struggle, a revolutionary moment, the fight for political and economic justice. I saw what can be achieved when people stick together. That's precious.

I am not a pacifist. Reluctantly and regrettably, that is where I am. What parent wouldn't protect their child from violence? My core conflict is that I stand over my actions and yet profoundly regret the hurt inflicted. It is an uncomfortable and often a difficult lived experience to attempt to justify. But I believe our struggle was necessary and *therefore* justified. War came to us. People were hurt. I hurt people. Enemies, yes, but even their loss and pain is a matter of regret.

For all that is lost in conflict – precious lives and potential, family, friends and comrades, the innocent and bystanding – we can honour by imagining the future and working to harmonise our efforts and vision. My greatest sense of hope for the future has always come from contact with the Other – the imagined Other – for faced with the shared reality of what we are and have in common, Otherness begins to lose its crippling hold. We need to transcend division, to leave Otherness behind as a useless, debilitating, myopic and mutually self-destructive state of mental negation. I think it is profoundly inappropriate to speak of winners when so many from all sides have experienced loss. Nobody wins until we all win. We are all reduced. Grief is a particular and a universal experience. This is our situation and where we begin.

Index